THE PSYCHOLOGY OF
Joss Whedon

THE PSYCHOLOGY OF
Joss Whedon

AN UNAUTHORIZED EXPLORATION OF *BUFFY*, *ANGEL*, AND *FIREFLY*

Edited by
JOY DAVIDSON, Ph.D.
WITH LEAH WILSON

BENBELLA BOOKS, INC.
Dallas, Texas

"Mal's Morals" © 2007 by Robert Kurzban
"'Darn Your Sinister Attraction!'" © 2007 by Carol Poole
"Free Will in a Deterministic Whedonverse" © 2007 by Thomas Flamson
"The Adaptive, the Maladaptive, and the Mal-Adaptive" © 2007 by Nicholas R. Eaton and Robert F. Krueger
"An Analysis of Slayer Longevity" © 2007 by Tracy R. Gleason and Nancy S. Weinfield
"How Buffy Learned to Confront Her Fears" © 2007 by Brian Rabian and Michael Wolff
"Terror Management Aboard *Serenity*" © 2007 by Wind Goodfriend
"Existentialism Meets Feminism in *Buffy the Vampire Slayer*" © 2007 by C. Albert Bardi and Sherry Hamby
"Dealing with the F-Word" © 2007 by Misty K. Hook
"'Stripping' River Tam's Amygdala" © 2007 by Bradley J. Daniels
"Buffy the Vampire Dater" © 2007 by Siamak Tundra Naficy and Karthik Panchanathan
"More Than Entertainment" © 2007 by Stephanie R. deLusé
"Buffy's Search for Meaning" © 2007 by Mikhail Lyubansky
"Psychology Bad" © 2007 by Ed Connor
"'There's My Boy . . .'" © 2004 by Joy Davidson, reprinted from *Five Seasons of Angel*
Additional Materials © 2007 Joy Davidson

BenBella Books, Inc.
6440 N. Central Expressway, Suite 503
Dallas, TX 75206
www.benbellabooks.com
Send feedback to feedback@benbellabooks.com

BENBELLA

Printed in the United States of America
10 9 8 7 6 5 4 3 2 1

Library of Congress Cataloging-in-Publication Data

The psychology of Joss Whedon / edited by Joy Davidson, with Leah Wilson.
     p. cm.
   ISBN 1-933771-25-9
   1. Whedon, Joss, 1964---Criticism and interpretation. I. Davidson, Joy. II. Wilson, Leah.

PN1992.4.W49P79 2007
791.4502'32092--dc22
                        2007030711

Proofreading by Paige Kimmel and Stacia Seaman
Cover art by Ralph Voltz
Cover design by Laura Watkins
Text design and composition by Laura Watkins
Printed by Bang Printing

Distributed by Independent Publishers Group
To order call (800) 888-4741
www.ipgbook.com

For special sales contact Robyn White at robyn@benbellabooks.com

CONTENTS

INTRODUCTION

GILES: But that's the thrill of living on the Hellmouth! There's a veritable cornucopia of . . . of fiends and devils and, and ghouls to engage. (*everyone looks at him*) Pardon me for finding the glass half full.
　　　　　　—"The Witch," *Buffy the Vampire Slayer* (1-3)

CORDELIA: If there's one thing I learned living on a Hellmouth: every day is precious, you never know when it may be your last.
　　　　　　—"Double or Nothing," *Angel* (3-18)

ANGEL: I keep saying that. But nobody's listening.
　　　　　　—"Epiphany," *Angel* (2-16)

Angel is wrong. Nearly *everybody* is listening—and not just to him. We're listening to all the heroic, fiendish, always complicated characters who populate the universes created by television impresario Joss Whedon. Listening to them is as close as we get to listening to Whedon—and we haven't stopped listening since that day in 1997 when the premiere of *Buffy the Vampire Slayer* kicked off a pop culture domino effect that hasn't yet subsided.

For Love of Joss

Maybe we started listening to Whedon because he was so darn much fun—but we kept listening, and we're still listening *hard*, because he forces us to peer into the remotest corners of our own morally capricious,

1

emotively turbulent world. And we like that. We like the scalpel's-edge intensity of the Whedonverse, the way it mirrors and makes sense of our own treacherous plane of existence. We like confronting our darkness, even if, in doing so, we think we're still just having fun.

Whedon's works are compelling, even addicting. They have bite and soul—a lot like the vampires we've come to adore. When we gaze down into the Whedonverse's fathomless abyss, the abyss always gazes back—lending the seductive illusion that we're never truly alone. The Whedonverse reveals our human condition in its most glorious and depraved variations, capturing our collective consciousness with unyielding pathos and rollicking humor. That, too, is why we keep listening, keep taking in more of that world, re-experiencing it over and over, through first runs, syndication, films, DVDs, and comic books.

Which brings us to Whedon's genius, and the source of our loyalty to him—both of which lie in his capacity to turn a translucent private vision into solid characters riddled with contradictions and emotional paradoxes. Joss gives us heroes who, amidst mesmerizing melodrama and metaphor, kissed by wit, are utterly human—especially when they aren't human at all. He gives us characters so fallible, so exquisitely flawed, that we are destined to love them and then immerse ourselves in the 'verse they inhabit.

Denizens of the Whedonverse, with their full complement of tangled relationships, are sweepingly iconic, too. They represent grand and pervading ideas that extend beyond their isolated selves: from feminism, spirituality, and Marxism, to mortality, passion, and sacrifice. The layered, near-epic quality of Whedon's work lends itself to serious study, much like the poetry of T. S. Eliot or the sonnets of Shakespeare. No other contemporary creator of media for the masses has aroused such academic *and* popular devotion to his original materials—with the possible exception of Gene Roddenberry. Publications that reflect upon the Whedonverse have mushroomed over the past half decade, spanning books aimed at fans as well as academic anthologies, professional journals, Internet journals, fan sites and blogs. University courses and international "Buffyology" conferences abound, while references to Whedon's works spring up in fields as diverse as literature, history, communications, media studies, women's studies, philosophy, religion, linguistics, music, cultural studies, feminist studies, masculinity studies, queer studies, transgender studies, sociology, architecture, and of course, psychology. Whether the discussion centers on the text, the characters, the social context, the audience, or the mythos, all are excavations of what it means to engage in life, to ponder existence, to desire, to love, to nurture, to despise, to risk, to fight . . . and to die. Thus, it's hardly a stretch to suggest that, in one way or another, all studies of the Whedonverse are studies in psychology.

Psychology in the Whedonverse

The breadth of the field of psychology is at least as colorful and variegated as the Whedonverse itself. Each subgenre beneath the umbrella of "psychology" is a 'verse of its own, uniquely endowed with history, culture, principles, dogma, traditions and traditionalists, rebels, villains, and heroes. Where strands of psychological sciences or arts intersect, they often do so tentatively, tiptoeing up to one another or accidentally bumping bits before glancing quickly away. Just as the *Angel*verse and the *Buffy*verse cross paths but do not breach boundaries, many schools of thought within psychology lean on or borrow from one another while maintaining distinct or somewhat conflicting identities.

The Psychology of Joss Whedon honors the diversity of psychology as an integrated, applied science. Blending theory, research, and clinical approaches, it offers a scientifically kaleidoscopic view of the Whedonverse. Yet readers needn't have a background in advanced science to thoroughly engage with each of the book's essays; they've been written for the Whedon fan, not the academic. Still, they cover an impressively wide swath of intellectual territory. Here's just a sampling of what we take on:

❖ We consider the question of free will in Joss's universes: Does it exist? Or might it be a necessary illusion that we mortals clutch just to get through each day?

❖ We highlight evolutionary psychology, a controversially deterministic theory embracing the idea that organisms are shaped by the forces of evolution to find pleasure in that which perpetuates the species. Are

3

we, therefore, especially drawn to Whedonverse residents who are "morally succulent," i.e., who appeal to our evolutionary survival instincts? How does a father-daughter bond (or lack thereof) merge with evolution's sexual selection processes to determine a woman's lust/love objects? How might evolutionary theory impact one slayer's romantic choices?

❖ We dive into Jungian depth psychology. Freud's disciple, Carl Jung, postulated that in each of our psyches' darkest corners there hides an entity containing our forsaken, denied primal urges. His theory suggests that we are most strongly attracted to others who manifest our secret, disowned traits. Does Buffy's explosive relationship with Spike reveal her shadow self? Is vampirism actually a metaphor for narcissism?

❖ We segue to traditional models of psychiatry, questioning the degree of pathology in two of the most forensically challenged males aboard *Serenity*: Mal and Jayne.

❖ We follow a cognitive-behavioral plan for healing adolescent anxiety and depression, and we ask: How can the experience of successfully challenging fear alter a young woman's faulty beliefs about herself? How, especially, can this affect an anxious Chosen One, whose every day could be her last?

❖ We're introduced to "terror management theory," an innovative field of psychology that seeks to explain how people cope with the daily threat of violent death. In studying terror management, what better living laboratory could we ask for than aboard the ship *Serenity*?

❖ We watch feminism meet existentialism as Sunnydale residents search for meaning in the perils of life on the Hellmouth. We see existential therapy—a clinical derivative of existential philosophy and psychology—help Buffy grapple with the prophecy that death would be her gift.

❖ We explore Joss Whedon's own assertion that he is a radical feminist. Along the way we dip into radical feminist theory, gender theory, social psychology, self-psychology, and feminist therapy.

❖ We turn our attention toward the realm of neuropsychology. How does messing with the brain change behavior and even alter human consciousness? Among all the dark arts practiced within the Whedonverse, could the science of brain-tinkering be the darkest of them all?

❖ We see the healing power of the Whedonverse when one brave author describes her own transformation from victim to real-life superhero.

And, finally, we enter the Whedonverse through Darla and Angel's sado-erotic *folie a deux*. I wrote this essay, the very last in this book, for an earlier BenBella volume: *Five Seasons of Angel*. "There's My Boy" focuses on the relationship that was Angel's most formative and karmic, yet it also revisits the core psychological themes introduced in this book's preceding essays, from shadow selves to narcissism, parental influences to found families, terror management to existentialism and the meaning of life. In fact, in *Angel*, I believe that Joss Whedon reveals how *he* sustains a sense of purpose in a tumultuously disturbing world. I think Whedon shares a perspective that could give added meaning to all the angst, all the pain, all the struggle—and even all the fitful growth—that he, his characters, and his fans inevitably confront. I believe that the creative genius, Joss Whedon, imparts his own existential secret, his own mantra, in the voice of Angel, the vampire with a soul.

But, please, *don't turn to the back of the book to seek that message!* I'm certain—and convinced Whedon would agree—that the end will be far sweeter if you pursue it slowly, relishing every ripe and juicy moment along the way.

—Joy Davidson, Ph.D.
New York, NY
August 2007

If you ask an evolutionary psychologist why you keep chasing blondes with big . . . er . . . hair, she'll decipher your urges with an eye toward human adaptations designed to replicate her genes. In fact, she'll decode every move you make, every breath you take, every vow you break in evolutionary terms—the cryptographic key to human nature. Granted, not all psychologists take so deterministic a stance on every tingle in your loins or shiver in your neocortex, nor do they all view moral development in neuro-evolutionary terms. But don't let that stop you from living large and rewarding your brain with Robert Kurzban's view of what makes that tingle-provoking Malcolm Reynolds so universally appealing to our sense of all that is right and good in the world.

MAL'S MORALS

Evolutionary Pornography

ROBERT KURZBAN

"You don't know me, son. So let me explain this to you once: If I ever kill you, you'll be awake, you'll be facing me, and you'll be armed."
—Malcolm Reynolds, "Serenity"

Malcolm Reynolds, captain of *Serenity*, is a man living on the brink of disaster. He ekes out a meager existence, taking jobs on both sides of the law. Such a man can afford, of course, few luxuries. Despite this fact, he indulges in at least three. As the opening quotation suggests, he indulges in the luxury of honor. Along with that, he indulges in the luxury of loyalty and, most expensive of all, the luxury of morality.

If you don't believe that these are luxuries, consider "The Train Job," discussed in more detail below. Mal could have simply set sail with a tidy profit. Instead, because of his sense of honor, he earned nothing for the job, except the ire of a powerful crime lord. These "profits" would accumulate interest and, eventually (in "War Stories"), cost him a profound sum of money (earned in "Ariel"), a horrific torture session, and an ear

7

(subsequently reattached).

Honor, loyalty, and morality are expensive. They cause you to make important—even life-threatening—sacrifices.

In some ways, you might think audiences would react negatively to such extravagance. We have only scorn for the penniless man who, finding a couple of bucks, buys a sixer of Stroh's. Isn't Mal *foolish* for such indulgences?

Perhaps. But that's not the point.

Such traits—in particular the last of the three—are, to coin a phrase, moral pornography.

And we like to watch.

Evolutionary Pornography

The answer to this mystery comes from a relatively new approach to understanding human nature, evolutionary psychology (Cosmides, Tooby, and Barkow 3).

One element of this approach allows us to think about a perennial mystery, the aesthetic sense. That is, it tells us about what we will find appealing.

And we already know some of the answers.

It's the sugar in your coffee. It's the salt on your pretzel.

It's the sun on your face, soft fur on your hand, and the aroma of fresh apple pie.

It's a sexy body, scantily, or perhaps elegantly, clad.

It's skiing, surfing, parasailing, and Space Mountain.

But it would be a mistake to think that it stops there.

It is also solving a puzzle. It's deftly penned prose, honed and polished to linguistic perfection. It's the tones of exquisitely played Beethoven. It's probably the parabolic touchdown pass.

And still it doesn't end there. It's seeing her name come up on your cell phone. It's when open arms and wide smiles welcome you as you stomp the snow from your boots in the doorway. It is seeing your name at the top of the chapter. Better still, on the dust jacket.

It is not limited to the concrete. It begins with these. Or, at least, it began with these. But it didn't stop. Not by a long shot.

THIS IS YOUR BRAIN ON PORN

In a recent study (Singer et al. 467), two people were asked to play a simple game, called the "Dictator Game." One person is given ten dollars, the other zero. The first person is faced with a simple choice: how much of the ten dollars to give to the second person, a stranger brought in just for the experiment. Thousands of participants from around the world have played variations on the Dictator Game.

This one was different. In this game, there was a third experimental subject. They couldn't participate, but could only watch. This subject was, however, somewhat special. This subject was watching the game from inside a multi-million dollar magnet: an fMRI machine. And while the subject was watching (via computer), their brain activity was monitored. In this particular version of the game, on occasion, a "selfish" Dictator who chose to give little or no money to the other person was punished.

When the selfish Dictator—who the person in the magnet had never met and would never meet—was punished, an interesting thing happened. For some subjects (men), an area of the brain associated with reward (left ventral striatum/nucleus accumbens) "lit up" more when the unfair person was punished compared to a control condition.[1]

In a similar study, people in a scanner were actually able to punish people who had acted in an untrustworthy fashion toward them. Taking revenge here activated an area associated with pleasure, the caudate nucleus (de Quervain 1256).

Your brain likes to take revenge, and it likes to see the bad guys punished.

Revenge, whether you administer it or someone else does, is rewarding.

It's the sugar in your coffee.

In other words, it's evolution's way of telling you that you're experiencing something GOOD.

Darwinian Aesthetics

If there is any basic principle in the history of psychology, it's that organ-

---

[1] This difference between conditions in the relevant brain regions did not occur in female subjects. It's unclear why this sex difference emerged.

isms tend to seek reward (and avoid pain). And if there is any basic principle in the history of biology, it's that organisms have been shaped by the forces of evolution via natural selection. Taken together, these two basic principles imply that evolution has equipped organisms to find things that are, evolutionarily speaking, GOOD for them to be rewarding.

It's easy to understand why certain things are rewarding. For many organisms, evolution has sculpted their nervous systems to direct them toward the Big Four F's: Feeding, Fighting, Fleeing, and Mating. If we could scan a mouse eating cheese, its brain would light up. If we could scan it winning a fight, if we could scan it escaping, if we could scan it in its more personal moments . . . same thing.

Evolution equips organisms with, roughly speaking, innate notions of what have been called "adaptive targets" (Cosmides and Tooby 459), things that are "GOOD" (again, in the evolutionary rather than moral sense) for the organism. Organisms' nervous systems are designed to seek these things, find them rewarding, and come back for more (Orians and Heerwagen 555).

You'd like to think we're different, but we're not. Natural selection equipped us to find things rewarding that, over evolutionary time, directed our ancestors toward adaptive behavior (Thornhill 543). Like rats pressing a lever, people play the slots, lick ice cream cones, and down vodka tonics.

Psychologists can take advantage of this. Sometimes the reward systems can be "tricked." Mice don't get a kick out of cocaine because mice that did cocaine left more offspring than other mice. However, to guide mice toward adaptive behavior, some sort of neurophysiological reward system is needed, and cocaine activates this same system. To put it somewhat crudely, because of this fact, you can "hotwire" mouse brains to give them the neurophysiology reward without the experience that, in a world without experimental psychologists, would only come with some spectacularly adaptive behavior, or perhaps not at all.

People in marketing take advantage of this as well. Things, services, and ideas sell in a free market because they satisfy evolved appetites. In this sense, the marketplace—from the grocery store to the theme park to popular media—is a window that looks onto our evolved preferences. Crucially, what sells are the not only physical things we enjoy, but also *representations* of things. Literature is a clue to aesthetic systems—what we like to read about are the people, situations, and events that we would like to be or have happen to us in our world (Carroll). Untold riches. Beautiful women. Resourceful men.

Evolution didn't equip us just to like the concrete, like a nice piece of cheese, a nice piece of cake, or, with apologies, a nice piece of ass.[2]

Human reward systems—our "Darwinian aesthetics" (Thornhill 561)—are not restricted to the concrete (Dutton 693). When our friend in the fMRI witnessed a selfish jerk getting punished, a complex social dynamic involving three people—jerk, victim, and punisher—his brain lit up because like sugar, coffee, and sex, *justice* is aesthetically appealing.

Like our lab rat on cocaine, human nervous systems can be "fooled" (Burnham and Phelan 246). We have brains that are designed to find certain things rewarding because they would have been adaptive in the past. We have various brain parts that lead to the experience of pleasure and pain. These brain regions are important because they're evolution's way of telling you that you're doing something right, and should do it again. These reward regions guide you toward doing things that, under normal evolutionary circumstances, lead you to leave more descendants than you would otherwise. So, we're wired to want to do, see, and smell certain things because our ancestors who did them did indeed leave descendents. The rest—the individuals whose brains were not wired up to guide them toward successful reproduction—those people are represented by those branches you see ending on evolutionary trees. Every generation is the result of particular individuals' reproductive success in the previous generation.

In the case of the human male, it's reasonable to design in an aesthetic appeal for a large number of sexually willing, very fertile young women (Malamuth 19). Larry Flynt discovered this, made a fortune, and was shot for his trouble.

Artists in various media discovered this as well, leaving us with da Vinci's painting, Shakespeare's wit, and Rodin's sculpture.

---

[2] Both the pronouns used here and the themes are somewhat andocentric. Forgive me. This is a meditation on Malcolm Reynolds, which provides an excuse, if not an actual reason.

The Aesthetic of Character

Like our friend in the machine, we love to read—or watch—as the Count of Monte Cristo gets his revenge. There is a grammar of social relationships—a way in which various kinds of behaviors are combined together. Some constructions are more appealing than others. Revenge—misdeed followed by punishment—is an appealing grammar. As endless authors have discovered, deserved altruism, reciprocated love, and self-actualization are all appealing aesthetic grammars.

But behind the grammar is yet another adaptive target, another Darwinian aesthetic. They are complexly interrelated, but distinguishable.

And now we leave the lab and re-board *Serenity*. We don't just love the story where the bad guy gets what he has coming. We don't just consume the story arc with pleasure.

We love the hero who brings him to justice.

Characters' attributes are the cocaine of good storytelling. In the same way that the male brain is attracted to representations of sexually available women because ancestors attracted to such things left descendants, the human brain is attracted to characters that display those features of abstract quality that would have made them GOOD to have around. In short, we love the good guys, in all probability, because wanting to hang around them would probably have been a GOOD idea.

This is not to say that things are so simple. Drawing characters who are GOOD is fairly easy. But some characters are relatively one-dimensional. They are defined by a simple trait, such as fighting for one's country. Captain America is great as far as he goes,[3] but some might argue that his character lacks a certain depth.

The art of character—both in the fictional sense and in life—is the inevitability of tradeoffs. At any given moment, we can choose to act selfishly, in our self-interest, or commit various acts of sacrifice, from small to large.

Malcolm Reynolds faces any number of such moments. Living on the brink of poverty, capture, and death, he could be forgiven for choosing

---

[3] As far as he *went*. During the writing of this chapter, he was killed by an assassin. (Of course, death is often a somewhat transient state for superheroes.)

self-interest. Remember: loyalty, honor, and moral principles are the luxuries of the wealthy. It is among the poor and desperate that they are remarkable.

LOYALTY

Loyalty is, with some imprecision, siding with and sacrificing for others, particularly in the service of those with whom one has deep social bonds, such as love and friendship. It is altruism directed toward those to whom it is "due." We value loyalty in our friends, and the lack of it—betrayal—can tear apart even close friendships. Members of a social species such as ours invest large amounts in a small number of people, some of whom are selected through no choice of our own—such as family members—and others who are selected through careful choices (Tooby and Cosmides 132). A key factor in these important decisions is expectations about others' loyalty. In our own lives, we prefer others to sacrifice in our interest. No self-respecting evolved creature could be expected to be otherwise. This preference is visible more abstractly—we admire (real or media representations of) people who sacrifice for those dear to them.

It could be argued that because Mal is captain and leader, loyalty is his central defining character trait. There is no denying that this is indeed important. In "Heart of Gold," we learned, eavesdropping on Mal's eavesdropping, that Inara's friend, Nandi, was in trouble, with no one to defend her against the nefarious forces aligned against her. Mal agreed to help. For free. As devotees of the series, we knew how unusual this was. Living from hand to mouth, the crew of *Serenity* could ill afford uncompensated work. We were surprised but delighted by Mal's, "You keep your money. Won't be needing no payment."

When Inara insisted on paying because she thought it was "important we keep ours strictly a business arrangement," we saw in Mal's face that abstract moment of beauty. We saw the connotation of character that made it clear that he did not want to help for the money, but rather from loyalty. That she viewed the act—or, at least, said that she viewed it—as financial revealed that Mal was not just *willing* to sacrifice for the woman who—we knew, if even he didn't—he loved; he was *eager* to.

Along the story arc, he caused her much more pain than her thoughtless remark caused him, by sleeping with Nandi.[4] In this moment, Mal, arguably, came as close to distasteful to the viewer as he ever did in the series or in the movie. We sensed that Inara's own words drove him from loyalty to selfishness, but, still, what we saw was a distinct lack of loyalty.

It is up to each of us as viewers—as judges of actions and character—to decide if Inara's tears were too high a price to be paid for the satisfaction of Mal's worldly appetites. Here, the metaphorical sugar of Mal's loyalty is tinged bittersweet. It is unclear if the revelation of Mal's ultimate humanity draws us to him—as with realist art—or away. Which do we prefer, the representation of the perfect but unbelievable hero, or the representation of the flawed man, realistically self-medicating his (emotional) pain by seeking (physical) pleasure?

Of course, sometimes we're treated to simple sugary goodness. In "Ariel," Jayne betrayed River and Simon to the authorities and Mal nearly killed Jayne in revenge. He stopped at the last moment, but here we saw loyalty practically naked. Tormenting Jayne for his betrayal, we saw Mal's loyalty to people whom he owed very little. This was important in the context of character, as Mal frequently pretended that he kept them aboard for practical reasons, rather than any genuine friendship. If this were true, he would not have risked his relationship with his hired gun, Jayne. As Jayne gasped for breath as *Serenity* ascended up into the thinning atmosphere, Mal's character was exposed before us.

It satiated our appetite for loyalty.

HONOR

The quotation that opens this chapter, taken from the pilot episode, denotes Mal's *honor*. Dictionary definitions vary, but generally honor refers to a sense of fairness and honesty. To see honor best is to see what it is not. A person of honor does not take advantage of someone who could be exploited. He does not profit from the misfortunes of others. And he ensures that in conflict, the playing field is flat—which is why he does not shoot someone in the back. Note that being honorable does

---

[4] On meeting Nandi, Mal said, "Any friend of Inara's is a strictly businesslike relationship of mine." This turned out to be a shot across the bow.

not necessarily mean being law-abiding. An honorable person might well not abide by an unfair law.

To return to "The Train Job," Mal and his crew were hired by one Niska to steal some cargo from the Alliance. All went well—or reasonably well—until Mal learned what they had stolen: medicine for sick people, including women and children. To keep the merchandise was to let these people die.

No person of honor could let this stand. Mal returned the booty and tried to return the payment for doing the job, thus losing all profits but obeying the strictures of personal honor. To keep the payment and deliver the goods to the (already wealthy) criminal mastermind would have made him a reversed Robin Hood, taking from the poor and giving to the rich. His return of the medicine and his attempt to return the payment for the job fit nicely into our aesthetic sense of honor. The deserving poor got their medicine, the malign rich were denied additional wealth, and all of this, recall, came with a decidedly high price tag.

It is important to note that when trying to return the money to set things straight with Niska, Niska's henchman, Crow, declined to accept the returned money. On his knees and bound, Crow was kicked into *Serenity*'s engine intake by Mal's boot. We saw here that Mal's honor has its limits. And, again, as viewers we are asked to evaluate—or even understand—Mal's conflict, and we are once again drawn into the texture of fiction that separates it from fantasy. Mal is honorable. He did the right thing. But he does not only kill people when the playing field is even. Nobility is sometimes trumped by the reality of the underbelly of the smuggler's lifestyle.

More importantly, it is sometimes trumped by the third and final element of Mal's character addressed here, morality.

MORALITY

It is easy to think that Mal's signature qualities are loyalty and honor. Whedon goes to great lengths to show us these features, setting the character's actions, often, in opposition to his lines. Listening to Mal, it would be easy to believe he is only out for himself and to heck with other people or a set of abstract principles. His loyalty and honor lie in what he does rather than what he says.

But it would be a mistake to think that loyalty and honor always win. If Mal were driven first and only by loyalty, for example, he would not put his crew in harm's way. And he certainly would not go out of his way to do so in the service of an abstraction such as moral principle.

Morality has frequently been equated with conscience—doing the right thing according to a set of principles. However, morality is much more than that. When Crow was liquefied by *Serenity*'s engine, this was really an act of morality; in particular, it was moralistic punishment. Crow, unwilling to abide by the equitable arrangement Mal had presented him, was subject to Mal's moral wrath.

The best illustrations of the conflict among morality and nobility and loyalty come from moments in the film, *Serenity*. First, consider the interplay of Mal's honor and morality. From the quote that opens this chapter, you might think Mal would be reluctant to kill unarmed men. There was Crow, of course. In the film, however, his moralistic outrage is in full swing; he shoots no fewer than three unarmed men, one in the process of trying to surrender. (Mal was, it must be said, pretty angry; the man was part of an attack in which Shepherd Book and the others in the settlement were killed.)

But the critical moment is when Mal discovers the secret of the planet Miranda. He is faced with a choice. He can skulk away. Or he can go toe-to-toe with both the Alliance and the Reavers, putting himself and his crew at risk so that he has the chance to make public the sins of the Alliance—the deaths on Miranda and the creation of the Reavers, along with the cover-up.

It's important to note that loyalty demands ignoring this political scandal. A single Reaver ship or Alliance cruiser is more than a match for *Serenity*, which is no military heavy cruiser, like *Enterprise*, but a small cargo vessel. And there is no profit in succeeding in this mission.

No profit, that is, other than the (arguable) cornerstone of morality: punishing those who have committed a great wrong, in this case the Alliance's crimes against an entire populace.

And, in the end, the price is paid. Simon is severely wounded, and Wash, Mal's closest friend's husband, is killed.

Morality trumps loyalty and honor. In the film, Mal fights dirty and uses his crew as human fodder in the service of a principle. And not only that, but punishing the Alliance might not even bring about a greater good. It certainly will not bring back the dead on Miranda.

Mal's loyalty has limits. It does not dictate all his actions.

And we adore him for it.

And this is part of Whedon's genius. In Mal we see a man continually beset by the exigencies of his morality, whose necessities preclude loyalty, as there are principles that pull with too much force to leave intact the bonds of friendship, even love.

Conclusion

Whedon's creations, of character in context, hold important lessons about our evolved aesthetic sense. From the appeal and success of his works, we can infer important lessons about what human psychology finds rewarding. The lights of *Firefly* illuminate human nature. In particular, they reveal something which is often only obvious at the level of the concrete. We do not find it particularly interesting or mysterious that we are drawn to Hershey bars. The evolved function of this appetite is relatively easy to understand.

But evolved aesthetics climb to higher levels, and we are drawn to representations of GOOD things. We enjoy pictures of landscapes, beautiful people, and cuddly babies. The function of these appetites is relatively easy to understand: Evolved creatures should be attracted to things that are GOOD for them.

Yet higher, we are drawn to representations of abstract principles. We like to see loyalty rewarded, love reciprocated, and justice done. The leap is longer, but it is easy to imagine that, like our friend whose brain found reward in seeing unfairness punished, our brains are built in such a way that they find these things rewarding.

In the domain of character, a similar explanation holds. We live (and our ancestors lived) in a world in which friends need to be chosen, alliances formed, and social bonds maintained. With only limited time and a limited number of people to ally with, surely we ought to be attracted to people who would make good friends and allies. Our minds should find the people who show these qualities rewarding.

If we imagine that the Good Guys are to these reward systems what pictures of young naked women are to male evolved mating psychology, we see that Mal's morality feeds these systems. To write such characters properly is more complex than writing a porn film. Our tastes in social relationships are more finely grained and more nuanced than male sexual appetites.[5]

Our Darwinian social aesthetics should be honed to draw us to characters with features that would have made them very appealing to have in one's social network.[6] They should have a diversity of positive features. Interestingly, because of the complexity of social life, they can't max out on all of them because some of them are in conflict. Sometimes, morality precludes loyalty. Sometimes, loyalty precludes nobility. Luke Skywalker, somewhat frustratingly, won't just kill the Emperor because Luke abides by a principle of nonviolence unless absolutely necessary (which, fortunately, is frequently enough for some good light saber duels). But our evolved systems are drawn to people with mixes of these qualities because these systems serve us well in guiding us—in real life—toward making good choices about our social lives.[7]

The genius of writing is establishing a character with a mix of these features and finding elements that make them excite the part of your brain that's telling you who to befriend and who to stay away from. This art tells us about evolved human social aesthetics. The characters we love are character pornography—they tell us what our system craves. In the same way that (some) men[8] would like to live in a world of endless sexually eager, attractive women, we would like to live in a world populated by the characters we are drawn to.

---

[5] Sorry, guys.

[6] Villains are an interesting wrinkle. So are horror movies. Neither villains nor horrific deaths are GOOD in the sense I've been talking about it. I won't delve into this here, but rather mention one of my favorite quotations from my father: "Rob, every experience you have should either be pleasurable or educational." Seeing villains and disasters might feed the human appetite for information about fitness-relevant features of the world, such as dangerous situations, predators, deaths, and so on. These things are "educational." And, in case you're wondering, yes, my father's words did help drive home the point that I should make sure I have the front door key with me when I go out to get the paper in subarctic temperatures while wearing pajamas.

[7] With notable exceptions. You know who you are.

[8] Not me, sweetie.

What would it be like to live in a 'verse populated by Mal Reynoldses? Unless circumstances were extreme (e.g., if a planet's population had been obliterated), you wouldn't have to worry about getting shot in your sleep. Or in your back. Or when unarmed. There would, however, be little respect for the law. Mals, as it were, have no particular patience for the laws of men. Laws are an inconvenience to be accepted when possible, bent when expedient, and ignored when necessary or, more importantly, Right. People would be honorable, loyal, and moral, and particularly the last.

In this sense, Mal is the kind of guy we would like around, a realistic and interesting mélange, making him, to mix some metaphors, morally succulent.

Because, in the end, it's not, actually, the sugar in your coffee.

It's the flavor of the beans, the fat in the cream, the sweetness of the sugar, and the warmth in your mouth, all in the right combination.

Evolved aesthetics are, to be sure, satisfying at their most basic. But woven into a tapestry, the complexity of aesthetic targets is the reason that we have the word "sublime."

And, finally, I hasten to add that it is not intended to be a criticism of *Firefly*, *Serenity*, or Joss Whedon to call Mal morally pornographic.

After all, it's really good porn.

ROBERT KURZBAN, PH.D., is currently an assistant professor at the University of Pennsylvania in the department of psychology. He received his Ph.D. at the University of California Santa Barbara, and received postdoctoral training at Caltech, UCLA, and the University of Arizona. His research focuses on evolved cognitive adaptations for navigating the social world in domains such as mate choice, friendship, morality, and cooperation.

REFERENCES

Burnham, Terry and Jay Phelan. *Mean Genes: From Sex to Money to Food: Taming Our Primal Instincts*. New York: Penguin Books, 2001.

Carroll, Joseph. *Evolution and Literary Theory*. Columbia: University of Missouri Press, 1995.

Leda Cosmides and John Tooby, "Toward an Evolutionary Taxonomy of Treatable Conditions," *Journal of Abnormal Psychology* 103.3 (1999): 453-464.

Leda Cosmides, John Tooby, and Jerome H. Barkow, "Introduction: Evolutionary Psychology and Conceptual Integration," in *The Adapted Mind*, eds. Jerome H. Barkow, Leda Cosmides, and John Tooby (New York: Oxford University Press, 1992), 3-15.

Dominique J. F. de Quervain, Urs Fischbacher, Valerie Terrier, Melanie Schellhammer, Ulrico Schnyder, Alfred Buck, and Ernst Fehr, "The Neural Basis of Altruistic Punishment," *Science* 305.5688 (2004): 1254-1258.

Denis Dutton, "Aesthetics and Evolutionary Psychology," in *The Oxford Handbook for Aesthetics*, ed. Jerrold Levinson (New York: Oxford University Press, 2003), 693-705.

Niel Malamuth, "Sexually Explicit Media, Gender Differences, and Evolutionary Theory," *Journal of Communication* 46.3 (1996): 8-31.

G. H. Orians and Judith Heerwagen, "Evolved Responses to Landscapes," in *The Adapted Mind*, eds. Jerome H. Barkow, Leda Cosmides, and John Tooby (New York: Oxford University Press, 1992), 555-579.

Tania Singer, Ben Seymour, John P. O'Doherty, Klaas E. Stephan, Raymond J. Dolan, and Chris D. Frith, "Empathic Neural Responses Are Modulated by the Perceived Fairness of Others," *Nature* 439.7075 (1992): 466-469.

Randy Thornhill, "Darwinian Aesthetics," in *Handbook of Evolutionary Psychology: Ideas, Issues, and Applications*, eds. C. Crawford and D. Krebs (Mahwah, NJ: Lawrence Erlbaum Association, 1998), 543-572.

John Tooby and Leda Cosmides, "Friendship and the Banker's Paradox: Other Pathways to the Evolution of Adaptations for Altruism," *Proceedings of the British Academy* 88 (1996):119-143.

Everyone knows that teenage girls are insufferably self-indulgent and self-obsessed, bursting from childhood with the panicked urgency of winged insects fleeing cocoons. Narcissism is almost synonymous with that period . . . but it passes. Usually. Buffy Summers was nothing if not an "ordinary" teenage girl when the series began. Then, things changed. Big time. Carol Poole hones in on the super-slayer's post-resurrection struggle and her obsessive relationship with bloodsucking bad boy Spike in season six, and asks us to consider the evidence that Buffy has narcissistic personality disorder. Poole offers a compelling analysis of the Jungian symbolism found in Buffy's tumultuous affair with Spike and in vampirism itself, giving dramatically dark and deep new meaning to the term "soul mates."

"DARN YOUR SINISTER ATTRACTION!"

Narcissism in Buffy's Affair with Spike

CAROL POOLE

*B*uffy the Vampire Slayer (BtVS) fans have long debated whether it was genius or the opposite that led the show's creators in season six to involve Buffy in a violently sexual affair with Spike, a vampire. Dark as it was, the story of their relationship impressed me as an insightful metaphor for the psychodynamics of narcissistic disturbance. As I will argue, Buffy's state of mind throughout her affair with Spike was a nuanced, accurate reflection of how it feels to suffer from narcissistic pathology.

In this view, informed by psychoanalytic and Jungian ideas, Spike was not simply an unhealthy boyfriend choice for Buffy; he was an image of her own shadow, a reminder of every greedy, primal need she had disowned for the sake of being a hero. Her affair with him was a mirror image of the disturbance in her soul, and yet it also represented a desperate, unconscious attempt to repair a split in her psyche by passionately tangling with her disowned self.

Buffy Hates Being Killed

Dying never brought out the best in Buffy. Twice in her seven years as Sunnydale's resident vampire slayer, Buffy died and was resurrected. In both cases, she went out like a hero but came back darker, more hurt, defensive, and self-absorbed.

Following Buffy's first death and resurrection,[1] she returned to Sunnydale High after a summer spent shopping, not sharing, with her dad in L.A. (He complained to her mother, "She was just, I don't know, um . . . distant. No brooding or sulking, just . . . there was no connection.") Soon she was sniping at her Watcher, Giles, and calling best friends Willow and Xander "losers." She cruelly used Xander in a sexy I-wanna-torture-somebody exhibition dance that inspired the high school's resident Mean Girl, Cordelia, to remark, "You're really campaigning for Bitch of the Year, aren't you?" ("When She Was Bad," 2-1).

Why was Buffy taking her rage out on her friends instead of directing it where it logically belonged, against demons like the vampire who killed her? In the *Buffy*verse, as in life, the psyche rarely follows a straight line, and psychologically her reaction makes a lot of sense. As Giles explained, her bitchiness was understandable in light of her traumatic experience. "She may simply have what you Americans call 'issues.' She's convinced herself that she's invulnerable" ("When She Was Bad").

The psychological defense of denial is one way we split the difference between what we need and want from the world, and what the world, in fact, offers us. Buffy couldn't change the reality that her world was full of monsters that could hurt her, but she *could* refuse to be aware of her vulnerability. Denial is considered a "primitive" defense by psychoanalytic thinkers because it first shows up in very early childhood, unlike other, more sophisticated defenses which develop later in life. In Buffy's

---

[1] In "Prophecy Girl" (1-12), at the climax of season one's finale, Buffy succumbed to the Master, an über-vampire with a repulsive, stained, puckered mouth like a lamprey's. (Buffy called him "fruit-punch-mouth.") Having been warned that she was destined to lose this fight, Buffy stoically embraced her duty and went off to fight the Master anyway. She got in a few good blows before he choked her and dropped her face-down in a puddle, where she lay dead for about a minute before Xander showed up to revive her with CPR—a possibility the prophecy didn't mention, but didn't preclude.

case, denial apparently protected her from feeling overwhelmed by terror and rage, but at the cost of cutting her off from her friends and from all the positive aspects of her own vulnerability. In effect, it was as though Buffy were saying, "To hell with being vulnerable! I don't need anyone, I can be everything to myself. I'm in control of my world, because I'm not going to allow anyone in it but me."

In "When She Was Bad," Buffy was not very entrenched in this stance. It only took her friends becoming endangered for Buffy to remember that she needed and loved them, which meant that instead of continuing to dump on her friends she had to take responsibility for her own feelings, painful as they were. In the episode's climax, Buffy—wielding a sledgehammer, and with her murderer's bones conveniently dug up for her catharsis—was able to demonstrate, weeping, what she still had no words for: just how much she *hated* being killed.

It was in her second death and resurrection that Buffy really got deeply into her "issues." If it was hard for her to return to life after being killed by a vampire, her dilemma was much more complicated when she was her own killer. In addition to her trauma and conflicted feelings about being vulnerable, on returning from her second death Buffy seemed to be suffering from a self-directed rage so intense she couldn't bear to feel it: feelings of traumatic intensity.

To recap how she got into that predicament: In season five's finale, Buffy made a heroic, selfless sacrifice of her life to save the world and in particular to save her younger sister, Dawn. In this climactic scene, the clouds parted and a radiance in the sky seemed to beckon Buffy upward as she leapt from a tower. Music swelled behind Buffy's final words to Dawn: "The hardest thing in this world is to live in it. Live!" ("The Gift," 5-22).

After the fall, Buffy lay dead but lovely, serene in a pale ensemble which, like her body, somehow made it through an epic battle without a mark.

During the preceding weeks, Buffy had struggled to protect Dawn from an emotionally chaotic and petulant "god," a villain far more powerful than the vampires Buffy ordinarily faced. As Slayer, Buffy was tough but no match for a god, so she felt torn between her duty to protect Dawn and her awareness that she might not be able to. Dawn might die; so might Buffy, because as a hero she could not allow herself even to imagine saving herself by abandoning Dawn. In "The Weight of the

World" (5-21), Buffy became catatonic in response to being torn so powerfully between love, guilt, and need.

She resolved this dilemma by transcending her own survival instincts, or so it seemed. "Death is your gift," Buffy had been told by a spirit guide, and Buffy apparently decided this meant her death was a gift she could give to others. She died so that Dawn and her friends and the whole world could go on living. But there were clues in "The Gift" that Buffy hadn't fully grasped the gift of her own mortality—that is, fully cherished her own existence, and grieved her losses.

A big clue is that the fight scene commenced with a dramatic shift in mood—and with the appearance of a second Buffy. The mood of much of the episode leading up to the final fight in "The Gift" was tense and hopeless, weighted by everyone's awareness that once the god began the ritual sacrifice, the only way to save the world would be to hasten Dawn's death—an option Buffy refused to consider. Her "rally the troops" pre-battle speech was comically grim:

> BUFFY: Hey, everybody knows their jobs. Remember, the ritual starts, we all die. And I'll kill anyone who comes near Dawn.
> SPIKE: (aside, to Giles) Well, not exactly the Saint Crispin's Day speech, was it?
> GILES: We few—we happy few—
> SPIKE: We band of buggered.

But the fight began on a note of excitement and surprise. Buffy faced the god and won a round. The god came back swinging and tore off Buffy's head—only it wasn't Buffy, it was a robot! The "Buffybot" appeared earlier in season five, and it was one of the gang's bright ideas to resurrect it as a decoy in this fight against an overwhelming threat.

Psychologically, the appearance of not one but two "Buffys" in this fight scene suggests a last-ditch psychological defense with a hefty price tag: splitting. In the fight scene, Buffy appeared strong, serene, untouchable. She died a mystical, heroic death that appeared to be painless. But then there was this "Buffybot," dressed in the same outfit Buffy had been wearing herself earlier in the evening. By the end of the fight, the

Buffybot was a mangled pile of scrap, which seems like an accurate image of how Buffy might have felt in the instinctive, embodied part of her that *hated* being killed. The blows would have hurt, but no one was home to receive the pain—because Buffy had dissociated, or split off from conscious awareness, her vulnerability.

Judging by how Buffy felt and behaved when she was brought back to life in season six, this traumatic split was an intensification of her "issues," a more profound retreat from reality than she had ever before needed. In dying, Buffy found the logical end to a wish for invulnerability.

Being Undead: Buffy, Vampires, and Narcissism

During the few months (of earth time) when Buffy was dead, her soul was in heaven, or something like it, while her body lay underground in a coffin. But her death was unnatural, and in the first episode of season six, "Bargaining," her friends found a mystical loophole through which they could bring her back to life—and time, and vulnerability, and pain.[2] (And they expected her to thank them?)

Buffy's experience of being split between heaven and hell resembles a current psychoanalytic understanding of how it feels to suffer from narcissistic pathology, which means a disordered sense of self. As Sigmund Freud noted, a narcissist is self-absorbed because his self is a source of pain (Freud 25).

The symptoms of "narcissistic personality disorder," as defined by the American Psychiatric Association's *Diagnostic and Statistical Manual of Mental Disorders Fourth Edition, Text Revision*, include the following:

- ❖ A grandiose sense of self-importance;
- ❖ Preoccupation with fantasies of unlimited success, power, brilliance, beauty, or ideal love;

---

[2] Buffy's return was about as traumatic as it could have been. Because her friends left the gravesite believing the resurrection spell had failed, she came to life alone in her coffin and had to dig her way out. Then almost the first thing she saw above ground was the Buffybot (repaired and back in service) being torn to pieces by demons. Here, the symbolism seems clear: the Buffybot is Buffy's vulnerable self, her body, torn apart by unbearable experience Buffy can't contain within her awareness.

❖ A belief of being "special" and thus entitled to associate only with high-status or "special" people;

❖ A hunger for excessive admiration;

❖ A sense of entitlement, that is, unreasonable expectations of special treatment or others' automatic compliance with one's wishes;

❖ A tendency to take advantage of others;

❖ A lack of empathy for others' feelings and needs;

❖ Envy of others, or a belief that others envy one;

❖ Arrogant or haughty behavior. (APA 717)

Fans of Joss Whedon should have no trouble recognizing vampirism as a symbol of narcissism (see Figure 1).

In season six, the show delved into deeper imagery of narcissism's internal states and dynamics, asking viewers to empathize as Buffy, the heroine, struggled with her own narcissistic issues.[3] In psychoanalytic thinking, the inner hallmarks of narcissistic pathology include self-loathing and a sense of inner deadness or emptiness. "What narcissistic people of all appearances have in common is an inner sense of, and/or terror of, insufficiency, shame, weakness, and inferiority" (McWilliams 171). Depending on how they cope with these feelings, narcissists may seem self-absorbed in a self-inflating or self-denigrating way, but really they feel dead inside, which is how Buffy felt through much of season six.

In the *Buffy*verse, people become vampires when they are sired—killed— by other vampires. In current psychoanalytic thought there's no such clear or simple explanation for why people become narcissistically disturbed, but most therapists find it helpful to think about both internal and external factors, including obvious or subtle traumatic experiences which may inform a person's deepest beliefs about self and world. Symington argues that narcissism is, in part, a choice to fundamentally reject life, including the vulnerability that is a basic condition of being alive.

---

[3] Narcissistic symptoms can be temporary and transitory, as they usually were for Buffy and her friends. (Willow and Xander had their own dramatic episodes, as for example when Xander, in "Real Me" (5-2), literally split into grandiose and depleted versions of himself.) Anyone's sense of self may be destabilized during times of unusual stress or change, including adolescence! Or, as was the case with most of the monsters and vampires in the *Buffy*verse, a personality structure may be chronically dominated by narcissistic pathology.

FIG. 1: VAMPIRISM IN *BtVS* AS A METAPHOR FOR NARCISSISM:
COMPARISON OF SYMPTOMS

Symptom of . . .	Vampirism	Narcissism
Insatiable hunger for . . .	Human blood	Human affirmation, admiration
Constant terror of . . .	Exploding into dust fragments when staked/beheaded	Emotional fragmentation
When self is suddenly exposed to daylight . . .	Bursts into flames	Feels burning sensations of shame
Own self-image . . .	Does not reflect in mirrors	Does not hold together or reflect in one's own mind; ergo, hunger for external reflections
Envies and hates . . .	Humans, because they are alive	Others, because they seem to have whatever one feels one is missing
Fantasizes about . . .	World dominance	Perfection, control of one's own world
In relation to others, believes self to be . . .	Evil, more powerful; special	Worse and/or better than others; special
Lacks empathy . . .	For victims	For others
Feelings of rage related to . . .	Hatred of the living, and of stakes, fire, and sunlight	Hatred of vulnerability
Sense of entitlement extends to . . .	Using others as meals, lackeys, tools, toys, etc.	Using others as extensions of oneself
At heart, feels . . .	Dead (literally)	Dead, empty (emotionally)
Time seems . . .	Immortality makes time seem irrelevant	Denial of mortality makes time seem irrelevant, unreal

(Sources: *BtVS*; McWilliams 168–187)

Another symptom of narcissistic disorders is to feel always apt to fall apart, and desperate to be held together. Psychoanalyst Otto F. Kernberg theorized that the narcissistic ego,[4] like Buffy at the beginning of season six, is split between two opposite, alternating states: the *grandiose* (or all-good) verses the *depleted* (or all-bad). "The sense of being 'good enough' is not one of [narcissism's] internal categories" (McWilliams 177).

---

[4] In psychoanalytic thought, the "ego" is a person's ability, through conscious awareness, to cope with and adapt to reality. To have a split ego implies a problem in one's everyday coping abilities, and especially in one's capacity for relationships.

Narcissistically fragile people are especially vulnerable to shame, which psychoanalyst Neville Symington defined as "the emotion we experience when we are aware of the parts of ourselves that are not integrated" (Symington 26). In narcissism, the ordinary fact of having needs and being vulnerable is not well-integrated into one's sense of self, so life feels like a minefield: everyday social pressures trigger painful feelings of shame whenever one feels one's hidden, "bad" self has been exposed to view.

In Jungian psychology, the "bad" self has a name: shadow. In research involving word-association tests, Swiss psychoanalyst Carl Jung found evidence that the psyche is made up of unconscious structures called "complexes," or knots of feeling and belief that function as "splinter psyches" below a person's conscious awareness (Jung 40). This concept went mainstream with the "inner child," but in Jung there's not necessarily only one "inner child." Rather, each person's psyche is a mysterious world, a microcosm made up of many different feelings and beliefs, inner children and adults and animals and imaginary creatures—far too much life and feeling for anyone to consciously know about all at once, but all integral to one's selfhood.

The "shadow," then, is a complex—part of one's personality—which one can't see very easily. It includes both positive and negative beliefs and feelings which have been disowned because they clash somehow with a person's "persona," or public identity. Persona and shadow are opposites in Jungian thought, yet both are integral to a person's ability to feel alive and whole (Schwartz–Salant 67-68).

It's a tenet of Jungian thought that whenever we feel strongly provoked or moved by others, it's because they remind us of some less-known aspect of ourselves—our own complexes. In Jungian psychology, we grow by gradually coming to know more consciously the hidden parts of ourselves we glimpse in others (Jung 122–123).

If Joss Whedon's *Buffy*verse has a psychological Isaac Newton, a theorist who best explains its laws of psyche, it might well be Jung. Buffy and her friends started out battling external demons, but they grew up by struggling with their own demons and learning to integrate increasingly generous understandings of themselves and each other into their everyday awareness.

"I can be alone with you here": Spike as Buffy's Shadow

When Buffy returned from the dead the second time, she tried to keep her pain to herself. Instead of being openly angry with her friends, she was overly polite and distant, a mask to hide her despair. Giles perceptively remarked that he was "far from convinced she's come out of this undamaged" ("Flooded," 6-4). As Buffy explained when compelled by a musical demon to sing her heart out, "I touch the fire and it freezes me . . . I live in hell, 'cause I've been expelled from heaven" ("Once More, With Feeling," 6-7).

Psychodynamically, we might imagine she felt dead inside because she could only feel safe in her scary world if she believed herself to be superhuman, but this belief cut her off from and set her at odds with her own humanity. Her numbness was a defense against traumatic feelings which were too intense. She was furious with herself for being so human, and for holding such demanding, superhuman standards for her own behavior. She hated being killed, she hated herself for acting against her own survival, and also for stubbornly existing, needing, and being vulnerable anyway— and here was a big irony. Her supposedly "weakest" qualities turned out to be so hard to kill. As she complained to the demon named Sweet:

> SWEET: But what if I kill you?
> BUFFY: Trust me, it won't help. ("Once More, With Feeling," 6-7)

It puzzled many of her fans when, later in the same episode, Buffy revealed what she sensed *might* help: the embrace of Spike, of whom Buffy herself later said, "He's everything I hate, he's everything that I'm supposed to be against" ("Dead Things," 6-13). But this pairing makes all kinds of sense from a depth psychology perspective. To come back to life, Buffy needed to integrate more of her shadow, especially her greedy, needy, selfish will to live.

In season six, Spike's relationship to Buffy shifted subtly from his season five stance as her unrequited lover and occasionally chivalrous helper to a new role as Buffy's shadow. The first frames in the opening scene of season six showed Spike taking Buffy's place in a typical opening sequence in a graveyard at night ("Bargaining, Part 1," 6-1). When

Buffy returned from the dead, Spike was the only one she felt she could talk to without reserve, because like her (and unlike her friends) he knew how it felt to be dead. While Buffy sleepwalked through the first several episodes of season six, Spike shadowed her.

> BUFFY: Why are you always around when I'm miserable?
> SPIKE: 'Cause that's when you're alone, I reckon. ("Flooded," 6-4)

This seems literally true; in much of season six, Buffy was alone when she was with Spike. Their dialogue in the season's first half often sounded like soliloquy. In these scenes, it appeared that Buffy was acting out with Spike the conflicts she felt within herself. One side—let's call it Grandiose Buffy—can be heard when Buffy told Spike:

> BUFFY: You're not a man, you're a thing.
> SPIKE: Stop walking away.
> BUFFY: Don't touch me! ("Smashed," 6-9)

Then again, there's a line which didn't make much sense directed to Spike—as he immediately pointed out—but which had a sharp poignancy if one imagines it as Depleted Buffy rebuking Grandiose Buffy for taking that dive in "The Gift":

> BUFFY: Get a grip. Like you're God's gift. ("Wrecked," 6-10)

Buffy's conflicted sense of needing Spike yet being above him was often humorously played up in season six. In "Tabula Rasa" (6-8), when Spike was pressing Buffy to talk about their kiss in the previous episode, she responded by telling him, "I will never kiss you, Spike, never touch you ever, *ever* again." Then, to save him from an attack, she grabbed Spike, threw him to the ground, and fell on top of him. After fighting to defend Spike, Buffy commented to herself, "If I would just stop saving his life it would simple things up so much."

Clearly she felt she needed him in some way, even though she despised herself for having this need. When she first kissed Spike, she acknowledged that it wasn't a "real" relationship for her, but that Spike somehow offered her a way to feel her own frozen feelings. As she said in "Wrecked," she was "using" him. This word seems especially apt because it appears that she was not "using" him in the sense of taking pleasure in her power over him. Though he offered himself to her at one point as "a willing slave" ("Once More, With Feeling," 6-7), Buffy seemed put off, not intrigued, by that scenario. Instead she was "using" him out of desperation to feel more whole; in other words, using him narcissistically, to complete her sense of self. It's as though she saw Spike as representing some part of herself she felt she couldn't respect, but needed in order to feel alive.

At certain low points, it was not hard to understand Buffy's disgust for her "inner Spike." In "Dead Things" (6-13), the infamous balcony scene showed Spike at his most vampiric, feeding Buffy's despair and her longing to withdraw from life as they both watched her friends on the dance floor below:

> SPIKE: You see, you try to be with them, but you always end up in the dark, with me. What would they think of you if they found out all the things you've done? If they knew who you really were?

What I love about this admittedly creepy scene is how well it represents the mood state of narcissistic self-absorption. The dance floor where Buffy's friends were bopping around stood for a world of emotional risk and commitment to relationships with other people, to the uncertainties of life on earth. Hating her life and especially hating to be vulnerable, in leaving her friends for the balcony, Buffy was withdrawing to a fantasy world where she was above everyone else: a place of emptiness where nothing could ever change, live, or die. The balcony in the Bronze was a near-parody of the "heaven" Buffy was pining for, a narcissistic retreat from life.

But there was obviously more to Buffy's relationship with Spike, just as there's such a thing as healthy narcissism, also known as self-love. Spike's love for Buffy eventually regained him his soul and confirmed him in his quest to become a man, not a monster. And it wasn't all bad

31

for her either. In season six, while he was still plenty monstrous, Spike was the one who repeatedly stopped Buffy from throwing her life away. When Buffy was on the verge of spontaneous human combustion (brought on by singing out her intense feelings about being reshuffled into her mortal coil), neither her friends, nor her sister, nor her Watcher found the words she needed to hear; but Spike did:

> Life's not a song
> Life isn't bliss
> Life is just this:
> It's living.

> You'll get along.
> The pain that you feel
> You only can heal
> By living. ("Once More, With Feeling," 6-7)

In this bit of song, Spike invoked a larger, richer sense of Buffy as neither all-powerful nor unbearably weak, but somewhere in the human middle. He sang to a Buffy who could be hurt, but who could also heal. At a time when Buffy couldn't see herself whole, Spike could, and in this he represented her positive shadow, the voice of her own disowned wisdom.

Buffy's affair with Spike began when she kissed him a few minutes after he called her back toward life with these words. Clearly, their sexual relationship represented more than an unhealthy self-absorption. It was a complex relationship, refreshingly ambiguous for television, in which Spike took on the role of Buffy's shadow, sometimes in negative ways, sometimes positively helping her to integrate more of herself into her conscious sense of who she was.

If Buffy's fights in general were metaphors for her struggles with her personal demons, Spike stood in for some of her ugliest demons as well as for certain disowned strengths and, oddly enough, her humanness.[5]

---

[5] Some of the oddness comes from the wide range of interpretations given to Spike in season six by the show's various writers. Some of his behavior was plainly sociopathic, while in other cases he showed a genuine devotion and a capacity for truth which were nothing if not soulful.

The metaphor here was about Buffy desiring to know herself more deeply. In sex with Spike, Buffy let herself feel what she *did* feel, but believed she should not feel. Since these were her own feelings, dark yet necessary parts of her humanity, there was an unconscious wisdom in her bad behavior.

Eventually, of course, Buffy needed to end the affair, which seriously clashed with her persona, her ideals. But unlike Spike, who always had a keen nose for self-deception, Buffy was often wrong about herself, and I think she was off-base when she told Spike that using him was "killing" her ("As You Were," 6-15). It's too bad, I think, that she wasn't ready to enjoy loving this greedy, selfish side of herself just a bit more— but then, sooner or later Buffy had to wake up from the mutual enchantment in which Spike seemed to speak to her from the depths of her own soul. She needed to grasp that Spike wasn't truly a part of her; he was a vampire, and she was the Slayer. This moment was symbolized by the return of Buffy's straitlaced ex-lover Riley, the military guy. In "As You Were," Riley shot Spike's subterranean love-nest to tatters, prompting Buffy to finally break up with Spike.

But before she did, Buffy spent some time getting to know her underground self a bit better. She discovered she could survive knowing she wasn't always heroic, and didn't always win. When high-minded heroism said her life was a gift to give away, something shadowy and greedy and necessary in Buffy fought back and insisted on feeling, and this low-minded protest helped bring her back to life from the dreamy, deathly isolation of her narcissistic defenses.

CAROL POOLE, MA, is a psychotherapist practicing in Seattle. A graduate of Pacifica Graduate Institute in Carpinteria, CA, she is fascinated by the way pop culture retells ancient myths and occasionally even comes up with new ones such as *Buffy*.

REFERENCES

American Psychiatric Association. *Diagnostic and Statistical Manual of Mental Disorders (4th Ed., Text Revision)*. Washington, D.C.: American Psychiatric Association, 1994/2000.

Freud, Sigmund. "On Narcissism: An Introduction." In Morrison, Andrew P., M.D., Ed. *Essential Papers on Narcissism*. New York: New York University Press, 1986.

Jung, Carl. *The Essential Jung: Selected Writings*. Princeton, NJ: University of Princeton Press, 1983.

Kernberg, Otto F. *Borderline Conditions and Pathological Narcissism*. New York: Jason Aronson, 1975.

McWilliams, Nancy. *Psychoanalytic Diagnosis*. New York: The Guilford Press, 1994.

Schwartz-Salant, Nathan. *Narcissism and Character Transformation: The Psychology of Narcissistic Character Disorders*. Toronto: Inner City Books, 1982.

Symington, Neville. *Narcissism: A New Theory*. London: Karnac Books, 1993.

Flamson takes a free-wheeling approach to freedom of will in the Whedonverse, suggesting that our belief that we have free will, even when we in fact don't, is part of what defines us as human and gives us our power to face adversity. He takes on the prophesies in Buffy *and* Angel *that entice characters to make the very choices that ultimately bring those prophesies to fruition, addresses Mal's predictability and freedom-fighting in* Firefly, *and reframes the climactic question raised between Jasmine and Angel in* Angel *season four: "Is free will more valuable than a world free of strife and suffering?" We readers, of course, are free to determine our own views on these matters. Or are we?*

FREE WILL IN A DETERMINISTIC WHEDONVERSE

THOMAS FLAMSON

Take my love, take my land
Take me where I cannot stand
I don't care, I'm still free
You can't take the sky from me
— Theme from *Firefly*

The works of Joss Whedon have addressed a number of the timeless questions raised by art and literature. Are women truly "the weaker sex"? Do past evil acts make one irredeemably evil? Can there be any realm more cruel and capricious than that of Fox Network Programming? (For those new to Whedon's career, the answer to all of those questions is "no.")

Another fundamental question that has been addressed by *Buffy the Vampire Slayer*, *Angel*, and *Firefly* is that of freedom. Or rather, two distinct but related questions: Can we ever be said to be truly free? and, Do people need to be free? in regard to the latter question, the answer has been an emphatic and unwavering yes. But in regard to the former, the answer has been much more equivocal. Despite the seeming contradiction of this state of affairs—how can freedom be worth fighting for if it may not even be available?—we will see that there is, in fact, no necessary contradiction.

The Feeling of Free Will

An inescapable conclusion of human life is that, for much of the time, we are the authors of our own destiny. Every day people experience freely choosing what to do next—whether to cross the street, eat dessert, or buy a house. Some choices may feel less free than others—ask anyone in the midst of quitting smoking—but the experience of willing our actions, even those we may later regret, is a hallmark of human life. And yet, the advances of science have continuously demonstrated that ours is a material world, and most everything in it follows deterministic laws of predictable outcomes, including our own behavior. To many, the claim that our behavior is determined by prior causal forces in just the same manner as the movement of planets or the behavior of insects is an alarming, if not frightening, prospect. To counter this, it is commonly suggested that humans are in possession of a special, acausal, and indeterministic force, known as free will, which exempts us from the seeming nihilism of a deterministic universe. For the religiously inclined, this is commonly cast as the human soul, given by our creator in distinction to all the beasts of the field. For those of a more atheistic bent, who still wish to see human existence as possessing some unique quality that makes us special kinds of volitional agents, the apparently indeterministic quantum processes underlying subatomic particles are seen as a possible means of getting free will back into the admittedly physical brain and body. Both of these positions are commonly supported with recourse to the apparently empirical argument that we *must* have free will, as we experience freely choosing our behavior all of the time.[1] However, recent psychological research has shown this feeling to be largely an illusion: the moment we think we make a decision, it has in

---

[1] I am, of course, vastly oversimplifying these arguments for expediency's sake. For an in-depth discussion of the problems with the indeterminist position, I refer the reader to Daniel Dennett's *Freedom Evolves*, where they are addressed with much more care and respect than I would provide anyway.

fact already been made.

In a series of ground-breaking experiments, Benjamin Libet and colleagues demonstrated that this cornerstone of human existence is, in fact, illusory: people only consciously experience choosing to do something after the neurological processes of doing so have already begun. Participants were asked to make the proverbial minimal conscious effort—lifting a finger—while monitoring a fast-moving clock, and to report the time at which they chose to do so. These participants were also outfitted with electrodes on their scalps and fingers, to objectively measure the brain and muscle activity. They found that the participants reported choosing to move their finger 500 milliseconds *after* the relevant brain activity began increasing. While half of a second[2] may not seem like very much time, this does show that the conscious decision is not the real source of action, but rather a report of a choice that has already been made. This means that our conscious experience of free will is not, in fact, as free as it appears.

It has also been shown that people cannot tell when their decisions are made for them, if they are not conscious of the external source of their decisions. In experiments by Ammon and Gandevia, participants were again asked to choose when to lift a finger, and also to choose which hand to use. By targeting either the right or the left side of the brain with magnetic stimulation, the researchers were able to induce the participants to choose their non-dominant hand eighty percent of the time, whereas unmanipulated participants chose their dominant hand sixty percent of the time. Despite this manipulation, the participants all reported having consciously chosen which hand to use. Similar results had been obtained previously in Delgado's slightly less controlled and more invasive experiments with a brain surgery patient, electrically stimulating portions of the exposed motor cortex during surgery to produce movement that, behaviorally, appeared normal (unlike the jerky movements produced by electrically stimulating muscles). When asked why he had made these movements, the patient reported consciously

---

[2] Subsequent experiments by critics and supporters have shown that the exact amount of time between the initial brain activity and the conscious experience of a choice varies, but all have maintained the fundamental finding that we only experience choosing after the choice has been made.

willing to do so, claiming he was trying to look under the bed or discover the source of a noise.

Beyond demonstrating the disconnect between the conscious experience of freely willing an action and the actual neurological activity underlying it, psychologists have also demonstrated that participants can be led to experience consciously willing an action that they are not, in fact, impacting at all. Matute found that participants asked to determine the level of contingency between an aversive noise and their typing numbers on a keyboard reported high levels of control over the outcome, despite the fact that the termination of the noise was entirely determined by the activities of another participant. Because they had no other source to which they could attribute control, they leapt to the conclusion that they must be the ones determining the outcome.

Further, research has shown that participants will report some volitional control for events with which they know for a fact they had nothing to do. Wegner, Sparrow, and Winerman had participants sit in front of a mirror while wearing a robe, with a research assistant placing his or her hands through the arms of the robe. A series of tape-recorded instructions (e.g., clap your hands, wave them back and forth) directed the assistant's movements. Afterward, participants were asked to rate how much they felt they had consciously controlled the activity. When the participants themselves did not hear the instructions, they provided very low responses (roughly one and a half on a seven-point scale). When they did hear the instructions, however, they reported mid-level responses (about three on the scale). While not claiming full authorship of the activity, it is remarkable that awareness of what the ensuing action was to be doubled the sense of volitional control for activities that every subject knew perfectly well they were not controlling. This suggests that our feeling of free will derives in part from the presence of cues to authorship, such as prior knowledge of the ensuing action and visual evidence that the action is being performed by our bodies. In this experiment, the participants who heard the recorded instructions and saw what looked like their own hands making the movements apparently received sufficient cues to experience partial authorship, despite being consciously aware that this was not the case.

Beyond the immediate illusion of freely choosing a given action, the entire industry of modern social science is largely predicated on the possibility of finding the underlying causal processes that lead people to make the choices they do, be they individual life history factors, cultural or social pressures, or genetic determinants. Most of the arguments in psychology, sociology, anthropology, and behavioral genetics today are not about whether external factors predictably determine behavior, but about which factors are the most important. It is the very nature of scientific investigations to posit that a given effect has some prior cause, which can be discovered through systematic elimination of candidate causes (Popper). In the case of human behavior, these causes may range from genetic predispositions or brain trauma to traumatic childhoods or an oppressively patriarchal culture, but they are nearly always "external," in the sense of being outside of the agent's control at the time the choice was made.

The Problem with Prophecies

In essence, then, it seems to be the case that humans are rather easily led to believe they have freely made choices which were actually the inevitable effects of prior causes. This is also true of the humans (and close facsimiles thereof) in the works of Joss Whedon. While the immediate evidence for illusory will described in these experiments is rarely seen, the deterministic nature of apparently free choices is commonly illustrated through the metaphor of prophecies. Indeed, it is nearly a truism of the Whedonverse that the attempt to avoid the consequences of a prophecy is precisely what causes its fulfillment. In season one of *Buffy*, Buffy attempted to circumvent a prophecy that the Master (an old and powerful vampire) would escape and kill her. Although she had resigned herself to dying, she hoped to prevent the Master's escape by confronting him directly in his prison in the subterranean ruins of a church ("Prophecy Girl," 1-12). It soon turned out, however, that killing[3] Buffy was the very thing that provided the Master with sufficient power to free himself; had she never gone to the Master's lair, he would not have been able to escape.

---

[3] It also turned out, of course, that killing her did not mean she would remain dead (Xander successfully revived her shortly after the Master drowned her). Prophecies often resemble legal documents in their adherence to the letter, rather than the spirit, of the content.

Similarly, in *Angel*, the Nyazian Scrolls prophesized the "Tro-Clon," a confluence of events that spread across several seasons, and foretold either the "purification" or the "ruination" of humanity, or possibly both ("Offspring," 3-7). Confronted with this prophecy, various characters attempted to prevent its outcome, and each attempt was essential to its actual fulfillment. First (in the chronology of the world, not that of the television episodes), the time-traveling demon Sahjhan learned that the Nyazian Scrolls foretold that the "one sired by the vampire with a soul" would be the one to kill him ("Forgiving," 3-17). In order to prevent this outcome, he froze Daniel Holtz, Angelus's nineteenth-century nemesis, and released him in the twenty-first century, where he manipulated him into attempting to kill Angel and Darla before Angel's son Connor could be born ("Quickening," 3-8). As Holtz did not do so, Sahjhan also changed the prophecy to warn that "the father will kill the son" ("Forgiving," 3-17), which in turn led Wesley to assist Holtz in kidnapping the infant Connor, whom Holtz then took to Quor-Toth, a hell dimension where time passed more quickly than in the normal world ("Sleep Tight," 3-16). Connor returned a few weeks later, having passed seventeen years in a hell dimension acquiring the skills necessary to eventually kill Sahjhan ("A New World," 3-20).

But that was not all. Another aspect of the Tro-Clon was that Connor had to father the "Power That Was" Jasmine with Angel's love interest Cordelia ("Apocalypse Nowish," 4-7), and the subsequent events (discussed in greater detail below) led to such despair that Angel *did* have to kill him, in a way—he slit Connor's throat in order to complete a spell performed by the evil law firm Wolfram & Hart that rewrote reality and placed Connor in a normal family, with memories of a normal childhood ("Home," 4-22). In the following season, Connor did return, now unknown to all but Angel, and did in fact kill Sahjhan in combat ("Origin," 5-18).

Again, the actions of each of the agents in this convoluted story, each attempting to avoid a prophesied outcome, led to that very outcome. Had Sahjhan not meddled with the original prophecy, or preserved Holtz to set loose upon Angel when Darla was pregnant, it is possible Wesley never would have helped Holtz kidnap Connor in order to avoid Angel's killing of him. Had that not occurred, Connor might not have acquired the skills needed to defeat Sahjhan, nor would he have lost the normal childhood that led to the despondency that, in turn, led to Angel's having to "kill" him in order to give him a new life. We see that, in the world of *Angel* and *Buffy*, it is not merely the case that decisions which were thought to be free had actually been predetermined, but that the predestination was only possible because of attempts to escape it. While these prophecies are always taken at face value, dictating in advance what events will transpire, they actually serve as triggers, leading the characters they speak of to pursue a predictable line of action, in turn creating the conditions that will actually fulfill the prophecy.

The essence of determinism is this predictability. Decisions are not made *ex nihilo*, but are the predictable outcomes of a mechanistic process, a long, traceable line of causes and effects. In the case of complicated agents like human beings, that is a very complex process, combining the personality or temperament of the actor, the past events he or she has encountered, and the immediate circumstances surrounding the moment of decision, but it remains strictly predictable, and anyone with access to enough information can calculate what will happen when person X encounters situation Y at time Z. In the mystical world of *Buffy* and *Angel*, gods and demons do have access to this information, and frequently employ it to determine the actions of our heroes. But we also see this determinism in the decidedly less mystical world of *Firefly*. While there is no prophecy detailing the future of Malcolm Reynolds, the captain of the smugglers' ship *Serenity*, other characters are frequently shown to be able to manipulate his actions by presenting him with information they know will lead to his doing what they desire. In "The Message" (1-12), for example, Mal and first mate Zoe's old war buddy Tracey manipulated them into assisting in his plan to escape the corrupt Alliance officer he was cheating out of the artificial organs he was hired to transport inside his body.[4] Tracey took a drug to feign death and had himself mailed to the *Serenity* crew along with a recorded message asking them to get his body safely back to his home planet, quoting the beginning of a meaningful maxim from their days in the war: "When you can't run anymore, you crawl, and when you can't crawl, you find

---

[4] I said "less mystical," not "less weird."

41

someone to carry you." Tracey was relying on their sense of obligation to comrades-in-arms to get him out of a problem he created for himself, and when things later went south, the reanimated Tracey told Mal that he picked him and Zoe because they were sentimental "saps," and therefore predictable.

Mal, in turn, avoided the worst outcomes of these "predestinations" by himself predicting what other people would do. He rightly predicted that local crime boss Patience would attempt to kill him while buying scavenged Alliance goods from him, and feigned trust while sending out his tracker and muscle Jayne to neutralize Patience's snipers ("Serenity"). In "Trash," he again predicted a double-cross, in this case expecting Saffron—a con woman by whom he had already been tricked once before—to attempt to steal the Lassiter, a valuable antique laser gun she had conspired with Mal to steal from its rightful owner. He sent another crew member, Inara, to await Saffron at the drop point and retrieve the Lassiter after Saffron's inevitable betrayal. Finally, in *Serenity* (the film, not the episode), Mal recognizes that Inara is being forced to call him into a trap by the fact that they do not fight during their conversation, which would have been the normally predictable course. Prepared for the Alliance to know his location, he removes the signaling beacon they would use to track and destroy his ship, throwing it to the Alliance operative just as that threat is made.

The ability of Mal and others to counter these predictions in *Firefly*, as opposed to the oedipal fulfillment of prophecies in *Buffy* and *Angel*, derives from the difference in their sources. Because the prophecies come from deities, with nigh-infinite access to information, they are able to foresee the countermeasures the characters will attempt, and incorporate them into the plan. When it is other humans making predictions, with our significantly more limited access to relevant information, every contingency is not planned for, and the characters are better able to grapple with the deterministic forces that confront them. To put it more provocatively, in the worlds of Joss Whedon, the greatest threats to freedom are the gods.

The Compatibility of Free Will and Determinism

This brings us to the core of the free will and determinism dilemma. The characters in Whedon's worlds are not free in the strict sense of being completely undetermined. In fact, they are eminently determined, making choices that can be predicted in advance with knowledge of their personality and the surrounding circumstances when they make that choice. However, this determinism cuts both ways, and means that the characters are also capable of predicting their opponents' behavior, and this capacity presents new information which changes those circumstances. In each of the cases where Mal avoided the trap set for him by an opponent who predicted his deterministic behavior, he did not in fact change that behavior; he merely added additional behaviors, making predictions in response to the fact of his opponent's predictions. Of course, his opponents may have predicted that prediction, and adopted their own countermeasures, leading to an infinite regress of second-guessing. At some point, however, this would become too cognitively taxing for any human being to engage in, and someone would eventually fail to predict the still causally determined choice of the other.

The set of all relevant prior conditions, and of all relevant present information, is too large for the future results to be calculated with certainty. And if our futures cannot be calculated in advance, then we are "free" in the very important sense of being able to behave in an unexpected manner. This is why the claim that our behavior is determined, in the sense of being the result of prior conditions interacting with present ones, need not lead to the nihilistic conclusion that we are slaves of predestination. In essence, we do not have the kind of free will we like to think we do—that the decision to act begins spontaneously when we hear ourselves thinking it, and has no prior cause that makes it predictable. But we do have the kind of freedom we like to attribute to other people—a fundamental responsibility for one's decisions.

This is because there is a distinction between the *fact* of free will, and the *feeling* of free will. We have an illusory experience of free will that makes us think we are not "meat puppets," our strings being pulled by a long line of materialistic, predictable, and therefore determined processes. This is, in an important sense, false, as what determinism really means is simply that there is a traceable chain of causes and effects underlying our behavior, and we do not simply do things out of the blue. To say that the conscious experience of free will is an illusion is not to say that we do not have free will, but merely that it does not work the way we feel like it does. The *fact* of free will is distinct from the *feeling*— and we are the ones making our decisions, even if they do not happen the way we feel like they do.

For while the experience of making choices through one's own free will may itself be illusory, it remains the case that, most of the time, we are the source of our behavior. Surely, it is the outcome of a number of forces, both internal and external, that have coalesced into our individual life histories, opinions, beliefs, and desires, but these remain ours; there is not another agent making those choices for us. Most of the time, the meat inside the puppet is the thing pulling the strings.

Using the Illusion

The illusory experience of consciously willed choices serves as a kind of cognitive shorthand, saving the conscious representational machinery the trouble of experiencing much of the "math" of decision-making, and instead presenting us with the "sum," the end-result decision that has motivated our actions, or lack thereof. It appears that this experience of being free to make one's own choices is not merely a cognitive simplification, but may be an important aspect of psychological health, suggesting that the normal functioning of human minds depends on that illusion. Glass, Singer, and Friedman demonstrated that merely believing one has control over the environment may enhance performance in stressful environments. Two groups of subjects were asked to complete a series of complex cognitive tasks while being subjected to random, loud bursts of noise. One group was given a button, which they were told could be used to stop the noises at any time, although the experimenter would prefer it if they did not. The other group was given no such option. Although no one in the button condition ever actually used it to stop the distracting noise, they showed a significantly higher performance on the tasks than their peers in the no-button condition, showing greater tolerance for frustration (in attempting to solve insoluble puzzles), and missing two-thirds fewer errors in a proofreading task. Further, they reported the noise to be less aversive, and expressed greater feelings of control than those in the no-button condition. Similarly, Taylor, Lichtman, and Wood have found that a belief in greater personal control than the facts technically suggest may improve responses to threatening information. Among breast cancer patients, believing one (or one's physician) could exert some control over the cancer was strongly associated with overall positive adjustment.

Further, the will to exert control over one's circumstances also seems to motivate greater achievement. In a series of experiments, Burger demonstrated that a strong "desire for control" (such as preferring to make one's own decisions, avoiding the loss of control, and taking on positions of leadership) is tied to a number of factors essential in achieving success. For example, despite showing no significant difference in *performance* in an anagram task, participants high in desire for control asked to be given more difficult subsequent tasks than those reporting a low desire. They also expressed greater estimations of their ability to complete simple but cognitively taxing tasks, such as connecting randomized numbers sequentially, yet made more accurate estimations of how successful they would be. In a timed proofreading task, high desire for control participants made a greater effort than lows, when the task was made more complicated by adding additional requirements (to note the number of appearances of the word "the" and of proper nouns). In all of these studies, it is worth noting that the desire for control was not related to a greater *ability* to perform the tasks, but rather a greater *motivation* to achieve.

These studies[5] all point to the conclusion that the factual accuracy of one's conscious experience of freely willing action and controlling one's destiny is not the only criterion for evaluating the utility of that experience. It seems that, in many kinds of situations, we may benefit from overestimating the extent to which we can consciously control the events that happen to us, and the desire to maintain that overestimation may be essential in driving the human race to produce the actual accomplishments we have. Even if we are not as free as we like to think we are, there may well be a very good reason for thinking so. As Gunn said after

---

[5] And many, many others—the study of "positive illusions" and "the illusion of control" has become quite a growth industry in social and clinical psychology over the last forty years.

being told about the external manipulation of everyone's choices to bring about the Tro-Clon:

> GUNN: The final score can't be rigged. I don't care how many players you grease; that final shot always comes up a question mark. But here's the thing: you never know when you take it. Could be when you're duking it out with the legion of doom, or when you're just crossing the street deciding where to have brunch. So you just treat it all like it was up to you—the world in the balance, 'cuz you never know when it is. (*Angel*, "Inside Out," 4-17)

Fighting for Freedom

It is not determinism that is the enemy of free will, but rather the coercive manipulation of determinism by other agents. By using some form of coercion—either a direct physical threat or a forceful modification of an agent's internal state—a coercive agent can remove another's free will by reducing the set of beliefs and desires available to the coerced agent to those which will deterministically produce the desired behavior. The latter form (commonly known as "brainwashing") has been a recurring topic in Whedon's work, arising most literally in cases such as the device implanted in the vampire Spike by the Initiative, a secret military organization, which prevented him from attacking humans, or in the Alliance's manipulation of River's brain to create a conditioned psychic warrior in *Firefly*. But much broader (and slightly less literal) brainwashing in order to produce social order has figured prominently in the works of Whedon, and is unequivocally cast as the wrong path.

Firefly, centering around the efforts of a group of distinct individuals all looking to escape the omnipresent arm of the galactic state known as the Alliance, helmed by two veterans of the losing side in the war to avoid governance by that Alliance, really could not be more about freedom if Whedon had flashed the words "Freedom is Neato!" on the screen every tenth frame. The incorrectness of removing freedom for the sake of order was a frequent theme in nearly every episode of the series, but becomes most pronounced in the film that followed its too-brief run, *Serenity*.

Rather than show the authoritarians—in the form of the Alliance itself or of the petty despots it lets run the outer planets—to be bumbling, selfish, or downright cruel, as in the series, in the film the motivations of the Alliance are cast more complexly as well-intentioned attempts to force the world to be a better place, which inevitably makes it incredibly worse.

For it turns out that the Reavers, a group of horrendously violent men who have lost all trace of humanity and whose attacks on ships and on the outer planets are so violent and devastating as to make them literally unbelievable to the civilized society of the Alliance's core planets, are actually the remnants of Miranda, a test-planet for the Alliance's social engineering. There, the Alliance mixed a chemical known as "the Pax" into the ventilation systems, intending for it to reduce aggression and make the planet free of violence and strife. That is, they attempted to circumvent people's free will by directly attacking the neurological substrates of conflict. The result was truly better than they hoped—people not only stopped fighting with each other, but stopped fighting for life itself. Ninety-nine and nine-tenths percent of the populace simply gave up, lying down and slowly starving to death, without any drive to accomplish even the basic requirements of life. And, as with most psycho-pharmaceuticals, a small portion of the subjects had an (even more) adverse reaction to their treatment, which hyperactivated their anger centers and turned them into the Reavers.

As Whedon himself says, the "film is really about the right to be wrong" (Whedon, *Serenity*). While the intentions of the Alliance to bring about better living through involuntary chemistry were aimed at doing good, their failure to account for the importance of free will not only massacred an entire planet, but unleashed a much more dangerous force upon the galaxy than the occasional bar brawl or robbery they were attempting to suppress. With *Serenity*, Whedon is not trying to say that those or other crimes are themselves good things, but that individuals need to be able to choose for themselves whether to engage in them.

The narrative arc of season four of *Angel* is Whedon's most direct treatment of the value of free will, threatened by the aforementioned Jasmine. Perhaps not coincidentally, he also considers it the best season (Whedon, "Season Four Overview"). One of the Powers That Be (deity-like beings who maintain a generally hands-off approach to the human realm), she decided to incarnate herself on Earth and bring about world peace by robbing everyone of their free will and uniting them in unconditional devotion to her. Although she initially enslaved Angel and his friends, as well, they broke free of her spell by coming into contact with her blood, and set about finding a way to end her domination of Earth. This season directly addressed the value of free will by casting the question in the most challenging terms—is free will more valuable than a world free of strife and suffering? The bliss experienced by Jasmine's followers contrasted sharply with the pain experienced by the members of Angel Investigations as they contemplated the loss of that happiness and, more importantly, of the confidence that everything would work out for the best because Jasmine said so ("Sacrifice," 4-20). After Angel managed to break Jasmine's spell, Los Angeles erupted into violence, as everyone lashed out in fear and confusion, having lost their sense of peace and happiness. They confronted each other, Jasmine berating Angel for having ended world peace by ending her control, directly addressing the season's moral—and the conclusion of this essay—in the following exchange:

JASMINE: I offered paradise; you chose this.
ANGEL: Because I could. Because that's what you took away
     from us: choice.
JASMINE: And look what free will has gotten you.
ANGEL: Hey, I didn't say we're smart. I said it's our right. It's
     what makes us human. ("Peace Out," 4-21)

THOMAS FLAMSON is a doctoral candidate in anthropology at the University of California, Los Angeles. His research interests include intentionality, theory of mind, and the role of emotions in risky decision-making. His current research focuses on the evolutionary origins of humor and aesthetic preferences, and their role in developing social relationships. Besides being a long-time fan of Joss Whedon's work, he was once served Cheetos by Seth Green ("Oz" from *Buffy* and *Angel*) at a party.

REFERENCES

K. Ammon and S. C. Gandevia, "Transcranial Magnetic Stimulation Can Influence the Selection of Motor Programmes," *Journal of Neurology, Neurosurgery & Psychiatry* 53.8 (1990): 705-707.

Jerry M. Burger, "Desire for Control and Achievement-Related Behaviors," *Journal of Personality and Social Psychology* 48.6 (1985): 1520-33.

Delgado, Jose M. *Physical Control of the Mind: Toward a Psychocivilized Society.* Harper Colophon Books, 1969.

Dennett, Daniel Clement. *Freedom Evolves.* London: Allen Lane, 2003.

David C. Glass, Jerome E. Singer, and Lucy N. Friedman, "Psychic Cost of Adaptation to an Environmental Stressor," *Journal of Personality and Social Psychology* 12.3 (1969): 200-210.

B. Libet, E. W. Wright, and C. A. Gleason, "Readiness-Potentials Preceding Unrestricted 'Spontaneous' Vs. Pre-Planned Voluntary Acts," *Electroencephalography & Clinical Neurophysiology* 54.3 (1982): 322-335.

Benjamin Libet, "Unconscious Cerebral Initiative and the Role of Conscious Will in Voluntary Action," *Behavioral and Brain Sciences* 8.4 (1985): 529-566.

Helena Matute, "Learned Helplessness and Superstitious Behavior as Opposite Effects of Uncontrollable Reinforcement in Humans," *Learning and Motivation* 25.2 (1994): 216-232.

Popper, Karl R. *The Logic of Scientific Discovery.* New York: Basic Books, 1959.

Shelley E.Taylor, Rosemary R. Lichtman, and Joanne V. Wood, "Attributions, Beliefs About Control, and Adjustment to Breast Cancer," *Journal of Personality and Social Psychology* 46.3 (1984): 489-502.

Daniel M. Wegner, Betsy Sparrow, and Lea Winerman, "Vicarious Agency: Experiencing Control over the Movements of Others," *Journal of Personality and Social Psychology* 86.6 (2004): 838-848.

Whedon, Joss. Commentary on *Serenity.* Dir. Joss Whedon. Universal Pictures, 2005.

Whedon, Joss. Commentary on "Season Four Overview." *Angel: The Complete Fourth Season*, Special Features. 20th Century Fox, 2004.

In the dystopian Firefly *'verse, the government itself is "antisocial." Were it possible for the "character traits" identifiable as the Alliance to coalesce within the body of a single individual, they would surely produce a pathological, even psychopathic character. In such a 'verse, how do we conceptualize "antisocial" behavior by citizens like Mal and his crew? Is rebellion against the status quo actually a healthy act? And if it is, how do we distinguish between one person's pro-social adaptation to a brutal world and another's genuinely delinquent behavior? Eaton and Krueger put Mal and Jayne into analysis and, using both conventional diagnostic methods and suggested improvements to the current system, offer intriguing answers to these questions.*

THE ADAPTIVE, THE MALADAPTIVE, AND THE MAL-ADAPTIVE

Personality Traits in Firefly

NICHOLAS R. EATON AND ROBERT F. KRUEGER

Although *Firefly* lasted only one season, it was filled with so much information that viewers could get quite an education. Those interested in learning interplanetary diplomacy, the art of seduction, or how to curse in Mandarin were not disappointed, and the breadth and detail of the *Firefly* universe allowed audience members with widely varying tastes to find something to their liking. The character development of the series was outstanding (especially given its brief run on television), and each of the *dramatis personae* became increasingly fleshed out as the episodes progressed. While several loose ends remained after its cancellation (e.g., what was Shepherd Book's past? Would Mal and Inara ever express their mutual affection? What possessed Wash to grow that horrible moustache?), most characters' personalities were explored to such an extent that we can describe their traits with relative clarity.

This is particularly true of Mal and Jayne. And although Mal and Jayne often showed similar traits—mostly when it came to criminal behaviors—close inspection of their personalities can allow us to differentiate them in psychologically meaningful ways and to make hypotheses about disorders they may have.

Personality Traits: The Good, the Bad, and the Ugly

Everyone has a personality—even people who seem not to because they are so bland (e.g., those who are not outgoing and friendly may be high in the "introversion" trait, while those who do not enjoy many activities may be considered low in "sensation seeking" or high in "schizoid" or "depressive" traits). Many of our personality traits are considered adaptive (that is, beneficial) to our survival. Individuals who are high on traits of conscientiousness are generally responsible, competent, disciplined, and concerned with duty—in short, the type of person you want as your engineer on long trips to the outer planets. Individuals who are high on agreeableness typically are pleasant to be around, giving, modest, and not manipulative—the way you probably want your shepherd to be.

This focus on *positive* personality traits may make it seem that personality traits are always adaptive, but this is not actually the case. Just as there are traits that may make someone's personality attractive and pleasant, so too are there traits that many people find repellant and abrasive. For example, individuals who show high levels of the trait hostility are probably less likely to be desirable as friends (unless you find yourself frequently in need of back-up in bar brawls). These maladaptive traits are often referred to as being "pathological."

Defining what makes a particular trait pathological is no small task due to a variety of factors that come into play. The most common conceptualization of pathological personality is that proposed by the *Diagnostic and Statistical Manual of Mental Disorders Fourth Edition, Text Revision (DSM-IV)*, a sort of symptom bible to which psychologists and psychiatrists refer when making diagnoses. The *DSM-IV* lists ten official sets of pathological personality features; these sets of features are referred to as "personality disorders." Although the personality disorders are differentiated by exactly which traits and behaviors are included in each (e.g., "persistently bears grudges"), they all share a set of common requirements necessary for them to be diagnosable, and these requirements provide a good start at defining exactly what is pathological personality.

Chiefly, the *DSM-IV* requires "an enduring pattern of inner experience and behavior that deviates markedly from the expectations of the individual's culture." This pattern must permeate many aspects of the person's life as well as numerous social situations. In addition, it must have begun when the individual was an adolescent or young adult and not changed over time. Finally, a pattern of personality traits is considered pathological when it leads to "significant distress or impairment in social, occupational, or other important areas of functioning" (689). For our purposes, we will consider this to be a reasonable definition of what makes a personality trait, or a pattern of personality traits, pathological.

Personality Traits: Constant as the Northern Star?

Although the definition above requires that pathological personality traits be rigid, inflexible, and stable over time, we have to ask ourselves if this has a basis in reality. Many of us like to view ourselves as a particular type of person across all situations (e.g., Wash might think "I'm always a funny guy"), but the fact of the matter is that we probably are not. Does your level of outgoingness change between when you are full of energy and when you are exhausted at the end of a day? Do you show the same degree of interpersonal friendliness and warmth traits when talking with your best friend as you do when arguing with someone you did not like in the first place? Of course not. Even Wash is serious now and then. To varying degrees, the expression of personality traits is situationally variable—that is, traits differ from one situation to the next. Although someone may *tend* to be a certain way in general, it is likely that he or she changes when extreme situational factors are present.

The characters of Zoe and River presented excellent illustrations of the principles of situationally variable and stable personality traits, respectively. During flashbacks of the war with the Alliance, Zoe was often portrayed as a cold warrior woman (e.g., in "The Message," she stealthily positioned herself behind an enemy soldier and remorselessly slit his throat); in her scenes with Wash, she typically showed a warm and caring side. Clearly, a warm and caring personality would not have served her well during the war, nor would the personality of a cold-hearted fighter be conducive to a good marriage (unless possibly she were married to Jayne). River, on the other hand, frequently showed the trait of behavioral disinhibition (i.e., she did not adequately control certain negative behaviors, such as randomly slicing Jayne with a butcher knife in "Ariel"), and her disinhibited behavior was not relegated to only one situation. In fact, what made it most troubling was that she could lash out at any time. While this led to considerable consternation among the crew (especially when she was brandishing a gun, as in "Objects in Space"), it provided an excellent example of a trait likely to be expressed regardless of the situation.

Mal's Personality as Captain: Maladaptive or Mal-Adaptive?

Another concept that proves problematic for defining pathological personality traits is that of maladaptiveness. As discussed above, personality traits do not occur in a vacuum (with space being the obvious exception), and a trait that might be pathological for one person or in a given setting might be beneficial for another person or in a different setting. Mal's behavior in his role as captain illustrates this point well. Captain Reynolds is a self-assured and arrogant leader who expects everyone to follow his instructions without questioning them; the *DSM-IV* calls this pattern of traits narcissistic personality disorder.

However, are these traits maladaptive? Clearly, as the commander of *Serenity*, it is necessary for Mal to be confident in his decision-making. Similarly, when he barks orders at his crew, it is of the utmost importance that they follow them without argument. For example, in "Out of Gas," Zoe was severely wounded by an explosion, and Wash, her loving husband, was steadfastly planted by her side. Mal ordered Wash to the bridge to help safeguard the other members of the crew, and when Wash refused to leave his injured wife, Mal made it clear this his order was not a request. Although Mal did not come off looking like the nice guy in this scene, the reasons for his behavior were clear: he was expressing an authoritarian trait, which, although interpersonally unpleasant, was ultimately adaptive in maintaining the safety of *Serenity*. For those reasons, Mal's personality seemed to be adaptive in this circumstance. Had an arrogant Mal told Wash to leave Zoe's bedside in a situation in which there were no serious threat to the crew, however, his order likely would have been seen as harsh, unnecessary, and heartless. This would have negatively affected the way his crew viewed him and would probably have represented the display of a pathological personality trait.

Mal and Jayne: The Brains and the Brawn

Almost every episode of *Firefly* depicted Mal and Jayne breaking the law in some way, whether through theft, physical violence, or deceit; in fact, both characters excelled at being outlaws in one way or another. That said, it seems likely that most dedicated viewers would say that Mal and Jayne, while similar, are very different—even with regard to their lawlessness. Two of the primary ways to account for these differences, which overlap well with issues hotly debated by personality theorists and researchers, are 1) the use of "dimensional classification" and 2) the relationship between antisocial personality disorder and psychopathy.

Exploring an Alternate Dimension

Most physical disorders are thought of as "dichotomous" or "categorical"—that is, they are either present or absent. Medical doctors typically diagnose a patient on a "yes-no" basis. For example, a patient either does or does not have a broken leg. With a few notable exceptions such blood pressure, it does not make much intuitive sense (nor is it very comforting to the patient) to receive a diagnosis such as "your leg is at the thirtieth percentile of leg brokenness." The classification of mental disorders, which developed out of the categorical tradition used in physical medicine, also tends to be categorical: a patient is determined to either have schizophrenia or not have it. Unlike physical medicine, however, psychologists and psychiatrists often find that a yes-no diagnosis does not provide enough information about a patient's functioning and disease severity.

In recent years, there has been a push to develop a dimensional model of psychopathology (i.e., mental disorders). The main idea behind dimensional classification is that a patient's psychological problem is evaluated on a sliding scale of severity. Such an approach can be helpful for thinking about at least some physical diseases (e.g., borderline hypertension), and many mental health professionals are now pressing for future editions of the *DSM* to conceptualize some mental disorders dimensionally. One area of psychopathology in particular seems to be leading the charge toward understanding the benefits (and limitations) of dimensional classification: personality disorders.

If we look at Mal and Jayne's criminal behaviors in the context of the current *DSM-IV* personality disorder criteria, it is clear that they both show significant levels of antisocial personality disorder. (Please note: although it is common to refer to someone who does not want to go to a party as "antisocial," psychologists and psychiatrists would describe this as "asocial" behavior, reserving the term "antisocial" for behaviors that are "against society" because they violate the rights of other people.) Table 1 shows how Mal and Jayne perform on the *DSM-IV* diagnostic criteria for antisocial personality disorder; to receive a diagnosis of this disorder, an individual must possess at least three of the main criteria, be at least eighteen years of age, and show evidence of childhood conduct disorder (more about that later).

TABLE 1: A DIAGNOSTIC CHECKLIST OF MAL AND JAYNE'S
ANTISOCIAL PERSONALITY DISORDER SYMPTOMS

A. Diagnostic Criteria	Mal	Jayne
1. Repeated behavior for which one could be arrested	X	X
2. Deceitfulness (e.g., lying, conning others for profit)	X	X
3. Failure to plan ahead or impulsive behavior	X	X
4. Aggressiveness (e.g., physical fights) and irritability	X	X
5. Disregard for the safety of the self or other people	X	X
6. Irresponsibility (e.g., not honoring obligations)		X
7. Lack of remorse, indifferent to stealing from/hurting others		X
B. Age		
The individual is 18 years of age or older	X	X
C. Conduct Disorder		
There is evidence of childhood conduct disorder	?	?

(Adapted from *DSM-IV*. These represent our best judgments about Mal and Jayne's behaviors across all episodes. As we are unable to interview the characters to better determine the appropriateness of each diagnostic criterion, this is a somewhat subjective exercise. Viewers could certainly make well-reasoned arguments about the presence or lack of several of these criteria.)

As we can see from the table, both Mal and Jayne meet more than the necessary three antisocial personality disorder criteria—Mal's behavior justifies meeting five of them, while Jayne, somewhat unsurprisingly, meets all seven.

For the sake of argument, we will assume presently that both Mal and Jayne meet the other *DSM-IV* antisocial personality disorder requirements (i.e., age and childhood conduct disorder) as well. This allows us to conclude that both Mal and Jayne are antisocial. Is this really the best way to understand them, however? Regular viewers of the series would likely note that although objectively Mal and Jayne's behaviors sound similarly antisocial, there is a distinct and meaningful difference in *how* antisocial they are. They were both aggressive, for example, but Jayne seemed much more interested in gratuitous violence, while Mal typically resorted to physical fights only when necessary. Similarly, both Mal and Jayne were deceitful. However, Mal tended to con the Feds into letting him slip by with stolen cargo while Jayne lied to Simon and River, his own crewmates, and turned them in to the police for a reward. It seems that while on the surface these behaviors can be accurately grouped together as "deceitfulness," on a deeper level they differ in severity. They may both be criminals, but which of them would you trust more to borrow your car?

The use of dimensional classification provides more information than simply lumping all individuals into a single category, as we have just done with Mal and Jayne. We can preserve more information about the behaviors of each, as well as how antisocial they are relative to each other, by placing them on a continuum of antisociality. The easiest example of this would be to use the seven *DSM-IV* diagnostic criteria for antisocial personality disorder but, instead of saying that anyone who meets three or more criteria is antisocial as we did above, we would utilize the actual number of criteria met. In this situation, Mal would be at level five of the antisocial continuum (because he meets five of the seven criteria), and Jayne would be at level seven (because he meets all seven). This scheme provides additional information that is lost in a yes-no categorical system, such as 1) both Mal and Jayne show high levels of antisociality, 2) Jayne shows more antisociality than Mal does, and 3) Jayne shows the maximum amount of antisociality possible.

To develop these ideas further, a personality researcher could create a more comprehensive measure of the antisociality dimension. She would likely include a much greater number of potential antisocial behaviors and break up the existing criteria into smaller parts (e.g., aggressiveness could be broken up into aggression toward people and aggression toward animals). This would allow her to cover a broader range of behaviors at a more specific level of analysis. Such an approach would also help prevent a "ceiling effect" (an inability to distinguish between individuals who score high, because the maximum score is too low), which is probably what we saw with Jayne's score of seven out of seven. It is likely that, with the seven-criteria system used above, both Jayne and the bounty hunter Jubal Early ("Objects in Space") would meet all seven criteria, where an antisociality continuum with more criteria would probably discriminate between the two of them.

Another issue with the system above is that if a person endorsed an antisociality criterion such as "I have hit someone when I was angry," it would add one point to his or her total antisociality dimension score. If another person endorsed "I have beaten someone to death when I was angry," he or she would also receive one point of antisociality. It is clear, however, that these two antisocial behaviors are of different severity. Thus, the researcher might also utilize a set of statistics (known as "item response theory") to determine the properties of each criterion, such as how severe each criterion is, and ensure that her system for measuring the antisociality dimension had criteria ranging in severity from very low to very high.

Mal and Jayne: Petty Crooks or "Psychotic"?

Inara referred to Mal, on at least one occasion, as a petty crook, while in the pilot episode, two other characters separately referred to him as "psychotic." Like "antisocial," the word "psychotic" is often used differently by mental health workers and lay individuals. In professional parlance, "psychotic" symptoms refer to those typically seen in disorders like schizophrenia, such as hallucinations or delusions. "Psychopathic" refers to traits and behaviors of certain individuals that are often associated with criminality. Note, however, that psychopaths are not commonly murderers or serial killers, as the word is commonly used, although they can be. While River clearly shows psychotic symptoms at times (in fact, Simon said she had paranoid schizophrenia in "Safe"), the question of psychopathy is herein reserved for Mal and Jayne.

There is a significant degree of overlap between psychopathy and antisocial personality disorder. In fact, the antisocial personality disorder diagnostic criteria were written in hopes of capturing some facets of psychopathy, if not the entire concept. Individuals with either disorder have a propensity for unlawfulness, as well as deceit, manipulation of others, and so on. However, there are important differences. Psychopaths tend to show a greater degree of emotional coldness and detachment from others. They are often superficial and fake in their relationships, presenting a false face that differs across situations—this trait led psychopathy research pioneer Hervey Cleckley to refer to psychopathy as the "mask of sanity." Research has shown that psychopathy and antisocial personality disorder differ in the frequency with which they occur in criminals as well. In studies conducted in prisons, a very large percentage of convicts typically meets criteria for antisocial personality disorder; a much smaller percentage tends to meet criteria for psychopathy. Findings such as these have led many researchers to claim that antisocial personality disorder is largely a disorder of criminals. Psychopathy, on the other hand, may be a separate entity with meaningful real-world implications distinct from those of antisocial personality disorder (e.g., psychopaths might commit crimes that are harder to detect because of their exceptional skill in deceit).

It seems that Mal and Jayne illustrate the difference between antisocial personality disorder and psychopathy to some degree. Mal, as discussed above, meets many of the criteria for antisocial personality disorder (but not all). However, it seems that his antisocial behaviors are closely tied to his criminal line of work. He actively shows empathy for others and interest in causes greater than himself (such as his participation in the war for independence). Mal tends to be calm and collected, but it is clear that he has close emotional bonds with Zoe, Inara, and Kaylee. Further, one could make a reasonable argument that Mal's criminality is the result of the Alliance's victory in the war and ever-tightening grasp over the united worlds. Mal seemed to have wanted to get as far "into the black" as he could to maintain his independence, and as such, had to resort to smuggling (and other antisocial behaviors) to survive. All of these points are underscored by Badger's description of Mal as "a man of honor in a den of thieves" in the pilot episode.

Jayne, on the other hand, not only meets all of the criteria for antisocial personality disorder, he also displays traits characteristic of a psychopathic personality. He seems to lack empathy and compassion, as when he turned in Simon and River in "Ariel" or when he wished to kill the neutralized government spy in "Serenity." Also in "Serenity," he very frankly told Mal that he did not betray him only because the money he was offered to do so was not enough. It would be "an interesting day," Jayne said, if he were ever offered an adequate amount to betray his captain. Jayne treats women as sexual objects, and only offered his help to the women under siege in "Heart of Gold" after he was told that they were professional "whores." He also tried to barter Mal's wife Saffron in exchange for a gun, pleaded to have sex with her, and noted that he never kissed women on the mouth in "Our Mrs. Reynolds." Additionally, Jayne's behavior is almost always wholly self-serving. He did not fight on either side in the war for independence, and he refuses to risk his safety without the promise of sufficient coin. He did not express forgiveness or understanding for River's mental condition, and he stole from the other crewmembers, cheated during card games, and tormented Simon regularly throughout the series. While it seems likely that Mal would have been a responsible (if somewhat reckless) citizen were it not for the rise of the Alliance, can we say the same thing about Jayne? It seems probable that Jayne would have always taken advantage of others (especially women) and used force to get what he wanted, while maintaining an emotional coldness and distance from those around him. For these reasons, it seems that Mal may be more antisocial, while Jayne may lend a psychopathic flavor to the crew of *Serenity*.

What Ever Happened to Baby Jayne?

Let us put our psychopathy discussion aside and once again focus exclusively on antisocial personality disorder. While Mal and Jayne both meet a sufficient number of criteria to receive this diagnosis (i.e., three or more) and both are eighteen or older, they cannot be diagnosed with antisocial personality disorder unless they also show *evidence* of childhood conduct disorder. The behaviors that constitute conduct disorder are divided into four categories: theft and deceitfulness, serious rule violations, destruction of property, and aggression toward people and animals. Each of these groups consists of specific behaviors in which the child may have engaged. To officially meet diagnostic criteria for conduct disorder, three of these specific behaviors must be present within a year span; that said, *DSM-IV* states only that evidence of childhood conduct disorder, not necessarily a diagnosis thereof, needs to be present for true antisocial personality disorder.

What is problematic in the situation of Mal and Jayne's childhoods, and is also commonly a problem when dealing with real-life individuals, is that we know little of their youths. In the case of real-life patients, early memories are not perfectly accurate, and individuals suspected of having a disorder that includes deceptive behavior cannot be expected to be honest and open anyway. Psychologists and psychiatrists who seek to make determinations about childhood conduct disorder often rely on information gleaned outside of the interviewing room. A helpful place to start might be to interview the parents, siblings, teachers, and childhood friends of the individual being assessed in hopes that their responses converge on whether problematic behaviors were present during the individual's youth. Another method is to search school, police, and court records. The benefit of this approach is that these records are not susceptible to memory loss or temptations to gloss over the truth.

Hypotheses made about the presence of childhood conduct disorder based on the content of the *Firefly* episodes can be tenuous at best, as very little explicit information was divulged about Mal's formative years. Mal mentioned to Saffron in "Our Mrs. Reynolds" that he was raised on a ranch by his mother and her workmen. In fact, he seemed to remember this as a pleasant experience and praised the benefits of living and working in such an environment. This may be indicative of a fairly typical childhood, which would fit well with the theory that adult Mal is only antisocial due to situational factors and a need for independence.

While we know little about Mal's childhood, we know nothing about Jayne's upbringing and family. In "The Message" he expressed pleasure upon receiving a hat from his mother, but this tidbit, although touching, is insufficient to weave a reasonable theory about young Jayne. However, our hypothesizing might benefit from the application of a psychological construct called the "externalizing spectrum." This spectrum consists of several "acting out" behaviors and traits that commonly co-occur. The externalizing spectrum is most typically conceptualized as a combination of pathological personality traits (e.g., aggressiveness, impulsivity), antisocial behaviors (e.g., stealing, violence, deceitfulness), alcohol and drug abuse, and, most importantly for our purposes, childhood conduct disorder. Research shows that the externalizing spectrum and its component parts arise from both genetic and environmental influences—that is, nature and nurture.

It is clear that Jayne meets the personality and behavioral aspects of the externalizing spectrum based on his antagonistic, uninhibited style and his theft, assaults, and lies. Jayne's frequent use of inebriating substances, often to the point of profound intoxication (as in "Jaynestown") indicates that he displays this aspect of externalizing behaviors as well. As Jayne's behaviors are so consistent with the externalizing spectrum—in fact, it would be difficult to find an example of something Jayne did that was *not* a form of externalizing—it seems reasonable for us to assume that he likely displayed other aspects of it as well. As childhood conduct disorder is closely related to the actions in which Jayne frequently engages, it is probably justifiable to believe that his childhood was marked by severe conduct problems.

To summarize, both Mal and Jayne's behaviors are criminal. That said, there are psychological distinctions that may prove helpful in understanding both the origins and rationales of each character's actions. While Mal may have shown traits associated with criminality, he seemed to be a man of conscience driven to a criminal lifestyle by difficult circumstances. While his behaviors hinted at the presence of antisocial personality disorder, the decisions he made and the ways in which he acted may simply have been a "Mal-adaptive" means of survival. Jayne, on the other hand, seems to be described better as a serial and career criminal. His reckless disregard for others and extremely callous nature indicate that his personality may be more pathological than Mal's. In fact, Jayne's behaviors might best be described using the concept of psychopathy—

an extreme, largely incorrigible disorder with profound negative consequences for the individuals he unremorsefully harms. Further, he demonstrates a wide range of externalizing spectrum psychopathology, which allows for the hypothesis that he likely was an oppositional, disobedient, and overall difficult child. Thus, his behaviors may represent a lifelong pattern of unlawful and unrepentant behaviors that will follow him from cradle to grave.

A Final Note

Although *Firefly* lasted only for a single season, the obvious care with which Joss Whedon crafted the characters contributed significantly to their humanity and psychological realism. Whether investigating the differences between antisocial personality disorder and psychopathy, or uncovering the possibly adaptive nature of seemingly maladaptive traits, *Firefly* provides excellent fodder for thought and discussion on this topic. Unfortunately, we have only been able to scratch the surface here. For further reading, we recommend Kenny and Kenny's highly readable and entertaining discussion of *normal* personality traits in "The Personalities of *The Simpsons*" chapter of *The Psychology of The Simpsons*.

The authors would like to thank Anthony Curtis, David Fask, Dane Kettwich, and Greg Mennemeier for their comments on this chapter.

NICHOLAS R. EATON is a graduate student pursuing a Ph.D. in clinical psychology at the University of Minnesota–Twin Cities; he received his B.A. from Washington University in St. Louis ('03). He once won first prize in a trivia contest at a regional *Star Trek* convention—a fact he neglected to mention when applying to work with Dr. Krueger. A friend suggested he watch a series described as "*Star Trek* meets the Wild West," which sounded horrible. His interest in disseminating psychological research to the public, as well as his subsequent love of that show, led to this chapter—a chapter that he sincerely hopes you have found to be informative and enjoyable.

ROBERT F. KRUEGER, PH.D., is professor of psychology at the University of Minnesota–Twin Cities and an associate editor of the *Journal of Abnormal Psychology*. Dr. Krueger has been honored with both early- and mid-career distinguished research awards from the American Psychological Association and the American Psychological Foundation. His professional interests include personality, psychopathology, statistics, and behavior genetics; that said, he feels slightly unnerved by the possibility that, ultimately, his most widely read publication might be about *Firefly*. Aside from his psychological endeavors, Dr. Krueger enjoys things like *The Simpsons*, jazz, science fiction, and video gaming. His top secret desire is that this chapter will become a citation classic and someday earn him the degree of Doctor of Science Fiction, *honoris causa*.

*A love affair gone drastically wrong, a death-defying accident, a humiliating pro-
fessional crisis: we've all experienced painful and even traumatic events that we
look back upon with a feeling that only a miracle pulled us through. In truth, the
real miracle is often the love and support of friends and family who were there
with a rope and a pulley when we were on the verge of hurtling over a cliff.
Gleason and Weinfield show us that we are actually hard-wired for love—that our
close relationships are indeed our strength, and that even a superhero's survival—
in body and soul—depends on a little help from her friends.*

AN ANALYSIS OF
SLAYER LONGEVITY

Relationships on the Hellmouth

TRACY R. GLEASON AND NANCY S. WEINFIELD

"A Slayer with family and friends. That sure as hell wasn't in
the brochure."

— Spike, "School Hard" (2-4)

The following report has been commissioned by a concerned party
who seeks to understand issues related to slayer effectiveness and
longevity. Once called, slayers, due to the nature of their mission,
have historically had short and brutal lives. One slayer, Buffy Summers,
has managed to survive well past the span of any of her predecessors.
Her endurance cannot be attributed to superior strength, discipline, or
training. Slayers are all imbued with the same strength, and all receive
thorough training by qualified Watchers. If anything, Buffy seems to
have been less thoroughly dedicated to the training mission of the Slayer
than those who came before her. Documented history suggests she never
studied the slayer handbook, and she failed to operate within the parameters of secrecy and separation from civilians that have been observed in
traditional slayer training ("What's My Line, Part 2," 2-10). What is
more, reports indicate that Buffy's training began much later than that of

the typical slayer. Unlike slayers Kendra and Kennedy, she was not identified and indoctrinated to her destiny in childhood.

Because Buffy's unusual effectiveness as the Slayer cannot be explained by unusual fighting prowess, this report focuses on possible psychological explanations for her success. After careful consideration of the evidence, we assert that Buffy's success as the Slayer can be explained precisely because she did not adhere to the slayer tradition of isolation. Buffy's relationships with her mother Joyce Summers, her Watcher Rupert Giles, and her friends Willow Rosenberg, Xander Harris, and the rest of a group described as the "Scooby Gang" were in fact not the liability that conventional lore about slayers would suggest. In the following report we detail how psychological research on relationships may explain the ways in which Buffy's emotional connection to family and friends made her the most effective and longest surviving of all the slayers to date.

Relationships Are Stronger Than Death

The psychological literature is quite clear: For normally functioning individuals, relationships are essential to success, both psychologically and practically. Our work, and the development of our personal strengths and qualities, are all done in the context of relationships and with the help, direct or indirect, of others. Slayers, in this respect, are no exception. As Buffy's longevity demonstrates, the Slayer needs her relationships to survive. In fact, our investigation has shown that Buffy's prolonged life was not the result of not dying; records reveal that she died twice. The intervention of Buffy's friends, in both cases, resulted in her return from the dead to continue as Slayer.

Understanding how Buffy's relationships fostered her superiority requires an understanding of some of the psychological benefits of close relationships. We begin, then, with the essential questions: What are close relationships? What do they do for people? Relationships are our emotional, interdependent ties to others, and they provide us with support, validation, nurturance, and guidance. In the context of our relationships we learn how to cooperate, negotiate, manage conflict, wield power, regulate our emotions, and help others (Berscheid and Regan;

Hartup). Our close relationships, especially early ones, give us a firm foundation from which to explore the world and face its intellectual, social, and emotional challenges (Weinfield, Sroufe, Egeland, and Carlson). Relationships teach us about ourselves, about intimacy, and about reciprocity (Hartup). In short, we thrive or falter, both interpersonally and individually, as a function of our relationships.

Perhaps the easiest way to understand what our relationships do for us is to think about what happens when they are absent or lacking in quality. Infants and children in desperate circumstances, who receive basic care like food and clothing but no nurturing, do not develop normally. Their development is compromised not only socially, but physically and cognitively as well (Zeanah et al.). For example, in a classic study in London in the late 1960s and early 1970s, Barbara Tizard and her colleagues compared four sets of children who were institutionalized for the first two to four years of their lives. One group was adopted between ages two and four, one group remained institutionalized, one group went back to their families between ages two and four, and one group was never institutionalized. The researchers found that the institutionalized group fared worse than the other groups on almost every measure they used, including in their behavior, cognition, and social interactions (Tizard and Rees 1974, 1975). Indeed, even into adolescence the institutionalized children showed elevated rates of aggression and antisocial behavior in comparison to their adopted peers (Hodges and Tizard).

Individuals with poor quality relationships, especially early in life, have difficulty managing their own emotions (Denham) and face compromises to their thinking and problem-solving (Pianta and Harbers). Moreover, these difficulties continue over time. In one study (Pianta and Harbers), mothers and their children were observed working together on a series of problem-solving games on the first day of kindergarten. Mothers who were not emotionally supportive with their children, and who did not provide good quality assistance to their children during the activities, had children who performed poorly on subsequent standardized school testing in second, third, and fourth grades. This prediction held up even as the researchers ruled out the mother's education level and the child's general cognitive ability at school entry as alternative explanations. Clearly, troubled early relationships do not facilitate the development of subsequent competence and high quality relationships, and are generally difficult to overcome.

Ultimately we need others—not only to survive, but to thrive and to realize our full potential. Slayers, despite their powers, are no exception to this rule. The expectation that the Slayer should isolate herself from friends and family—even if putatively for her safety and theirs—may actually work against her survival. Strength, power, and even independence are fostered by attachments to others (Feeney). In a longitudinal study of relationships and development, researchers have found that individuals who had a high quality, supportive attachment to a caregiver in infancy continued to show signs of power and independence over time. In preschool these children were rated as highly independent by their teachers (Sroufe, Fox, and Pancake). Observations of peer interaction also revealed that these individuals were less likely to fall victim to bullies at school than were children who had poor quality early relationships (Troy and Sroufe). By adolescence, those who had high quality early relationships were the most likely to emerge as leaders during decision-making activities with their peers (Englund, Levy, Hyson, and Sroufe). Other research with adult couples (Feeney) has demonstrated that adults whose romantic partners were accepting of their need for support and occasional dependency were more likely to work independently of their partners on challenging tasks, and more likely to pursue important personal goals over time, than were individuals whose partners rejected support and dependency needs. Perhaps not surprisingly in light of these findings, our investigation revealed that Buffy's greatest successes were shared with, and in many cases even dependent upon, her relationships with others. The greatest failures she and the Scooby Gang endured came at times when they were apart, psychologically if not physically. Emotional distance from others creates vulnerability. The compromises of isolation are clearly seen in the cases of other contemporary slayers, Kendra and Faith, whose unfortunate failures we address later in this report as a contrast to Buffy's success.

Close relationships come in different forms, such as those with parents and those with friends, and each type of relationship provides both overlapping benefits and unique advantages. Just as normal individuals avail themselves of multiple sources of relationship support, we assert that Buffy drew her power from her relationships both with her parent figures and with her friends. Below, we detail some of the ways in which Buffy's relationships ensured her effectiveness as Slayer.

Parents Are Sources of Strength

In psychological terms, parents are our first "attachment figures." Research on both humans and non-human primates has established that attachment figures protect their offspring physically and emotionally, nurture them, and watch over them while encouraging them to explore the world and face its challenges (Cassidy). In psychological terms this is called a "secure base" (Bowlby); in colloquial terms attachment figures are our rocks to lean on. Having a secure base emboldens us to make friends, to confront the unknown, and to take chances, because we have a safety net. When things go wrong our attachment figures comfort us and still believe in us, preparing us to go out and try again. Buffy, emotionally, had two "parents" who served as secure bases for her—her mother, Joyce, and her Watcher, Giles. Our investigation confirms that they protected Buffy and nurtured her as a daughter. She had slayer strength, but Joyce and Giles gave her the self-assurance to wield her power to its full potential.

Both Joyce and Giles provided physical protection for Buffy. For example, Joyce protected Buffy from Spike, knowing that he was a killer yet unaware of Buffy's status as the Slayer. Disregarding the danger to herself, Joyce smacked Spike in the head with an axe when he threatened her daughter's safety. Giles sought to protect Buffy as well. In "Helpless" (3-12), the Watchers' Council ruthlessly deprived Buffy of her slayer strength in order to test her skills. When the test became too dangerous, Giles revealed all to Buffy to try to protect her. He followed her into danger to save her, and was ultimately fired for, as the Council explained, loving her like a daughter. Despite Buffy's charge to protect the world, and unlike other slayers historically, Buffy had people who instinctually protected her.

Joyce and Giles's protection of Buffy extended beyond her physical well-being, and into the realm of her emotional well-being. They saw what Buffy needed emotionally, and acted to make it so. Giles worked to help Buffy let go of her secret—that she killed Angel, not Angelus. He understood that she had to come to this confession herself, and could not be forced, just nudged. He concocted a story about doing a binding spell for Acathla, and needing more and more details about Buffy's final moments with Angel. Buffy complied to assist with the spell, and Giles's gentle prodding for details eventually freed her of the secret that Angel's soul was restored before she had to kill him. Similarly, Joyce realized that Buffy, in an idealized teenage way, was holding on to the unrealistic idea of making a life with Angel. Joyce knew that Buffy needed ties to the normal, mortal world, and asked Angel to be the one to break it off. Here Joyce protected Buffy in a different way, ensuring that Buffy got what she needed rather than what she impulsively wanted. In each case, Joyce and Giles intervened to guarantee that slaying did not leave Buffy emotionally hardened and/or disconnected from others.

Buffy also turned to Joyce and Giles for support, and for the emotional strength to perform the most difficult of her slayer duties. Buffy could face down literal demons, but she still needed parents to help her manage her psychological demons when she lost Angel and knew she had to kill him. When Giles talked with Buffy about Angel turning evil, she was blaming herself. He comforted her and told her that all she would get from him was support and respect, not blame. She went home and sought comfort from Joyce as well, who held her daughter and stroked her hair, knowing only that Buffy needed her. Later, when Giles was nearly killed trying to avenge Jenny's death, Buffy first punched him then hugged him and cried, telling him she could not lose him because she could not face fighting Angelus without him. Unlike other slayers, Buffy was permitted to express her doubts and fears and to receive comfort, which subsequently gave her the strength to continue the fight.

Friends Fight by Our Sides

While parents guide us into the social world, providing a safe haven if things go wrong, our study of Buffy's success as the Slayer suggests that her relationships with Joyce and Giles were not the only ties that kept her going. Her friends, commonly referred to as the Scooby Gang or

Scoobies, also provided support of many kinds. As mentioned, although Buffy died twice, in both instances members of the Scooby Gang (first Xander and then Willow) brought her back to slay once more. While resuscitation is an extreme example of the kind of help and support friends can offer, it is an apt metaphor for the way in which these relationships are also critical as we face the challenges, large and small, of our daily lives.

Friendships, like the ones between the Scoobies, teach us about negotiation, cooperation, and perspective-taking (Bukowski, Newcomb, and Hartup). In contrast to parents, who are authority figures in their children's lives, friends interact with each other on the same level. Neither member of a friendship is inherently more competent, although, of course, each may have individual strengths and weaknesses. Our analysis of the members of the Scooby Gang revealed that each had something to contribute: Buffy had power, Willow had technical expertise, and while Xander worried that he did not have a role to play, his presence proved pivotal in many instances (e.g., see above reference to bringing Buffy back to life the first time). Part of the beauty of friendships is that they give us a chance to both give and receive support, improving our social skills and raising our self-esteem (Hartup and Stevens). Compared to people who do not have good friends, those who do are more sociable and cooperative and have more comfortable interactions with others in general (Hartup). Forming a social network of close friends is a key to healthy psychological functioning.

Of course, friends are more than just promoters of good behavior and a healthy psyche. Friends often help us manage life transitions. For example, adolescents who maintain high quality relationships with their best friends as they start college have an easier transition than adolescents whose high school friendships begin to fade away (Oswald and Clark). Our investigation suggests that despite her status as the Slayer, Buffy was no exception to this rule. When she started college at UC Sunnydale she had a rough time, largely because her group of friends was dispersed. Although Willow and Oz attended with her, they were often off together and Willow was so in her element that she left Buffy behind. Xander was away, Angel had left, and Giles was both newly out of work and preoccupied with a visiting lady friend. Consequently, not only did Buffy have a hard time getting started academically, but she did the unthinkable—she ran away from an ordinary vampire. Not until the Scooby Gang was reunited was she able to recommit herself to slaying.

Buffy was at her strongest when united with her friends. On one occasion, this unity was literal. Toward the end of her freshman year of college Buffy battled Adam, a combination human, demon, and machine focused on creating a human/demon master race. Part of Adam's plan to weaken Buffy was to put her and her friends at odds—an assignment executed by Spike. The Scooby Gang, however, realized in time what had happened, and they performed a spell that combined their strength into Buffy herself. Giles and his knowledge of Sumerian (for reciting a spell), Willow and her magic, and Xander as the heart merged with Buffy and her slaying powers to enable her to defeat Adam.

Isolation Leads to Darkness

Our assertion that Buffy's unusual longevity and power as the Slayer are a function of her relationships is clearly supported when contrasted with the isolation and slaying careers of Kendra and Faith. Isolation from peers is connected to negative outcomes such as antisocial behavior, compromised thinking (especially about relationships), aggression, and delinquency (Parker and Asher). Consequently, we would expect to see rather dire consequences of Faith's emotional isolation and Kendra's social isolation. Both Faith and Kendra worked with the Scoobies, but never quite successfully. In Faith's case, reference was made to her original Watcher, who was killed before Faith arrived in Sunnydale. The loss of her Watcher, and a difficult upbringing before that, had an enormous impact on Faith, who was thereafter compromised in her ability to work with Buffy and the others despite her initial charm. When her new Watcher, Gwendolyn Post, turned out to be evil and told her she was an idiot, Faith felt guilty for being taken in and resolved further to depend only upon herself. Even as Buffy encouraged Faith to trust her, Faith made her position perfectly clear: "*I'm* on my side," she said, "That's enough" ("Revelations," 3-7). After Faith accidentally killed the deputy mayor she withdrew further, rejecting every effort by the Scoobies to bring her back into the fold and offering her services to the evil mayor.

She ended up in a coma, only to wake up a year later and wreak more havoc before leaving town. Her subsequent reformation and return to help Buffy battle the First Evil years later was met with skepticism and suspicion by the Scoobies, even as they recognized that they needed her help. As in all social networks, a reputation, once earned, is difficult to overcome.

Although Kendra's social isolation never resulted in a move to the dark side, systematic scrutiny of her performance as Slayer reveals the effects that a paucity of relationships had on her abilities. Kendra's family had given her to her Watcher so early in her life that she had no memories of them. She had grown up believing that family and friends would be a distraction from her focus on slaying, and had thus avoided forming relationships. The closest thing she had to a companion was her favorite stake, Mr. Pointy. Kendra was appalled at the number of people who knew that Buffy was the Slayer. At that time, Buffy noted that her own emotions and emotional attachments fostered a level of creativity and power that made her a more flexible fighter, and ultimately a better slayer, than Kendra. Unfortunately, Buffy's observation proved prescient. Kendra, despite flawless training, was killed by Drusilla a mere year after she was called. Drusilla's mind-control abilities were similar to those the Master used on Buffy, which Buffy was able to overcome through a combination of resuscitation by Xander and subsequent creativity in fighting. Kendra's adamant adherence to the traditional slayer rules may well have been her downfall.

Conflict and Loss Lead to Despair

The evidence suggests that the practice of isolating slayers from friends and family is contraindicated. Success as the Slayer, as for any person, is supported and maintained by close connections to others. Indeed, we need only look at times in Buffy's life when her relationships were problematic in order to be convinced. After Angel lost his soul, Buffy found herself at odds with those closest to her. She found little sympathy from Giles and the Scoobies after Angelus had terrorized and harmed them. At the same time, Joyce discovered that Buffy was the Slayer and dealt badly with that revelation, rejecting her daughter's true identity. Faced with feelings of isolation and grief after having killed Angel, Buffy ran away from Sunnydale and from her life as the Slayer, leaving the Hellmouth unprotected. When she returned she faced anger and disappointment (and eventually forgiveness) from her mother and from the Scoobies, both for having abandoned her duties and for failing to realize that although relationships have ups and downs, she could turn to them for anything.

Buffy's second return from the dead is another excellent example. Having been ripped from heaven by Willow's magic spell, Buffy found no common ground with her friends and was lost in her attempts to reestablish her life. To make matters worse, Giles left her in an attempt to force her to take on more adult responsibility, a mistake for which he later apologized. Without those connections, Buffy had trouble figuring out how to cope with running a household and taking care of her little sister, Dawn, and almost lost custody of Dawn in the process. The Geek Trio, a group of comically bumbling evildoers, was effective in harassing her in a way that would never have worked when she was more effectively connected to the Scoobies and had Giles as her Watcher. Ultimately, her only way to cope in this world was by communing with someone who was equally disaffected from it. Spike, no longer human but unwelcome in the demon world as well, had an odd understanding of Buffy's confusion, and she was drawn to him for the comfort and commiseration he could offer.

The death of a loved one is one of the most difficult losses anyone can face, even as an adult. It leads to sadness, grief, and a period of struggling to reorient oneself to the world and to carry on (Bowlby). Being the Slayer didn't change that reality for Buffy. Joyce died while Buffy was in college, and Buffy's world crumbled. Although Buffy was surrounded by death on a daily basis, her own mother's death was a profoundly different situation. She didn't feel ready to face adult responsibilities without Joyce there to back her up. Records suggest that after she went to college, Buffy hadn't even seen Joyce regularly. The fact that, technically, Buffy was old enough to manage her life without her mother didn't ease this pain. Buffy lost her purpose and couldn't shake her despair. Both her self-confidence and her slaying suffered as she struggled to understand her own connection to death, which the apparition of the First Slayer cryptically described as her gift.

Conclusions and Recommendations

Finally, the impact of relationships on Buffy's work as Slayer, and the importance of relationship connections for all slayers, was most apparent in the success she had in the monumental task of closing the Sunnydale Hellmouth. All who had fought alongside Buffy in the past—Willow, Xander, Giles, Spike, Anya, Faith, Dawn, and even Angel—and those who had joined her ranks more recently—Andrew, Principal Wood, and the Potentials—worked together to conquer the local forces of evil forever. This army was not a faceless mass of identical soldiers, but a social network functioning as a single unit. They did more, however, than win that battle. Buffy's insight that the slayer power could be shared by all potential slayers, and Willow's spell to bring that to fruition, resulted in a permanent change in the slayer line. Now the Slayer is not "one girl in all the world" ("Welcome to the Hellmouth," 1-1), but one of a network of girls who fight together.

In sum, our assessment is that Buffy owed her success as Slayer to her failure to operate in isolation. Her relationships with family and friends played a positive role in her psychological functioning in the same manner they do for non-slayers. The rule that someone with superhuman powers must function outside of a social context appears to be an outdated, and even dangerous, requirement. Perhaps the record of Spike's words to Buffy, when she asked him how he had killed slayers in the past, say it best: ". . . And now you see, that's the secret. Not the punch you didn't throw or the kicks you didn't land. Every Slayer . . . has a death wish. Even you. The only reason you've lasted as long as you have is you've got ties to the world . . . your mum, your brat kid sister, the Scoobies. They all tie you here but you're just putting off the inevitable" ("Fool for Love," 5-7).

We assert that realization of the slayer death wish is not inevitable. The isolation of sequential slayers has ended, but our investigation indicates not only that the slayers should not fight in isolation; they should not live in isolation. We hereby recommend that slayers be encouraged to develop healthy relationships with parents, Watchers, and a civilian friendship network.

TRACY R. GLEASON, PH.D., is an associate professor in the department of psychology at Wellesley College, which is where Buffy, and particularly Willow, should have gone to college. She received her Ph.D. from the Institute of Child Development at the University of Minnesota in 1998. Her contributions to this essay provided a lovely forum for combining her research interests in relationships and imagination.

NANCY S. WEINFIELD, PH.D., is a developmental psychologist and an assistant professor in the department of psychology at the University of Virginia. She received her Ph.D. from the Institute of Child Development at the University of Minnesota in 1996. Her research focuses primarily on parent-child relationships, attachment, and the strategies individuals use to cope with emotional pain, thus making her a natural fan of Joss Whedon's work.

REFERENCES

Berscheid, Ellen, and Pamela Regan. *The Psychology of Interpersonal Relationships.* New York: Prentice Hall, 2005.

Bowlby, John. *A Secure Base: Parent-Child Attachment and Healthy Human Development.* New York, NY: Basic Books, 1988.

Bukowski, William M., Andrew F. Newcomb, and Willard W. Hartup. *The Company They Keep: Friendship in Childhood and Adolescence.* New York, NY: Cambridge University Press, 1996.

Jude Cassidy, "The Nature of the Child's Ties," in *Handbook of Attachment: Theory, Research, and Clinical Applications,* eds. Jude Cassidy and Phillip R. Shaver (New York, NY: Guilford, 1999), 3-20.

Denham, Susanne A. *Emotional Development in Young Children.* New York, NY: Guilford Press, 1998.

Michelle M. Englund, et al., "Adolescent Social Competence: Effectiveness in a Group Setting," *Child Development* 71 (2000): 1049-1060.

Brooke C. Feeney, "The Dependency Paradox in Close Relationships: Accepting Dependence Promotes Independence," *Journal of Personality and Social*

Psychology 92 (2007): 268–285.

Willard W. Hartup, "Social Relationships and Their Developmental Significance," *American Psychologist* 44 (1989): 120–126.

_____, "The Three Faces of Friendship," *Journal of Social and Personal Relationships* 12 (1995): 569–574.

Willard W. Hartup and Nan Stevens, "Friendships and Adaptation across the Life Span," *Current Directions in Psychological Science* 8 (1999): 76–79.

Jill Hodges and Barbara Tizard, "Social and Family Relationships of Ex-Institutional Adolescents," *Journal of Child Psychology and Psychiatry* 30 (1989): 77–97.

Debra L. Oswald and Eddie M. Clark, "Best Friends Forever?: High School Best Friendships and the Transition to College," *Personal Relationships* 10 (2003): 187–196.

Jeffrey G. Parker and Steven R. Asher, "Peer Relations and Later Personal Adjustment: Are Low-Accepted Children at Risk?," *Psychological Bulletin* 102 (1987): 357–389.

Robert C. Pianta and Katrina L. Harbers, "Observing Mother and Child Behavior in a Problem-Solving Situation at School Entry: Relations with Academic Achievement," *Journal of School Psychology* 34 (1996): 307–322.

L. Alan Sroufe, Nancy E. Fox, and Van R. Pancake, "Attachment and Dependency in Developmental Perspective," *Child Development* 54 (1983): 1615–1627.

Barbara Tizard and Judith Rees, "A Comparison of the Effects of Adoption, Restoration to the Natural Mother, and Continued Institutionalization on the Cognitive Development of Four-Year-Old Children," *Child Development* 45 (1974): 92–99.

_____, "The Effect of Early Institutional Rearing on the Behaviour Problems and Affectional Relationships of Four-Year-Old Children," *Journal of Child Psychology and Psychiatry* 16 (1975): 61–73.

Michael Troy and L. Alan Sroufe, "Victimization among Preschoolers: Role of Attachment Relationship History," *Journal of the American Academy of Child & Adolescent Psychiatry* 26 (1987): 166–172.

Nancy S. Weinfield, et al., "The Nature of Individual Differences in Infant-Caregiver Attachment," in *Handbook of Attachment: Theory, Research, and Clinical Applications*, eds. Jude Cassidy and Phillip R. Shaver (New York: Guilford, 1999), 68–88.

Charles H. Zeanah, et al., "Designing Research to Study the Effects of Institutionalization on Brain and Behavioral Development: The Bucharest Early Intervention Project," *Development and Psychopathology* 15 (2003): 885–907.

Whose teenage years didn't blaze with angst? Whose every waking moment—every pimple, every heartache, every misguided or brilliantly navigated plot to express independence—wasn't haunted by fear? Not mine, not anyone's I've ever known, and certainly not Buffy's. While everybody gets older, nobody—including Buffy—can grow UP until they face their own big bads and do battle with the constant urge to deny them, escape them, or submit to them. Rabian and Wolff remind us that picking off hell's demons was merely a sidetrip on Buffy's arduous journey. How she transformed her inner demons into a power so big she could first change destiny and then save the world is the real story, and it's applicable to anyone who wonders if she'll make it through her own turbulent times, or whether it's worth the pain to keep trying.

HOW BUFFY LEARNED TO CONFRONT HER FEARS

. . . and Lived to Tell about It

BRIAN RABIAN AND MICHAEL WOLFF

Atypical reaction to fantasy series, especially one with such beautifully crafted horror elements as *Buffy the Vampire Slayer*, is to wonder, "Who thinks up this stuff?" The implication, of course, is that it requires a twisted, perhaps demented, mind to create such deliberately frightening images of demons, vampires, and the like. We'll give Joss Whedon, creator of *Buffy* and its spin-off *Angel*, the benefit of the doubt and assume that his mind is neither twisted nor demented. For now, he gets a free pass; we'll even pat him on the back for his bottomless well of creativity, sense of humor, and understanding of the human condition. In *Buffy*, Whedon created such rich dialogue and such deep characters that his brainchild did the unthinkable—it lasted for an extended run on what would then have been described as a wannabe cable channel. Today it is common for non-network cable channels to run original series that earn both critical acclaim and respectable television ratings, but this was not the case when Whedon blazed a trail with his vampire-fighting teenager. So, for Whedon, we'll acknowledge that he has demonstrated for us genius rather than madness.

But the characters he created don't get off that easy. They come riddled with emotional turmoil, including angst, self-doubt, fear, envy, lust, and longing. (Sounds like adolescence.) Even those characters whose supernatural status might lead one to assume they would be free of such human frailties are tormented or impaired. But rather than creating distance with viewers, such qualities actually serve as the bonding agent that keeps viewers tuned in for more of the struggle. The most popular superheroes historically are those whose invincible public persona is counterbalanced by an ongoing private struggle for self-understanding, acceptance, and possibly even love. Superman is as invincible as any superhero, but can be brought to his knees by a package from home (i.e., kryptonite) or by his own unfulfilled longing to share his identity with Lois Lane. Batman, in his original inception, was a man trying to come to grips with the murder of his parents and meting out lots of revenge along the way. What kept us coming back to *Buffy* season after season was not the opportunity to watch another fight scene in which a vampire ended up getting staked, plentiful as they were, but rather the opportunity to watch more common human fights: the fight to maintain relationships, the fight to find one's place in the world, the fight against self-doubt. In retrospect, the weekly vampire stakings were often cheesy and weakly choreographed, and really served largely as a bridge between other, more mundane struggles facing Buffy at the time.

One popular pastime for hardcore fans of *Buffy the Vampire Slayer*, or *Buffy*philes as they so happily and proudly call themselves (okay, as we so happily call ourselves), is to dissect the seven seasons of the show with a focus on the iconic qualities of its hero Buffy Summers. Numerous authors have considered Buffy's importance as a feminist (or is it post-feminist?) icon, a conceptualization that has been supported by the show's creator himself, who makes no bones about the fact that Buffy was written through a feminist lens (Havens 6). Buffy's character symbolizes many feminist traits, including strength, egalitarianism, and autonomy, and while her self-doubts and vulnerabilities were salient throughout the series, Buffy maintained her dynamic identity as a potent feminine heroine.

Other common dissections of *Buffy* center on the religious threads that ran through the series, and interpret Buffy as a modern day savior. The opening montage during season one instructed us that Buffy was the "Chosen One," born to stand against the forces of darkness. It does-n't take too hard or long a look to notice that Buffy Summers came replete with apostles—Xander, Willow, Oz, and sometimes Cordelia and Anya—who helped to spread the good word that she was on the scene; an all-important resurrection (several, in fact); and an army of Potentials who could achieve immortality through her. Furthering the conceptual-ization of Buffy as savior was her overt act of sacrifice in the episode "The Gift" (5-22), when she launched herself off a tower in order to save her sister, Dawn.

But look beyond the iconic imagery and you'll also see something else: a pretty anxious young girl who had to work very hard over seven or so years of her life to fully conquer the emotional turmoil that beset her. It's been said by others that Joss Whedon loves anguish (Havens 3), but it would be just as accurate to say that Whedon loves anxiety. Because of its horror theme, *Buffy* is a treasure trove of fearful characters fleeing the monsters that torment them—and looking to hide behind Buffy's strength for protection. But less obvious, and sometimes lost in the interpretations of Buffy as a paragon of all that is good and sacred, are Buffy's own credentials as an anxious, fearful, and sometimes depressed human being. Her status as Slayer did not free her from the developmental challenges she faced as a teenager—namely figuring out her place in the world, how relationships are supposed to work, and what she was going to be if she ever grew up—and Buffy wore these bur-dens heavily.

The question of whether Buffy meets diagnostic criteria for a mental disorder is open for debate but not one that we will attempt to answer fully here. She certainly presents with a full complement of symptoms that fit under the umbrella of the term "negative affect," which refers to the spectrum of negative emotions one can experience, including anxi-ety, sadness, anger, depression, guilt, and irritability. Buffy's own collec-tion of negative affect indicators seems sufficient to intermittently inter-fere with her ability to do the things that she wants or needs to do, which would suggest psychopathology, or the presence of a disorder. But, to her benefit, she also presents with a balance of positive traits and emotions, such as happiness, strength, enthusiasm, pride, and determi-nation. At a minimum, Buffy is what child psychologists would refer to as an "internalizing" child, meaning that what negative emotions she does experience are largely expressed through processes internal to her, such as thoughts, feelings, and physiological upheaval, and which are therefore not regularly on public display. In other words, Buffy doesn't walk around agitated and screaming at people, but instead tends to withdraw and contemplate. Her emotions go largely unnoticed, except to those with whom she is very close.

For contrast, the character of Faith was introduced to Sunnydale in season three and represents the "externalizing" child. Whereas Buffy is introspective, thoughtful, and prone to torment from within as easily as from outside, Faith is defiant, oppositional, and often acts out, her pathology on ready display. When Buffy and the other Scoobies resisted Faith's rebellious approach to life and slaying, she sought reinforcement elsewhere, finding it in the company of Sunnydale's mayor. It was the equivalent of the schoolyard bully seeking out a gang of supporters when their traditional victims start standing up for themselves.

Faith's past is largely unknown to us, but it was hinted at frequently that it was not a good one. Consequently, Faith would not allow herself to get attached to Buffy and her friends or to find comfort in the family atmosphere they had created in the school library. Buffy's upbringing, although not as damaging as Faith's, similarly prevented her from fully recognizing her friends' love and appreciation. Her relationships with the Scooby Gang and with Giles were often turbulent, with Buffy waffling between relying on her friends to help her manage the burden of her responsibility as Slayer and wanting to keep them at a distance in order to simplify the job in front of her. This attempt to keep things simple, to reduce ambiguity and complication, is a hallmark of almost all anxiety disorders, and in Buffy's case, a good argument for the presence of Generalized Anxiety Disorder (APA 472). Anxiety and worry are more easily managed when ambiguity is reduced. Virtually every battle Buffy anticipated led her to seek out Giles for information, and she was often sent away, at least initially, without reassurance.

And what are Buffy's primary fears? That she will die in the midst of battle? That she won't be good enough to save herself, or her friends, or the world? That she is not worthy of being the Slayer? That she won't be loved? Understood? Accepted? That she is not wanted? All of the above? The episode "Nightmares" (1-10) provided evidence about her relationship fears when Buffy admitted to Willow that she worried that the stress caused by her trouble at her previous school compounded her parents' marital problems and led to their eventual breakup. Even more striking was Buffy's nightmare later in the episode, during which her father reinforced these worries by rejecting her:

> HANK: Having you. Raising you. Seeing you every day. I mean, do you have any idea what that's like? . . . all you ever think about is yourself. You get in trouble. You embarrass us with all the crazy stunts you pull, and do I have to go on? . . . You're sullen and . . . rude and . . . you're not nearly as bright as I thought you were going to be. . . . Hey, Buffy, let's be honest. Could you stand to live in the same house with a daughter like that? . . . Speaking of which, I don't really get anything out of these weekends with you. So, what do you say we just don't do them anymore?

Buffy's worries about being wanted and accepted were further evident in her ambivalent relationship with Angel (in which she could justifiably be described as "clingy") and in Angel's eventual rejection of her (as Angelus) in "Innocence" (2-14), in her vulnerability to the rejection of freshman lothario Parker in "The Harsh Light of Day" (4-3); and in her inability to accept Riley's unconditional love for her during seasons four and five.

Buffy's more general vulnerability to doubt—about herself, about her abilities, and about the world— was on display in such episodes as "Lie to Me" (2-7), in which she asked Giles to reassure her, after killing her recently sired friend Ford, that life will get easier:

> GILES: What do you want me to say?
> BUFFY: Lie to me.
> GILES: Yes, it's terribly simple. The good guys are always stalwart and true, the bad guys are easily distinguished by their pointy horns or black hats, and, uh, we always defeat them and save the day. No one ever dies, and everybody lives happily ever after.
> BUFFY: Liar.

Yet no amount of reassurance or convincing could dissuade Buffy from her doubts and worries, which is another characteristic of anxiety when it rises to the level of pathology. Anxiety cannot be reasoned away. In part, this is because worry serves an adaptive function. Even when worry is so overwhelming and it results in an inability to act, it is still serving an adaptive function by saving you from making difficult decisions: if you are so absorbed by worry that you are unable to break out of this cycle, you don't have to make efforts that could lead to failure and despair. Buffy herself fell into complete paralysis in the "Weight of the World" (5-21), when Dawn was taken by Glory; Buffy slipped into a catatonic state in which she was a young child, free of the present world's burdens.

Decades of psychological research suggest that most anxiety disorders and many forms of depression have a significant heritable (i.e., inherited) component. Thus, it is not by coincidence that anxieties, fears, and worries tend to run in families and are often transmitted across generations. Anxious parents beget anxious children. Add to this our understanding within a behavioral framework of the way in which parents model and subsequently reinforce anxious behaviors in their children, and it seems that Buffy's mother, Joyce, would be a good starting place in understanding Buffy's anxiety.

Although Joyce Summers does not stand out as a uniquely anxious person, throughout her time on the show she displayed what might be considered a worrisome nature. Joyce's response to the trouble Buffy found herself in at her previous school included persistent reminders about the importance of the new start they were making in Sunnydale and concern that any sign of trouble signaled a repeat of problems:

> JOYCE: (about cheerleading) I'm glad you're taking that up
>   again. It'll keep you out of trouble.
> BUFFY: I'm not *in* trouble.
> JOYCE: No, not yet. ("Witch," 1-3)

Throughout seasons one and two Buffy struggled to get out from under her mother's watchful and worrisome eye (e.g., crawling out the window to see Angel), eventually leaving home when her mother couldn't accept her announcement that she was the Slayer ("Becoming, Part 2," 2-22).

Although leaving Sunnydale may best be seen as Buffy's own anxious avoidance of her responsibilities as Slayer, her choice to leave the house to begin with, despite Joyce's insistence otherwise, was the first real step Buffy took toward managing her own life. It was, however, hardly the last. Once Joyce was aware of Buffy's role as Slayer, Buffy found herself having to overcome her mother's complicating involvement in her slaying. In "Gingerbread" (3-11), for instance, it was Joyce who organized other parents for a school rally when two children were found murdered, leaving Buffy to not only fight the true killer, but struggle against her mother and the other parents to do so.

Joyce always meant well, but so do most anxious parents who inadvertently reinforce anxious behaviors in their children by overprotecting them from the challenges they must face in order to grow. In Joyce's case, she was anxious that Buffy would fall under the influence of bad peers, but her need to involve herself in Buffy's daily activities no doubt also reflected her anxiety about being distanced from her only post-divorce living companion. Eventually, Joyce realized that Buffy's role as Slayer meant that she (Joyce) must contain her own anxiety. By the end of season three, she was able to acquiesce to her daughter's request that she leave town before the Ascension, so that Buffy wouldn't be distracted by worrying about her mother's safety.

At the same time that Joyce was coming to the realization that Buffy needed her independence, Buffy herself was working to get her own worries under control. The good news is that Buffy found her way into a successful seven-year management program for her negative affect. The bad news is that most commonly used interventions for anxiety today can be started and finished within a couple of months (though her fans aren't complaining). In "Prophecy Girl" (1-12), the Master foreshadowed Buffy's eventual process in overcoming her fears when, while instructing Collin, the Anointed One, on the power of fear, he said, "It is the most powerful force in the human world. Not love. Not hate. Fear." The Master told Collin that fear was in the mind, and that like pain, it could be controlled. "If I can *face* my fear, it cannot master me." Notice that the Master said, "If I can face my fear," not, "If I can *think* about my fear," or, "If I can just convince myself that. . . ." The foundation of most well-established treatments for anxiety and depression are new skills that assist in facing real-life situations that the patient had previously avoided. But while those skills might include new, more adaptive ways of thinking about the world, the real benefits of treatment come when the recipient is put in a position to gain new experiences that make the retention of long-held maladaptive beliefs impossible.

Attempts to change long-held beliefs through persuasion or reasoning alone usually fail. Beliefs tend to change when experiences force change. Buffy could be reassured repeatedly by Giles and her friends with little change in the way she thought. Buffy actually suffered from a number of significant cognitive distortions that contributed to her ongoing doubts and fears, including the expectation that she must be perfect and the belief that she was solely responsible for her success or failure. Her friends were always at the ready to support her, often making convincing arguments about how their participation would benefit her, but Buffy frequently forced them out of the fight, behavior that garnered resentment in several episodes. When Willow first announced to Buffy that she had decided to stay and attend college in Sunnydale in "Choices" (3-19), Buffy's initial response was, "I won't let you"—to which Willow replied, "Of the two people here, which one is the boss of me?" Buffy's eventual recognition of her friends' value to her set up one of *Buffy's* most touching episodes, "Checkpoint" (5-12), in which the Watchers' Council arrived in Sunnydale to test Buffy's development as Slayer, only to have Buffy ultimately reject the idea that they had the right to do so. It was not Buffy's defense of herself that was striking, but rather the way that she defended her friends to the Council, outlining their individual importance to her fight and reinforcing how much she needed them to be successful as Slayer. This was Buffy's acknowledgment that she was not alone in her fight, and that she could rely on the support of others to accomplish her goals.

Cognitive-behavioral therapies ask the recipient to become a detective of sorts, looking for actual evidence in his or her life to refute or support maladaptive beliefs. The accumulation of evidence against these beliefs, either through an examination of past experiences or through generating new experiences, leads to a necessary point at which the recipient must modify his or her beliefs to accommodate that evidence. Buffy's rebuke of the Watchers' Council came after an encounter with that season's archvillain, Glory, in which Glory only seemed to want to talk. Glory was more powerful than Buffy; Glory could have taken her out at any moment. Since she did not, Buffy was forced to wonder why. What Buffy realized was that she had something Glory wanted, and that gave her power. The Watchers' Council, Buffy realized, was similar — without her, the Slayer, they had no purpose. As with Glory, they needed her. Her encounter with Glory forced her to reconsider what she thought she knew, resulting in newfound confidence, and making her more effective as Slayer.

Although Buffy herself had little control over the timing of her real-life experiences, and subsequent shifts in thinking, there was a gradual and hierarchical nature to them from the start. This not only makes for good storytelling, with Buffy's stature as heroine developing as she faced and defeated more dangerous threats, but is also consistent with cognitive-behavioral models of treating anxiety, which prescribe that new skills for overcoming fears should be forged through a measured, step-by-step exposure to what frightens you. Buffy did not begin her journey as the slayer by taking on the First Evil, for instance, a challenge for which she would have been completely unprepared. Her first real exposures were to run-of-the-mill Sunnydale vampires, whose job, it appeared, was largely to interfere with Buffy's attempts to meet her friends at the Bronze. After dusting off a fairly large number of vampires, Buffy was ready to take on the Master, clearly a large first "formal" step for a shaken Buffy who, after saving the world, felt the need to confront the defeated Master's bones in "When She Was Bad" (2-1) before she could move on. Over the course of the next few years, Buffy sacrificed Angelus, disposed of the mayor, and triumphed over Adam, a government-created composite. With each experience, she grew in confidence and skill.

Even in the last few seasons of the series, Joss Whedon found ways to continue raising the stakes in Buffy's accumulation of real-life experiences. The goddess Glory and then the First Evil were, by far, the biggest challenges Buffy had ever faced, but by the time she was forced to take them on, she had already made significant strides in controlling her doubts and fears. The worry and anxiety she experienced facing the Master and the Annointed seem almost laughable in comparison.

With each new experience, it was more and more difficult for Buffy to continue with her concern that she was not worthy of being Slayer.[1] During this time, Giles served as therapist for Buffy, continuously educating her about the challenges ahead, providing support when self-doubt crept in, reinforcing Buffy for her accomplishments, and exhorting her to sharpen her skills for future challenges. Accordingly, Buffy's reliance on Giles diminished as her independence grew, punctuated by Giles's deliberate withdrawal of support when he felt that Buffy turned to him for help in handling difficulties with Dawn rather than dealing with them herself. In treatment, once skills are learned and beliefs are challenged through successful experiences, the therapist becomes somewhat obsolete. When cognitive-behavioral intervention is successful, control is essentially transferred from the therapist to the patient, who is after treatment capable of any challenges that come their way with ongoing practice.

Over the course of seven seasons, Buffy went from a girl pushed into action, to one who not only carried out the fight, but who was able to research and plan the fight independently. Just think of her transformation in the final stages of battle with the First. Buffy was no longer the student but the teacher, transforming the Potentials into future slayers, and preparing others for battle. She was calm and confident when she gave her last speech to the Potentials in "Chosen" (7-22):

> BUFFY: I hate that there's evil. And that I was chosen to fight
> it. I wish a whole lot of the time that I hadn't been. I know
> a lot of you wish I hadn't been either. But this isn't about
> wishes. This is about choices. . . . What if you could have
> that power . . . now? . . . I say we change the rule. I say my
> power . . . should be our power. . . . Every girl who could
> have the power . . . will have the power . . . can stand up,

---

[1] The only season that didn't fit neatly into this nice progression of foes was season six, in which Warren, Jonathan, and Andrew were the regular antagonists. Even if we concentrate on the final episodes, in which the loss of Tara drew out Willow's dark side, it was not Buffy who brought Willow's rampage to a halt, but rather Xander. The demons Buffy fought in this season were less literal, and thus could be seen as a break from the show's usual use of metaphor to portray the process of growing up.

will stand up. Slayers . . . every one of us. Make your
choice. Are you ready to be strong?

More impressive than this speech alone is the fact that Buffy was able to
take charge of the Potentials after friends, family, and potential slayers
alike lost faith in her leadership and ejected her from her own house.
She was curled up in an abandoned house, doubting herself and her abilities, until Spike found her and reminded her of who she was and all she
had overcome. Several seasons earlier, Buffy might not have recovered
from the blow to her ego. But, in the end, she had learned to believe in
her own abilities. She no longer wanted or needed someone to lie to her
in order to believe that she and the world she fought to protect were
going to be all right.

———————————

Born in New York and raised in Delaware, Brian Rabian,
Ph.D., is currently a faculty member in the clinical psychology program at Penn State University, where he serves as assistant director of child and adolescent services in the Penn State
Psychological Clinic. He received his BA in psychology from
the University of Delaware, and his Ph.D. in psychology from
the George Washington University. Clinically, he supervises
doctoral students in the use of cognitive-behavioral interventions for children and adolescents. His research focuses on the
identification of risk factors for anxiety, and on the relationship between sleep and daytime functioning.

Michael Wolff, Ph.D., is currently a faculty member in the
psychology department at Penn State University, where he
teaches undergraduate and graduate psychology courses and
is a staff psychologist at the Penn State Psychological Clinic.
He received his BS from Penn State University, his master's in
counseling psychology from Antioch New England Graduate
School, and his Ph.D. in counseling psychology from Penn
State University. His research interests include psychotherapy

processes (alliance, relationship, therapist factors, etc.) and their impact on outcomes.

REFERENCES

American Psychiatric Association. *Diagnostic and Statistical Manual of Mental Disorders Fourth Edition, Text Revision*. American Psychiatric Association; Washington DC, 2000.

Havens, Candace. *Joss Whedon: The Genius Behind Buffy*. BenBella Books; Dallas, 2003.

"Thanatology," the formal study of dying, grief, and the psycho-social aspects of losing a loved one, was the foundation for Dr. Elizabeth Kubler-Ross's ground-breaking research and bestselling classic, On Death and Dying. Kubler-Ross studied a world of comparative innocence—before 1967's Six-Day War turned into a thirty-year siege, before that unforgettable day in September when the world learned that terror and paranoia knew no borders. Like today's real world, innocence is long gone aboard Firefly-class ship Serenity, where the specter of violent death—whether from space marauders, the Alliance, or the terrible mayhem of the Reavers—resides. As a theoretical lens through which to observe the crew's struggle with death, the safer world of thanatology has been usurped by "terror management"—not a macabre oxymoron, but a newer area of psychological study that Wind Goodfriend contends has chilling significance for Mal and his crew.

TERROR MANAGEMENT ABOARD *SERENITY*

WIND GOODFRIEND

"On that day, you will finally meet the man."
—Shan Yu, as quoted by Shepherd Book, "War Stories"

Death is a fundamental aspect of life, something with which every culture and every human must somehow come to terms. In the series *Firefly*, death is something that cannot be denied. Typically, we think of death as the worst imaginable situation. However, there is a benefit to death that is not typically acknowledged: death makes us who we are: soldiers, lovers, and friends. We learn this lesson in a very blatant way in the episode "War Stories," which was filled with torture, pain, and death. Twice, characters discussed the works of Shan Yu, a psychotic Chinese dictator. As Shepherd Book explained to Simon at the episode's beginning, "[He] wrote volumes on war, torture, the limits of human endurance. . . . He said, 'Live with a man forty years, share his house, his meals, speak on every subject. Then tie him up and hold him over the volcano's edge. And on that day, you will finally meet the man.'" The crew of *Serenity* lived on the metaphorical volcano's edge every day. Because of this, we truly met them. Their personal identities, relationships, and ideologies would not have been so strong without constant reminders of their mortality.

We can all relate to the ways in which death can change us. We have all experienced either the death of a family member, the death of a close friend, or the fear of our own death. Recently, the field of psychology has produced a highly innovative and controversial theory which attempts to explain what men and women experience, mentally, when they cannot escape the thought of death. This theory is called Terror Management Theory (hereafter referred to simply as TMT). Clearly, characters in *Firefly* could be used as an interesting application of the theory—do their lives serve as evidence of the hypotheses put forth in TMT? First, we must understand the basics of TMT and what it suggests.

Terror Management Theory

Terror Management Theory was created in 1984 by three men named Tom Pyszczynski, Sheldon Solomon, and Jeff Greenberg. Simply put, TMT attempts to explain human coping mechanisms in the face of death's inevitability and, sometimes, imminence. There are several tenets to TMT, and they build on each other. Here is a basic outline of the theory's ideas:

1. All living things want to continue living.
2. Humans are unique in that they realize immortality is impossible—we will, eventually, die.
3. Humans can imagine what the physical experience of death will be like.
4. The thought of death is terrifying.
5. To avoid thinking about death, we embrace "worldviews," or ways of giving meaning to life, such as culture, religion, or some kind of legacy.
6. These worldviews allow us to believe that even though we personally will die, there is some permanent reality, which we can contribute to in a lasting way.

In other words, we can avoid the terror caused by death by clinging to our culture or religion (and hope that this culture or religion will go on forever). In the words of the original creators of the theory, "Symbolically . . . humans can attain a sense of immortality by contributing to art, science, the building of magnificent pyramids or commanding skyscrapers, or, more modestly, by making some small but lasting contribution to ongoing life. . . . And they can sustain some sense of immortality simply by being a valued part of a larger collective unit such as a tribe . . . or nation" (Pyszczynski, Solomon, and Greenberg 20).

So, we avoid thinking about death by distracting ourselves and by trying to leave some lasting mark on the world. But the question arises: What happens when we cannot avoid death? Times when thoughts of death are unavoidable are called times of *mortality salience*—death is there, smacking you in the face. The Alliance is trying to kill you, or Reavers want to eat you for a light snack. What do you do? TMT argues that when death is at the doorstep, you will embrace your worldviews even more.

Research has shown that at least in the modern U.S., this tendency is strong. A good example of worldviews is the belief that established laws are useful and need enforcing—especially if you happen to be a court judge. In a study conducted in 1989, twenty-two municipal court judges filled out a survey. Half of the judges were asked to write an essay about what would happen to them when they physically died, including both physical and emotional changes. Next, all the judges read a hypothetical legal case briefing about a prostitution trial (something most Americans' worldviews consider negative and immoral). Judges who were reminded of death through writing the essay suggested a penalty bond of $455 for the defendant, whereas the judges who had gone through the exact same procedure minus the death essay suggested only $50. Clearly, thoughts of death increased the judges' desire to enforce laws and the moral standards of their culture (Rosenblatt, Greenberg, Solomon, Pyszczynski, and Lyon).

In their book *In the Wake of 9/11*, the original TMT researchers discuss how mortality salience affected Americans (and the rest of the world) after the terrorist attacks. Examples of the aftereffects of 9/11 ranged from the incredibly positive (the generosity of thousands of people who gave blood to the American Red Cross or donated money to the various 9/11 charities that were created) to the incredibly negative (the increase of prejudice against Arabs and Muslims). Another example is the increase in sales of engagement rings after the attacks. All of these phenomena show, again, people clinging to their own worldviews and what they find important in life. When death is on our minds, we more greatly value what makes life worthwhile.

Given this, consider again the life of the crew aboard *Serenity*. Mortality on *Serenity* is certainly as salient as it can be, when its crew must deal with not just making enough money to survive in a practical sense, but also avoiding an Alliance who would rather they were dead and Reavers who would like to make them into jackets. Their situation is a perfect one to help us understand how unavoidable death thoughts will lead to intensified worldviews. Specifically, we can see the effects of death in three areas: personal identity, close relationships, and ideological conviction.

Personal Identity Aboard Serenity

TMT suggests that in a world of mortality salience, one's personal identity should become very strong. Individuals will have well thought-out worldviews, which will lead them to a strong sense of self. Sometimes, they will also cling stubbornly to a pre-formed identity. We saw this perhaps the most strongly and consistently with Captain Mal Reynolds. Mal started his career as a sergeant, a leader against the conformist Alliance, and he lives his life according to specific codes of honor that he has created in his own mind to deal with the fact that he was on a losing side of a war, and remained on the losing side even after the war ended. Specifically, that code might be summed up in the following rules: (1) The crew and the ship come first; (2) The crew does not argue with the captain; (3) Never leave a crew member behind; (4) Never give up.

We see these rules guiding Mal's life in practically every situation. Even though the war is over, Mal is still fighting; he even named his ship after the final battle. His stealing and cheating, especially in regard to the Alliance, also show that he is raging against a system he sees as an evil regime. Mal's personal identity is a rebel, a fighter, and just because the war is ended doesn't mean he was going to give up this sense of self. He often made statements such as, "We don't vote on my ship," and, "Don't ever tell me what to do" ("Serenity"). He only kills people when absolutely necessary. And, as he explained to Simon, "If I ever kill you, you'll be awake. You'll be facing me, and you'll be armed" ("Serenity"). He also protects the innocent—in "The Train Job," he sacrificed a large profit and the personal safety of his crew when he chose to return stolen medical supplies to a town in need.

Why is Mal the man he has become? His guiding principles were formed at least in part during his time in the military; we see the structure and the implicit chain of command that he holds dear. However, at the same time, he delights in breaking the rules set by authorities he doesn't acknowledge. If the Alliance tells him to do it, he'll immediately do the exact opposite. Why? Fighting the Alliance, Mal knew that his life was most likely going to be brutish and short. The fact that he could die at any moment would have led him to the decision that if he was going to die, he was at least going to *choose* how he died—he wanted to die with meaning. He wanted to be worth something.

Kaylee, the innocent yet brilliant mechanic, chose the exciting and dirty life of a ship's mechanic, and clearly loves her role. We saw several instances where her feelings were hurt when others insulted this chosen identity. In "Shindig" she became upset when Mal suggested she didn't belong in a pink fluffy dress. (Later in the same episode she proved that she could be herself, even wearing something impractical and feminine, when she impressed all the men at a party with her mechanical knowledge.) In "Safe," when Simon complained that his life was horrible, their ship was junk, and following the captain's orders was asinine, Kaylee was deeply insulted: "If that's what you think of this life, then you can't think much of them that choose it, can you?" Something very similar occurred in "Jaynestown," when Mal found Kaylee asleep on top of Simon. Embarrassed, Simon blurted out, "Nothing happened! . . . We certainly didn't . . . I would never . . . not with Kaylee!" Kaylee was justifiably insulted. She has to believe that her life is good and meaningful—she has to embrace her worldview. Although she is certainly not in denial about her dangerous lifestyle, Kaylee is the only member of the crew who always tries to live optimistically, facing the possibility of death with a smile and (whenever possible) ripe strawberries to go along with it. Kaylee's identity is based on her ability to find the sunshine in a storm. It is likely that she would not be so chipper were she not around death all the time; otherwise, she could pace herself. Kaylee's cheerfulness is her defense mechanism in a world of mortality salience.

Inara chose the life of a beautiful and cultured Companion. She is comfortable with her identity in this profession, and is annoyed when people imply that her choice was immoral or unethical—although she is careful not to show this annoyance with clients. We saw a glimmer of this in "Serenity" when a client accused her of rigging her clock so that she was paid for more time than she actually gave. Her smile slowly faded, but she said nothing in response. She only voices her indignation when Mal insults her—but these comments likely hurt her the most, because they come from the man she loves. Before Inara boarded *Serenity*, her life was full of confidence and luxury. However, once she became part of a crew that regularly faced danger and death, Inara began to question some of her choices. She was sure of herself and her life before; on *Serenity*, mortality salience caused her to doubt what she really wanted and who she really was. The presence of death can make one question one's priorities.

Jayne is perhaps the character most focused on survival—at any cost. Jayne is *Serenity*'s hired gun (he is the brawn, whereas pretty much anyone standing next to him, by comparison, would be the brain). He does not apologize for this or for any actions that arise from his need to survive. The first time we saw Jayne, the crew had just barely escaped Alliance boarding after an illegal salvage job. Jayne's statement after their narrow escape epitomized his philosophy: "Any one you walk away from, right? Long as we got the goods, I call this a win" ("Serenity"). Later in the same episode, Jayne considered working with the Alliance federal agent on board to turn in River and Simon for a hefty payoff. His only question was, "Does helping you out mean turning on the captain?" Jayne ultimately decided to be loyal to the captain, because "the money wasn't good enough."

Jayne was willing to follow the captain's orders, because he knew that in the long run this course of action was his best bet for survival. His choices are guided by an avoidance of death. Later, he told Kaylee that he was confident the captain was going to turn them in himself and make them all rich ("The Train Job"). Later in the series, though, Jayne had the opportunity to turn over Simon and River, get the reward money, and not endanger the rest of the crew. He took it—from Jayne's perspective, the situation was perfect (until he was betrayed by the federal agents, that is). It is important to note that this decision to turn in Simon and River was motivated not only by money and the convenience of having them off the ship, but by a recent altercation in which River had slashed him across the chest with a nine-inch knife ("Ariel"). This physical danger, the knowledge that River could kill him in his sleep, was what sealed the deal in Jayne's mind. When physically threatened, Jayne showed his true self.

Other than, perhaps, Jayne, all of the main characters were examples of relatively positive (or at least likeable) reactions to mortality salience. However, *Firefly* did show us the darker side of identity solidification in "Bushwacked." In this episode, the crew rescued a man whose ship was destroyed by Reavers. The effect of witnessing death and torture were too much for this man to take. As Mal explained, "He looked right into the face of it, was made to stare. . . . They made him watch. He probably tried to turn away, but they wouldn't let him. You call him a survivor—he's not. A man comes up against that kind of will, the only way to deal with it, I suspect, is to *become* it."

The "survivor" took on the identity of a Reaver, killing others and mutilating himself. This man couldn't handle the death brought by Reavers, so his identity completely changed to become death itself. The Reavers were created by the Alliance in a world where almost everyone on the planet died a slow death. This creation was explained as a neurological effect, but imagine the psychological effect of being one of the people who didn't die in that situation: everywhere you go, people you've known for years are dying right in front of you. The entire landscape is a morbid, mottled field of decomposing bodies. Even without the benefit of Alliance drugs, would you not fundamentally change who you were? It is possible that the Reavers' transformation happened in part because they couldn't psychologically handle a plague of these proportions. The Reavers *became* death—their worldview was nothing *but* death, so they embraced that and helped it spread. They slit their tongues and dressed in blood. They wore the skulls of their neighbors. The survivor in "Bushwacked" did the same. Any of us might have done the same. The Reavers were, after all, human.

Close Relationships Aboard Serenity

On a lighter note, mortality salience will often strengthen interpersonal bonds. We saw the awkward love of Inara and Captain Mal develop aboard *Serenity*. It was clear that they wanted to be with each other; however, their strong identities (as established above) got in the way. If they were to acknowledge their love, Inara would have to find another profession, and Mal would have to give up the ship and crew as his first priority. Mal also demonstrated behavior that indicated he felt inferior to the educated and classy Inara—that he felt she was "out of his league," so to speak. To get around this he insulted her whenever possible, calling her names like "whore" and implying she was common, in an ill-designed effort to make them more like equals. However, it was when death was salient that their true feelings came out—the terror of death solidified their yearning. For example, when the Reavers were chasing them in "Serenity," Mal softly touched her shoulder and ordered her off the ship for her own safety.

We saw their true feelings most clearly in three situations. The first was in "Shindig," when Mal caused trouble at a party because of his jealousy over Inara's date. When he was challenged to a duel by this man, who was clearly more skilled than Mal, Mal and Inara reached out to each other because they feared that Mal would die. This fear of death caused them to value the time they still had together. Second, when Inara believed Mal had been killed in "Our Mrs. Reynolds," her relief in discovering he was only unconscious led her to kiss him, overcome with passion. Finally, their relationship, in many ways, came to an end in "Heart of Gold." Here, Mal and the crew helped a house of prostitutes defend themselves against a local rancher. Mal took out his sexual tension over Inara with the house madame, but only after Inara told him that she wanted their relationship to be "professional." But Inara was clearly just pushing him away, because she was extremely hurt when she found out he had slept with someone else. As in most episodes, this one ended with everyone getting shot at and several people dying. It was during the aftermath of this experience that Inara told Mal she was leaving the ship for good. She understood that their feelings for one another either had to come out in the open, or end.

Kaylee and Simon shared a similar dilemma, in which they were interested in each other but not quite sure how to go about expressing it. Simon was more responsible for this relationship's failure than Kaylee was, but only because another close relationship—with his sister River—had to be his priority until River was safe. This sibling relationship was extremely strong (perhaps the strongest relationship aboard the ship). When Simon told the story of River's life to the crew in "Serenity," he smiled and spoke in a soft tone of love. He clearly did not regret sacrificing his entire life for her safety. In "Safe," we saw that Simon gave up everything, including his medical career and relationship with his parents, to keep River from pain and possible death. In this episode he even stood with River, ready to die with her, when local villagers tried to burn her as a witch; being faced with River's mortality strengthened the love he felt for her. However, we see the same thing when he faces his own and Kaylee's death at the end of *Serenity*. About to be raped, murdered, and eaten by hundreds of Reavers, he tells Kaylee that his only regret is not having been with her.

Firefly's only successful romantic relationship was the marriage between Zoe and Wash. When really put to the test, it was clear that either would sacrifice anything for the other. Zoe would have chosen Wash over the ship or her friendship with Mal, and Wash couldn't bear to be away from Zoe, especially when she was hurt or in danger. In "Serenity," as Reavers hovered overhead, Zoe and Wash held hands, literally reaching out to each other in this time of mortality salience. Later in the same episode Wash stated his concern for Zoe's safety explicitly: "Zoe's out on a job, I always worry." When the crew got back from the job safely, successfully outrunning the Reavers on their tail, Zoe's first thought was of grabbing Wash and making love. Being physically intimate with her husband was how she wanted to work off the built-up death anxiety. Wash was happy to help.

Interestingly, we learned in "Out of Gas" that Zoe didn't like Wash when he first came aboard. It's possible that she was immediately attracted to him, and this made her uncomfortable (as a strong and independent woman), and that is why she didn't like him. However, another possibility is that she just really didn't like him. In this scenario, they would have been drawn together only because of mortality salience. A smaller and older theory in psychology is "misattribution of arousal." You can become physiologically aroused for any number of reasons: fear, excitement . . . or, of course, anxiety arousing from potential death. In this situation, your heart is beating, you are sweating, and you feel light-headed. The misattribution of arousal comes in when you project these physical reactions onto someone nearby, interpreting your body signals as physical attraction to the other person. The symptoms are certainly similar. Thus, it's possible that being in mortal peril all the time led Zoe and Wash to be attracted to each other. It's also possible that constant danger made them yearn for something happy and meaningful in life—such as the passionate embrace of a lover.

Ideological Conviction Aboard Serenity

Finally, mortality salience and the threat of death often increase one's ideological convictions. As described above, Mal is a true solider, still fighting for the cause of Independence even though the war is over and his side lost. His belief in that cause was made clear repeatedly. However, we also saw Mal's conviction come through in other ways. One of these was his strong belief in the military philosophy that you never leave a man behind. In "Safe," it looked as if Mal would leave Simon and River behind when they were kidnapped by a village in need of a doctor. However, Mal later arrived at the last minute, and saved them both from being burned at the stake. When Simon asked him why he came back, he answered simply, "You're on my crew." Mal also went to great lengths to bring back Simon and River after Jayne turned them in to the feds ("Ariel"). When Jayne didn't understand why Mal was upset with him (after all, Jayne didn't endanger Mal), Mal explained, "You turn on *any* of my crew, you turn on me. . . . You did it to ME, Jayne, and that's a fact." The only reason he kept Jayne on the crew afterward was that Jayne asked Mal not to tell the rest of the crew what he'd done, indicating that Jayne really did care what they thought of him—especially when he thought he was about to die. Jayne wanted to leave a lasting impression that was positive, and that was the focus of his attention with death quickly approaching.

Another example of Mal's conviction came in "The Message," when they picked up a soldier who fought with Mal and Zoe in the war. Tracey had been a private under Mal's command, and he was relatively incompetent. Mal and Zoe attempted to help him when he was running from a deal gone bad, but Tracey betrayed them, shot at Wash, took Kaylee hostage, and insulted all of them. He endangered them as well by putting them in the path of dangerous men. Mal clearly has no patience for betrayal, and he cannot stand it when others threaten his crew and ship. Mal attempts to convince others that he is an uncaring, brazen rebel. So why didn't Mal turn Tracey over, or just shoot him out of the airlock? Most people in this situation would have done just that. But Mal is more complicated than he likes to admit. Mal knows that he is nothing without friendship, and the reason he cannot bear betrayal is because he so fiercely values loyalty. Mal remained loyal to Tracey, facing the threat of death by choosing to protect his friend and bring him home. Mal's code of honor remained true. He could only live with himself if he knew that he was the better man.

Ideological conviction defined Shepherd Book. His past was never fully explained, but he was certainly more than he appeared. He described himself in humble terms: "I'm a Shepherd. . . . Been out of the world for a spell; like to walk it awhile. Maybe bring the Word to those who need it told" ("Serenity"). Despite leaving his monastery, Shepherd Book was still preaching and reaching out; he still believed in God, and believed that faith would set you free. When an Alliance spy attempted to arrest Simon in the first episode and ended up shooting Kaylee instead, Book punched him in the face and disarmed him, but prevented Jayne from actually harming the man. He thus protected the crew, but also protected the man himself, showing that even in the face of death, he would hold to his beliefs.

In "Bushwacked," *Serenity* came upon a ship ravaged by Reavers. Most of the crew wanted to get rid of the survivor they found there, perhaps even kill him, but Book defended the man's right to live and find solace. Shepherd even argued that Reavers are just "men, nothing more. . . . Too long removed from civilization perhaps, but men. And I believe there's a power greater than men. A power that heals." When confronted with Reavers and the slaughter that comes with them, Shepherd's religious conviction only became stronger. He also argued that he should go over to the ship to provide prayer and death rituals to those who had been killed. Shepherd Book believed—he had to.

Book's faith was true—but that doesn't mean it was unquestioned. He seemed to have a crisis of faith after only a few hours on *Serenity*. After an ordeal that we can only assume initiated more feelings of mortality salience than he'd experienced in a long time, he confessed to Inara, "Is this what life is? Out here? I've been out of the Abbey two days. I've beaten a lawman senseless, fallen in with criminals. I've watched the captain shoot the man I swore to protect. And I'm not even sure if I think he was wrong. I believe I just . . . I think I'm on the wrong ship." It is possible that this was the first time Book had questioned his choices. Death made him confront what he always believed to be true. It was only after two days of danger and guns that he asked himself what he really believed. Inara knew this was an important point in his life. She answered, "Maybe. But maybe you're exactly where you ought to be" ("Serenity"). Faith is not something that should be based on blindly following what you've been told to believe in. True faith is based on questioning what you have learned, then really *agreeing* with it. You can't truly believe in something unless you've doubted it. This experience, which would not have happened if Shepherd had not faced death, is what made his faith stronger than ever.

But the person with perhaps the strongest ideological conviction in the entire *Firefly* universe is the movie's antagonist, the Operative. This man caused death; he killed hundreds in his quest. He was an assassin. But what was his personal ideology? What was his quest? Did he blindly follow orders from the Alliance, as a simple-minded drone? Quite the opposite—the Operative wanted a better world, and he was willing to do anything to get it. "A better world" was his worldview, his mission, his conviction.

In some ways the Operative was death incarnate. For him to be at peace with this choice of profession (which he clearly was), he had to reconcile in himself that death was the *way* to achieve his worldview, instead of his worldview serving as a distraction from death. This is a unique position. In fact, the Operative knew that what he was doing was evil—he believed that he had no place in a better world. Killers are not part of a better world—unnecessary death is not part of a better world.

It requires quite a bit of mental gymnastics to believe that what you are doing is horrible and evil, but also, at the same time, *right*. How could the Operative use death while simultaneously abhorring it? It seems impossible. However, it is a stance that many people would agree with.

Think about some examples. What if no one ever died? Assuming that people still procreated, the world would very quickly consume itself in a flood of overpopulation. We *need* death. In addition, thousands of people are in favor of the death penalty for criminals. Again, according to this philosophy, we need death, or at least are warranted in using it in some situations, if we so choose. Even people who do not agree with the death penalty often admit that if we could go back in time and kill people like Hitler before the Holocaust, murder would be justified. If these decisions seem rational, why not the decisions of the Operative? He lives in a world where death is not something to be feared, but instead something to be used.

In the end, the Operative decided that River needed to stay alive to create that better world; he broke his allegiance to the Alliance. This emphasized that the Operative was a thinking man, not a mindless drone. Perhaps because of his unique view of death, he was the character with the strongest ideology of all—he would do anything for a better world, even if he could not enjoy that world himself. Terror Management says that we all want a better world—it's just that for most of us, the best world is one that includes us. Perhaps our fear of death blinds us to any other possibility, and the Operative is one of the rare individuals who can really see.

WIND GOODFRIEND, PH.D., is an assistant professor of psychology at Buena Vista University. She earned her Ph.D. in social psychology in 2004 from Purdue University. Her areas of research expertise are gender stereotypes and romantic relationships, focusing specifically on positive and negative predictors of relationship stability over time. In her final year of graduate school, Dr. Goodfriend received both the "Outstanding Teacher of the Year Award" and the

"Outstanding Graduate Student of the Year Award" for her research. Since then, she has been nominated for and won several more research and teaching awards.

REFERENCES

Pyszczynski, Tom, Sheldon Solomon, and Jeff Greenberg. *In the Wake of 9/11: The Psychology of Terror*. Washington, DC: American Psychological Association, 2003.

Abram Rosenblatt, Jeff Greenberg, Sheldon Solomon, Tom Pyszczynski, and Deborah Lyon, "Evidence for Terror Management Theory: I. The Effects of Mortality Salience on Reactions to Those Who Violate or Uphold Cultural Values," *Journal of Personality and Social Psychology* 57.4 (1989): 681–690.

Despite the threat of drive-bys and lone gunmen, Bardi and Hamby remind us that no classroom on Earth can rival Sunnydale's—where, as they point out here, "every school day has a body count"—for sheer preponderance of death anxiety. In exploring Buffy the Vampire Slayer's *fiercely feminist approach to using heroic action against existential angst, they suggest that Whedon's genius lay in giving a cute blond chick physical prowess beyond any living man's. With this single device he evolved a premise through which to incubate increasingly complex layers of existential dilemmas—and not just Buffy's, but all the characters' within her sphere. These not only sustained the series for seven world-saving seasons, but ensured its meaningful afterlife beyond the gaping maw of cancellation.*

EXISTENTIALISM MEETS FEMINISM IN *BUFFY THE VAMPIRE SLAYER*

C. Albert Bardi and Sherry Hamby

A growing corner of psychology has devoted itself to the study of "terror management," or how people protect themselves from the knowledge of their own mortality. One of the experiments in this field sounds like something from an episode of *Buffy the Vampire Slayer*. Participants in the study are given the problem of nailing something to the wall and the only useful thing lying around is a crucifix. The results of the experiment show that participants are less likely to use the cross if they are first made more aware of death (made "mortality salient"). According to the researcher Greenberg and his colleagues, participants don't want to denigrate their meaning-making religious symbol, especially when they are confronted with the reason they need religion in the first place, death. (This particular setup only works with Christians, naturally, but similar results have been found with other groups.)

Of course, Buffy and her Scooby pals, and in fact all of ironically named Sunnydale for that matter, are ultra mortality salient. No one is confronted with death more than the Slayer and her associates. As a consequence, Buffy and friends should be struggling more than your average mortal to solve the basic riddle of existence: How do we find meaning when we are all doomed?

Thus Buffy, stake in hand, plays out one of the great existential metaphors of modern times. Existential psychology, especially as expressed in the work of Ernest Becker (from which terror management theory is derived), asserts that humans are ultimately motivated by their fear of death. And in *Buffy the Vampire Slayer*, Joss Whedon has explored all the great existential issues—angst, meaning, the limitations of existence, and the striving for immortality.

In our world, one important means of reducing death anxiety is through heroism, because heroism, like other solutions to death anxiety, offers some partial immortality through the chance to be remembered beyond the grave. Unfortunately, heroism as a path for the existentially despairing has generally been reserved for the male version of the death-conscious *homo sapiens*. Buffy, with her ability to kick some real undead butt (and despite her unassuming teenage persona), takes the usual heroic cultural solutions to the problem of meaning—which have been heretofore mostly supplied from a patriarchal perspective—into new, compelling feminist directions.

In *Buffy the Vampire Slayer*, Whedon enthralls the viewer by using each character—Buffy, Giles, Willow, Xander, Spike, and even some evildoers—to illustrate the highly individual and even idiosyncratic ways humans deal with the problem of meaning in the face of death. Even more compelling is that *Buffy* weaves gender into this subtle allegory, showing us that existential solutions can be thwarted, shaped, or encouraged by a highly gendered, patriarchal society.

Buffy and the Surprising Problems That Aren't Solved by Power

Here's a cold fact of our world: Women, on average, are less physically powerful than men. Although some feminists reject such essentialist notions of male and female, existential feminists such as Simone de Beauvoir assert that women's lives are heavily influenced by the biological differences between males and females. Through Buffy, Joss Whedon forges an entire anti-patriarchal universe from one creative act—giving a girl physical power beyond any living man. Forget the vampires. While they and other demons generate fuel for the plot, it is Buffy's power that makes the story.

You would think such power might solve those pesky old existential dilemmas once and for all. Buffy's solution to the problem of meaning would seem as easy as stone-etched destiny: Given you're the only one who can save the world, and given the world badly needs saving, then saving the world is what you do—Q.E.D. The rub is that Buffy is still a girl becoming a young woman.

When we first meet Buffy in the film, her goals are simply to maintain her popularity and appearance. Why would she want to give up the easy assurances of being cool and attractive for some icky, bizarre vampire-slayer destiny? But this is not a point of existential choice for Buffy, it is destiny. It's not long before Buffy begins to revel in her phallic power (yes, phallic—don't forget the omnipresent stake). Early on it seemed that Buffy had become convinced that her slayer destiny left her with no decisions to make. While her friends were completing career aptitude tests, Buffy bemoaned the futility of considering career options given her unique and permanent vocation. She's the Slayer, and she just needed to fake the civilian life stuff so that she could continue to save the world. In this respect she seemed just as trapped as a *Father Knows Best*–style homemaker—her role had been prescribed by forces outside of her with little input on her part.

Human realities and the Hellmouth interfere with such simplicities, both for good and ill. Buffy's power is not necessarily an asset in the quest to find meaning, and is sometimes even a liability. Her heroic solution did not provide existential peace. She was ambivalent about her role and constantly wondered whether the sacrifices were worth it. Her successes against the legions of death did not seem to count much in the lives of those she loves. The show was known for its human, as well as demon, death count, and for these lost people there was nothing that Buffy could do. Her mother died, not from some demonic or magical influence, but from something as inscrutable and meaningless as a brain tumor. And when Buffy made the ultimate sacrifice and gave her life for her friends and family, they resurrected her after a few months, ripping her from heavenly bliss. Buffy's existential dilemma persisted even when an eternal life in heaven was assured.

107

Yet, even as it offered only a partial solution to existential dilemmas, her heroism also seemed to close off opportunities for other sources of meaning and comfort: enduring romantic relationships. Another important body count in the series was the number of men that either couldn't handle Buffy's power or were forsaken by her for the greater good. Her superhero life is too much for mere mortals, even for Riley, who was about as close to a superhero as an actual human gets. The non-humans didn't work out any better. Perhaps one of Buffy's most poignant turning points came when Angel, her first lover, lost his soul because of their moment of pure bliss. Even though he eventually regained his soul, the relationship could not continue. She tried again with mortals and immortals alike, but it seemed that in the area of love, her powers were of no help.

As the series marched toward its end, and the darkness got stronger, we saw Buffy struggle to hold on to her role as Slayer and to develop as a leader and teacher. Her house was filled with potential slayers, who she was trying to train for an all-out war with an army of demons. Potentials and friends alike challenged her authority and her decisions. As with us all, she was forced to accept the consequences of both destiny and choice. Although, as existentialists point out, in some respects we all ultimately walk alone, there is also the challenge of finding the balance between independence and interrelationship, and this is one of the clearest examples of the way that Whedon has used feminist principles to stretch existentialist ideas. The final note of the series emphasized the latter, when Buffy's best friend, Willow, was able to awaken all the potential slayers across the world and ignite their slayer power. Together the Sunnydale team fought off the demons and sealed the Hellmouth. The earth was renewed with the common strength of Buffy and her sisters.

So, Giles, You Just Watch?

Every Dracula needs a Rehnquist, and every slayer needs a Watcher. No one can escape the existential yearning to be the hero of their own story, yet the Watcher, the Slayer's *sensei* and demon expert, has to completely and utterly abandon selfish projects and settle for a backstage pass. Oh sure, he knows all the secrets and he is seldom far from the real action. Yet, as a character in a supporting role, Giles had to bear the existential costs of pouring his entire selfhood into his slayer.

Early in the series we had no sense that behind Giles's scholarly persona there was a wish to be anything but an unsung hero. In fact, it is only when the Scoobies discovered that Giles did, literally, sing (Clapton, in a—gasp!—*public* café) that it occurred to the Slayer and the Scoobies that this tweedy bookworm had a personal life. Nevertheless, while youth may get fooled by the repressive efforts of adult meaning-making, the truth will out and it was not long before Whedon treated us to Giles's personal brand of angst.

It is tempting to say that Giles eschewed the normal male routes for immortality—career and family. In fact, when we met Giles he demonstrated many of the characteristics of the corporate climber and distracted father. He unquestioningly obeyed the Watchers' Council. He was also the emotionless *paterfamilias*, who held high performance expectations while too often ignoring his slayer's emotional needs. In Giles's defense, he was, like all elders, more aware of grave realities. Nobly, Giles worked ceaselessly to train Buffy. At the same time, he tried to protect her from the reality that she would, in all likelihood, die young. He simultaneously tried to train her to stand independently and to protect her.

In neither our world nor the *Buffy*verse are these interpersonal dynamics stable states of affairs. Any self-respecting Slayer with her own immortality projects would have gotten annoyed by all that *watching* before long, and Giles became more and more frustrated with Buffy's choice to run off, stake in hand, rather than study and train. Initially this dynamic solidified Giles's role, and existential choice, as representative of the patriarchy. Yet on any existential path, one is inevitably faced with dilemmas. Do we rigidly cling to our best-laid plans for meaning, or do we transcend them when they become worn? For Giles the moment of truth came when he was instructed by the Watchers' Council to subject Buffy to the Cruciamentum, a test of her slayer abilities that involved deceiving her, using drugs to strip her powers, and locking her up with a bloodsucker. To our dismay, Giles went through with the plan, yet at the last minute he rushed to help Buffy. For his loyalty, Giles was punished by the Council and lost the two life-devotions he had: his job as

Watcher, and his protectorship of Buffy.

Later in the series, of course, this corner of the Whedon world was put right: Buffy eventually took full control of her destiny and demanded that the Council knock off the stealth maneuvers and quit interfering with Giles assisting her. In name he became her Watcher once more, but Giles was no longer Boss or Daddy. As Buffy matured even further, Giles increasingly turned to other pursuits, both intellectual and interpersonal. He appeared to have achieved some sense of peace, having made his contribution to saving the world (the rest of us should be so lucky to have such a literal impact on that goal), and to have accepted his evolving role in place of static privilege handed to him by a male establishment.

Willow and the Question of Limits

Human beings are finite, limited creatures. When we first met Willow Rosenberg, she seemed almost distressingly comfortable with limits. She was a good, well-behaved student who largely conformed to the restricted roles made available to female high school students. In existential terms, the early Willow demonstrated many classic signs of what Ernest Becker called "fear of life." She was modest and unassuming even though she demonstrated computer prowess that would make Steve Jobs proud. She spent a lot of time fretting that she was not achieving in the domain of relationships—the accepted preoccupation of middle-class white females. Her personal power was not much in evidence and, like many youth, she seemed to have little sense that she could be turning her energies to more meaningful pursuits. She was rather unremarkable from either an existential or feminist point of view, and her first glimmers of power did not fundamentally alter this profile. Even when she exhibited extraordinary powers, as when she resurrected Angel's soul, she remained blithely unaware of it. She was comfortable as a limited being and had barely begun to ask what being so limited meant.

It's no surprise that someone so repressed would be ripe for problems with addiction. As her dabbling in magic turned to a serious interest and then almost to obsession, Willow abandoned nearly every aspect of her former conventionality. She explored her sexuality and began a lesbian affair with Tara, her partner in witchcraft. She started taking little short-cuts, breaking little promises, and then even began ignoring her friends' pleas to control her power. She thought she could get away with any-thing, even altering Tara's memories. She pushed and pushed against limits until finally the world, represented by Tara, pushed back. She tried to control herself but temptation was ever present. The desire to ignore limits—not only the laws of physics but the physical integrity of others—became the central issue of her life.

One limit with which Willow wrestled repeatedly was death itself. She literally resurrected Buffy at the beginning of season six to assuage her own grief, never stopping to think whether this was something that Buffy would want as well. Willow, and Xander, too, refused to face the prospect of continuing without Buffy. When Tara died, Willow was thwarted from completing another resurrection, and nearly destroyed the world in her anger that she could not control all of life's tragedies.

Willow struggled with the temptations of power right up until the end of the series. When she finally harnessed and expressed her full power it was once again with the goal of defying limits, this time ones that had been in place for centuries, by breaking the rule that limited slayer power to one girl in every generation and helping all of the potential slayers to achieve their full power simultaneously. From a feminist point of view, it is a great metaphor for casting off the constraints of patriar-chal society. From an existentialist point of view, one wonders if there are limits to casting off limits.

Sorry, Xander: Phallic Power Is Not Worth Much in Whedon World

In childhood we feel the helplessness of existence but still have faith in adults' power to protect and comfort. In adolescence, however, we first glimpse the absurdity and futility of the various solutions to the prob-lem of finding meaning. We begin to see caricatures of all the adult paths that can be taken. Teens do what adults do: they pick up habits, stum-ble through relationships, switch cliques, and suffer mindless employ-ment. They make their choices, yet they make them with the casualness of someone who is both newly self-conscious and with the shortsighted-ness of those for whom death seems distant and mostly unreal.

Some young adults just avoid acting altogether. Xander couldn't be a better example of this. All around him were kids who had something going on, while he had neither a special power nor a special group. He wasn't smart enough to be a nerd, athletic enough to be a jock, cool enough to be popular, or geeky enough to be a total loser (despite Cordelia's insistence). With no power, no path, and no group-supported claims, Xander's existential dilemma was this: How do I fit in a world where even all the women are more powerful than me?

Xander's often immature pursuits of women—including but not limited to Buffy, Cordelia, the Mummy Empada, the demon Anya, and other women who too often turned out to be demons—were all ill-considered attempts to solve his existential problem with a standard male sexual solution. Once, his project even resulted in the poetic justice of every woman in Sunnydale lusting after him with violently vicious force. Yet we knew that he was doomed to fail, as all are who would seek to solve psychological issues purely with sex. And when Xander finally got his wish to have sex with a slayer, it was not with Buffy but with Faith, and she afterward tossed him aside.

How was Xander saved from his adolescent existential stasis? We could say it was the commando training (which he retained from the Sunnydale Halloween where people became their costumes), which gave him the special skills he never had. We could also say that he finally found the courage to fight vampires using his own mettle. Or we could suggest that Xander came into his own as the Scoobies' heart and soul in this reverse-gendered *Buffy*verse, where the only man of the superhero group became the caretaker and cheerleader. But it may be most on the mark to say that like so many privileged, aimless males in our real world, Xander ultimately developed in the course of a challenging relationship.

It is Xander's passionate, mercurial, and downright freaky relationship with the demon Anya that helped him find his path to meaning. Throughout their relationship, Anya was involved in a twelve-step-like recovery from hundreds of years of addiction to power and vengeance. It was no surprise that when Xander became involved with Anya, she was going through the process of learning how to behave herself around people. This is where Xander shines. For even though he showed many signs of (again, standard male) commitment phobia—reluctance to get a steady job, resistance to leave his parents' basement, terror at the idea of getting engaged—Xander came into his own as an apologist for humanity. As the series progressed, episode after episode treated us to scenes where Xander was teaching Anya about the most crucial of human powers—loyalty, courage, and hope. It was in his role as her helpmate that he grew beyond his adolescent alienation to greater maturity, finding active meaning *in relation*, rather than sexual conquest.

Spike: Even Immortals Endure Existential Dilemmas

When we first met Spike, he was your basic happy-go-lucky evildoer. He relished every wicked act and delighted in the prospect of widespread suffering. It wasn't long, though, before Spike's insecurities become apparent. As with many men in our society, Spike's sense of self was wrapped up in competitive outcomes. When Angel reverted to Angelus, an almost immediate contest between him and Spike ensued, both for Drusilla's attention and the position of alpha vampire. Although not really sincere in his affections for Drusilla, Angelus met with success in both competitions. In his injured condition, Spike turned to drink and some excessive displays of angst. He had been stripped of two high-status roles, at least in the vampire community, and had a crisis in meaning. Apparently even soulless immortals are not beyond the reach of existential dilemmas.

Spike's crush on Buffy at first seemed little more than a rebound from his losses. It was so wildly improbable and so actively discouraged by Buffy that it hardly seemed a fruitful path to reestablishing meaning in his (un)life. At first his attempts to connect with Buffy vacillated between expressions of affection and reversions to violence and violation. Although slowly he more clearly and consistently aided Buffy and the Scoobies, at first his "help" (at the end of season two) was purely self-serving—the enemy of his enemy is his friend. Spike's true choices then became obscured when the chip prevented him from hurting any living thing was inserted in his brain. Even with the crushing pain caused by acts of evil, he could not completely control his violent outbursts. He was dispossessed of one tool of male competition—violence—yet he was still plagued by the aggressive impulses. Still, despite these existential ambiguities, his new role as sometime-helper provided a modicum of meaning and gave him exposure to the side of good.

When Buffy was resurrected he undertook a highly dysfunctional sexual relationship with her. Although he understood at least partially that he was being used, he so longed for closeness he continued the relationship anyway. When Buffy finally broke it off, he at first reverted to violence and attempted to rape her. His quick regret (at least compared to your typical rapist) led to the realization that he had not gone far enough to regain some measure of his lost humanity. He successfully regained his soul and, in the waning hours of the series achieved a truly heroic sense of purpose. Spike became an actualized being who was willing to make the ultimate sacrifice for love and the greater good. That's as close to an existential solution as any of us ever get. (Yes, we know he rematerializes in Los Angeles for the final season of *Angel*. In TV the charismatic seldom really die. The rest of us won't be so lucky.)

Would You Murder for Immortality?

Even the least charismatic vampires still have the great existential prize—immortality. There is just the teensy problem of having to become a serial murderer in order to achieve it. Most vampires, at least in the *Buffy*verse, can say that they weren't trying to become vampires—they became vampires because they caught the eye of someone who already was. But it is also true that virtually all of them, with the notable exception of Angel, kill humans to live and to slake their demon appetites, even though they could subsist on other blood. A few episodes of *Buffy the Vampire Slayer* explicitly broached the appeal of this Faustian bargain for the general public.

One of the most telling *Buffy* episodes, from an existential point of view, was "Lie to Me" (2-7). A group of adolescents had decided to become vampires so that they could achieve immortality and "stay pretty." Most seemed blithely unaware of the danger they were courting. They were dabbling in the camp of vampire culture as it is portrayed in old movies—all capes, pointy hair styles, and candlelit rooms. They didn't really appreciate that they were actually going to die, much less be

replaced by demons. They didn't understand that you have to be selected to become a vampire; otherwise you're just dinner. Their naïveté
about the costs of immortality almost exacted the price of their lives.
Only one of them, Ford, beset with terminal cancer, was truly earnest
and evil enough, even in his pre-demon state, to seek immortality at any
cost. He betrayed Buffy; but Buffy, of course, prevailed, and was waiting
to stake Ford upon his emergence from the grave.

In psychological terms, the surviving youth in "Lie to Me" experienced growth and increased ontological awareness. Somewhat unusual-
ly for people of such a young age, they had directly felt their yearning
for immortality. As adolescents, they were also willing to break rules and
engage in taboo pursuits. These are actually behaviors that are associated with repressed death anxiety, so their behavior was in some regards
an expression of the conflict between partial existential awareness and
typical adolescent death repression. With the exception of Ford, by the
end of the episode these teenagers had made psychological progress on
both of these fronts. Regarding their yearning for immortality, they had
come to terms with some of the parameters of human existence. In a
Beckerian analysis, it seems likely that they would now pursue some of
the more traditional paths to immortality—achievement, family—and
reject trying to obtain it literally. Chanterelle (later Anne), although initially somewhat lost after this encounter, did find more meaning in her
later appearances in *Buffy* and *Angel*. As with many adolescent brushes
with death, these youths' too-real encounter with vampires also led them
to value the life they had.

The Answer to the Problem of Existence?

Writers of books on existential psychology are plagued by a tricky issue:
If they pose the question of how meaning can be found in an ultimately
meaningless existence, people will be searching for a solution in the
back of the book and may be quite disappointed if they don't get one. In
his book *The Denial of Death*, Ernest Becker addresses this issue by first
slashing through some pat answers—longer life through medicine
(hah!), living more in your body rather than your head (double hah!)—
and then challenging the reader to find the best solution he or she can.

How should we each evaluate the quality of our own solutions? By how much life *and* death we take in—or in existential lingo, how much being and non-being we encompass. The catch is that the more real being you take in, the more non-being you get. Buffy received more power, thus Buffy received more meaning, more joy, but clearly more suffering, too. Xander finally reached adult maturity and came to care for Anya, only to lose her in the final battle. Willow came to a more mature and relational understanding of her power, but then had to humble herself with endless hours of practice to learn its judicious use. Every character's true growth can be traced this way, because being and non-being are the essential and ultimately inseparable yin and yang of existence.

Whedon reminds us, however, that even though we are free to choose a greater, more-encompassing circle of living (and more dying with it), culture, here in the form of gender, must be confronted in making those choices. In Xander's search for greater purpose and meaning, he had to overcome the narrow definitions of his male role. Spike, too, had to find a way to grow beyond his macho survival-of-the-fittest perspective.

Existentialism has always been a fairly macho pursuit. The ideals of existentialism are characteristics like courage (Rollo May) and idealized exemplars like Nietzsche's "superman" ("übermensch" in the original German). Existentialists often argue that we are essentially alone and disconnected. Can't get much more masculine than that. But Joss Whedon has helped show that you can address the big existential questions of meaning and purpose—and do so with courage—without hypermasculinity. The ultimate intersection of gender and existence is presented in the final episode of *Buffy the Vampire Slayer*: the forces of evil defeated through the expression of female power. Nonbeing was not vanquished—losses were endured, the future was uncertain, and other bulwarks of evil were yet to be challenged—yet hope was kindled. The ending of *Buffy* was the ultimate melding of clarity of purpose and the power of interrelationships—a beautiful expression of both existentialist and feminist ideals.

C. ALBERT BARDI, PH.D., is associate professor and chair of the psychology department at St. Andrews Presbyterian College in Laurinburg, North Carolina. He received his doctorate in clinical psychology from the University of North Carolina at Chapel Hill in 1996. His scholarly and clinical interests include existential psychology, the immigrant experience in America, Latino psychology, American Indian psychology, and the measurement and correlates of optimism and personal entitlement.

SHERRY HAMBY, PH.D., is research associate professor in the department of psychology at the University of North Carolina at Chapel Hill. She is co-author of *The Conflict Tactics Scales* handbook, and author or co-author of more than fifty other publications on victimization, assessment, and other topics. Dr. Hamby is a recipient of awards from the National Register for Health Service Providers in Psychology and the American Professional Society on the Abuse of Children. She has been principal investigator on grants from the National Center for Health Statistics, Indian Health Service, and other agencies. She is also a licensed clinical psychologist.

REFERENCES

de Beauvoir, Simone. *The Second Sex.* Trans. Howard Parshley. New York: Knopf, 1953.
Becker, Ernest. *The Denial of Death.* New York: Free Press, 1973.
Jeff Greenberg, Jonathan Porteus, Linda Simon, and Tom Pyszczynski, "Evidence of a Terror Management Function of Cultural Icons: The Effects of Mortality Salience on the Inappropriate Use of Cherished Cultural Symbols," *Personality and Social Psychology Bulletin* 21.11 (1995): 1221–1228.

Feminism has undergone numerous incarnations over the past century, splitting off into various "waves" over time, and within each wave, dividing into camps, such as liberal feminism, Marxist feminism, sex-positive feminism, and radical feminism. Joss Whedon has stated in the press that he is a radical feminist, believing that gender oppression, rather than class, race, or religious oppression, is at the root of most social ills. Can we take Joss at his word? Misty K. Hook puts the Whedonverse in the spotlight to see if his body of work is really as radical as the man himself claims to be.

DEALING WITH THE F-WORD

Joss Whedon and Radical Feminism

MISTY K. HOOK

Much has been made about whether the work of Joss Whedon is feminist. Books have been written, blogs composed, honors given, and arguments created on the premise that the 'verses of *Buffy*, *Angel*, and *Firefly* are feminist. All this talk about the feminism in his work is interesting, but the truly fascinating story rests with Joss himself. Some may wonder why a man would publicly proclaim himself a feminist; even in twenty-first-century America, the term "feminist" is often greeted with discomfort, even derision, and Joss describes himself not just as a feminist but as a *radical* feminist. All feminists believe in the equality of women, but radical feminists take it a whole lot deeper. Radical feminists believe that the cause of women's oppression lies deep in the entire gendered system (Tong). Thus, being a radical feminist means believing that fundamental changes to that system are necessary in order to bring equality (Steinem). Consequently, feminists tend to work within the existing system while radical feminists question the foundation of society itself.

Joss has located himself squarely within that paradigm. This is quite unusual. It's understandable that some women would hold radical views,

119

but a man? What causes a white, heterosexual male, who it is hard to imagine has suffered the kind of discrimination that would make him sympathetic to radical feminism's cause, to think and behave so far outside of the box?

To answer such a question, you have to think about gender. In our culture, certain traits tend to be considered either masculine or feminine. Someone who is ambitious and assertive would be labeled masculine, while a nurturing and gentle person would be categorized as feminine. And this gender stereotyping is the main reason why many of the characters in popular culture are one-dimensional. Strong women tend to become "men in a skirt," while men who embody feminine characteristics (and there are precious few of those) become objects of ridicule. However, current research indicates that femininity and masculinity are not a group of personality traits but are instead ways of looking at the world (Lips).

Thus, we all have what Sandra Bem (1981) calls gender schemas, which are cognitive structures that determine the way someone detects, evaluates, and organizes incoming information about gender. People who have "weak," or simple, gender schemas do not pay much attention to gender and simply adjust their behavior to fit in with the stereotypical gender norms and expectations of their culture. In contrast, people with "strong," or complex, gender schemas focus heavily on gendered information. While they are aware of stereotypical gender roles, they do not impose "masculine traits" on men or "feminine traits" on women but instead utilize personality traits for both sexes. And this is what I believe Joss does. He pays a great deal of attention to gendered behavior and information, and then sifts through it to emerge with his own conclusions about how people are and should be—which fits nicely within a radical feminist framework because it challenges the status quo.

One of the amazing and unique things about the work of Joss Whedon is that his characters are not gender stereotypes. Both his female and male characters defy expectations. Buffy, a popular adolescent girl, becomes a leader in fighting evil. Spike, a vicious killer, breaks down and weeps at the death of someone he loves. Cordelia, a beautiful young woman, is direct and confrontational without apology. Simon, a talented and ambitious physician, gives up everything to keep his sister safe. Instead of having his characters follow the rules of behavior for their respective gender, Joss unravels the contradictions of gendered behavior (e.g., Why can a young girl not be powerful? Why can a man not be vulnerable?) and gives voice to what is possible (Fine and Gordon). Thus, through the behavior of his characters, Joss demonstrates the richness and strength of people who encompass aspects of both masculinity and femininity.

Given the controversial, even threatening, nature of his work, one might wonder how Joss views his own gender affiliation. Does he consider himself masculine? Boys and men who reject typical masculine traits often become objects of derision; could this have affected his self-image? Gender schema theory, however, suggests that people are adaptive; they do not have to adhere to what society says is masculine or feminine but can instead incorporate changing cultural expectations to forge their own definitions (Bem). As a result, Joss is probably very secure in his own gendered behavior, and it is this very security that would allow him to be unafraid in challenging cultural dictates.

So okay, the strong gender schema allows Joss to notice and process information about gender in a radical way but how would he have learned that this was an acceptable thing to do? Socialization can be quite persuasive, and our male cultural ideal is very strong. We elect presidents and deify celebrities on the basis of that ideal. Where did Joss get the strength to defy such dominant cultural expectations?

In the small amount of research done on profeminist men (Vicario), it's been found that most tend to have a close relationship with a woman, strongly identify with women's disempowerment through their own marginalization, and know strong men who model profeminist ideals. Joss has all three. First and most importantly, Joss had a very close relationship with his mother, Lee Stearns. Their relationship had such a profound effect on him that he credits her as the inspiration behind his strong female characters. Reportedly, when Roseanne Barr asked him how he could write so well for women, he replied, "If you met my mom, you wouldn't ask." Second, Joss has talked about feeling alone, about feeling like a pariah because of his distance from others. He also has labeled himself as a nerd, a category that by definition sets one apart from the mainstream. Thus, Joss has experienced rejection because of who he is. Finally, Joss has mentioned his father, a strong and witty man, as someone who helped guide him in his feminist journey.

Consequently, with Joss's path toward feminism firmly established by his parents and his own experiences, he likely began to use feminists, probably radical feminists, as his reference group. A reference group is a group with which we identify, a group to which we look for ideals and perhaps approval (Tajfel). When one of "our" groups is criticized, we become defensive; when one is successful, we are delighted. Both these things are true because our personal identities are strongly connected to our social identities. This may be why Joss keeps identifying himself as a feminist in both interviews and through his work.

While it is easy to *say* one is a radical feminist, the proof is really in the pudding. Just how radically feminist is the work of Joss Whedon? Keeping in mind the necessities of catering to networks and appealing to the mass market, the answer is that his work is indeed pretty radical. The women in his 'verses stand the traditional power dynamic on its head. They take care of themselves and are either leaders or integral parts of the team, whether that team is villainous or heroic. Few prominent women, even those who initially appear to be weak (e.g., Dawn, Tara, Fred, *Firefly's* "Mrs. Reynolds"), are true victims.

This shift in the power dynamic can also be seen in the ways female characters persuade others to do what they want them to do. Women stereotypically gain influence via indirect strategies—dropping hints or asking leading questions—while men tend to use the more powerful bilateral and direct strategies (Falbo and Peplau). Bilateral strategies are methods that require a lot of mutual engagement, such as arguing or bargaining; direct strategies are ones that are open and clear, such as straightforward requests or orders. Joss himself has talked about trying to please everyone when he first started his career as producer and director. We can imagine that, as he gained experience and self-confidence in using more direct strategies, he was able to transfer that learning onto the female characters he created.

However, some of Joss's female characters have used bilateral and direct influence strategies from the very beginning. Zoe always clearly and calmly states what she is thinking and what she wants. Inara also doesn't hint around—at least when she's off the clock. When negotiating to lease one of *Serenity's* shuttles, Inara firmly told Mal what she would pay for rent (direct) and argued with him that having her aboard would increase his status (bilateral). Cordelia, too, uses powerful influence strategies, as she is always direct. When she was having financial difficulty in the first season of *Angel*, she simply moved in with Angel, telling him, "Hey, you can just dump my stuff on your couch or let *me* have the bed, whatever you feel good about" (*Room W/A Vu*, 1-5). Whatever else can be said about Cordelia, she never beats around the bush.

Not all of Joss's female characters used powerful influence strategies, but those who didn't soon learned how to negotiate from a position of strength, as though his characters were following his own process of unfolding. As he grows in his understanding of gender, his characters also evolve and develop, a sort of parallel process. Thus, Buffy began her tenure as Slayer using indirect strategies, but as she gained self-confidence and grew into a leader (much like Joss), she started using direct and bilateral influence strategies instead. Early Willow only hinted as to what she wanted or, if driven to more direct outbursts, backed down if confronted. However, she too learned that direct strategies garnered her more power, and by the time she was halfway through her freshman year of college she was sufficiently equipped to help Tara as Tara learned how to abandon her own indirect communication strategies and become a more powerful and effective person. Even River's transformation can be seen as a more extreme dramatization of this process: because of the Alliance's experiments, she had trouble with coherency, much less directness, for the series and much of the film, but fights through the trauma to identify Miranda and eventually take full control of her own abilities. By the end of the film she, like the other female characters in Joss's worlds, knows how to get what she wants. And in creating such powerful women characters who make no apology for their strength, Joss is signifying his acceptance and support of dominant women.

Similarly, Joss's female characters reclaim their sexuality. Instead of letting their sexuality be used to control them, these women use sex to empower themselves. In uniting sexually, Willow and Tara increase both their magical abilities and their self-confidence. Both Cordelia and Zoe use sexuality as part of their strength. Kaylee owns both her innocence and her sexuality equally, and her enjoyment of the latter doesn't take away from her expression of the former. And then there is Inara. Her character completely flips our traditional perceptions of sexuality. Her vocation as Companion celebrates both aspects of the Madonna/whore dichotomy (Messner and Montez de Oca): she is the dizzying combination of the high status woman your parents want to welcome into the family and the sexualized fantasy woman you want in your bed. Inara never permits her sexuality to constrain her (she sleeps with whomever she wants), nor does she accept poor treatment because of it. Thus, especially with the character of Inara, Joss shows his desire that rigid gender roles and the sexual scripts that often drive them be a thing of the past.

While Joss's vision for women does personify radical ideals, it is his depiction of men that is truly revolutionary. While many (correctly) bemoan the stereotyped portrayal of women in the non-Joss world, it should be pointed out that the rendering of men is equally as rigid. Many strong male characters in popular culture embody what Herb Goldberg described as the "male harness," the idea that men be successful, emotionally controlled, competitive, and independent. As part of this circumscribed ideal, adult men do not cultivate intimate friendships with other men, but instead rely primarily on their female romantic partners and friends for companionship and support. Joss himself seems to break out of that mold. Joss's emotions tend to be broad ranging; he frequently makes fun of himself, lavishly praises the work of others, and forms collaborative working relationships.

The one trait of the harness that Joss does possess is success—yet he uses that success to make the fruits of capitalistic accomplishments (our Western definition of success) seem bitter. Almost all of the men in Joss 'verses who are successful are the villains. Adelai Niska tortured Mal and Wash in "War Stories" *because* he valued success so much. He was afraid that if Mal got away with double-crossing him, he would lose his competitive edge. Lindsey McDonald and Holland Manners, both powerful lawyers for Wolfram & Hart, were so invested in succeeding that they were willing to sell their souls to the devil (in Holland's case, quite literally) in order to do so. In almost every instance, the men in Joss 'verses who work to obtain vocational success are depicted as evil and, fundamentally, truly lost.

In contrast, none of his main male characters are successful in the traditional sense. Giles, though arguably at the pinnacle of success in his chosen field of Watcher (he is, after all, the guardian of *the* Slayer), never seemed troubled by having to masquerade as Sunnydale High's librarian—a position of little power or prestige. Further, his reaction to being fired during season three appeared to hinge more on his concern for Buffy than his professional "failure." Angel is more concerned with redeeming his soul than making money. Even when he agrees to take the reins of Wolfram & Hart, it's not for financial gain but to help his son. Mal isn't trying to get rich with his thieving; he's just trying to survive. And Simon, the most vocationally successful good guy in any of Joss's 'verses, gave up a lucrative career in medicine in order to save River. Giving up his success is what *made* him a good guy; if he hadn't, if he'd left River to the Alliance when he could have saved her, he'd have become a villain.

Joss also ensures that his male characters are not totally independent. Traditional masculinity dictates that a "true man" is an island: he needs no one. In contrast, the men in the Joss 'verses are both connected and collaborative. They all work as part of a team, and seem to have no problem taking orders, even if those orders come from a woman. Giles may have begun the *Buffy*verse as Watcher, the man who was in charge of Buffy, but as she developed into a leader, he allowed her to take charge and accepted his role as part of her team. Angel headed up Angel Investigations, but after finding himself in a bad place emotionally, asked to become an employee under Wesley's leadership. Even Mal seeks advice (from both Zoe and Book), works collaboratively with other leaders (as he did with Nandi in "Heart of Gold"), and followed River's orders without (much) question to defeat Jubal Early in "Objects in Space." The independent trait of the male harness just isn't a part of any of the Joss 'verses.

In direct opposition to the male harness, Joss employs the radical technique of showing what could be: he allows his male characters to be mentally healthy. Study after study has found that the masculine stereotype promotes emotional distress (O'Neil, Good, and Holmes), violence, substance abuse (Addis and Cohane), illness, and early death (Courtenay). At its core, traditional masculinity is pathological because it is so restrictive. The emotions and vulnerabilities that women are expected to express are still there, but they are forced to rage beneath the surface. Joss cleverly exposes this gendered contradiction through the metaphor of monsters. Oz is the epitome of the stoic, emotionally contained male, yet his wild feelings are released while in his werewolf state. The ability of vampires to conceal their "true" faces—which are associated with rage, lust, and other strong emotions coded more masculine than feminine—can be read similarly. In this way, Joss demonstrates the unhealthy, even violent, outcome of leashing emotions until they can no longer be contained.

A better approach to good mental health is to allow people the option of expressing traits associated with either genders (Brems), and this is what Joss does for his male characters. (Mal isn't even afraid to don a dress when necessary.) None of the men in his worlds (even those with monstrous dual identities) is a true "manly man." All of them demonstrate a range of emotions, and instead of those emotions being viewed as weaknesses, they often are used to guide the characters toward deeper self-knowledge and acceptance. Spike may be the best example of this. His devotion to Buffy—which Xander, standing in temporarily for traditional masculinity, mocks him for—becomes the motivation for his transformation, and culminates in his winning his soul and sacrificing himself to save the world.

But perhaps the biggest reason that Joss's work is so radical is that he understands on a basic level that equality impacts not only women *and* men individually, but also how they function in relationship to each other. Radical feminists want to free both women and men from the rigid gender roles that society has imposed upon them, yet this is rarely depicted, even on so-called "feminist" shows. All too often, strong female characters, whether in film or on television, do not have relationships with equally strong men (same-sex relationships are a different story). Usually, the strong female character is attracted to a strong male character and sparks fly, but when they get together romantically, even if the woman remains strong (in itself a rare occurrence), either the man becomes ineffectual or the couple fights incessantly. One reason behind this tendency toward unequal relationships is that men who value stereotypical masculinity do not function easily into intimate affectionate relationships (Pleck, Sonenstein, and Ku). Healthy relationships require emotional sharing, compromise, and sharing of power, all things that are difficult for a traditionally masculine man (Whitehead and Popenoe). As most television and screenwriters deal in stereotypes, depicting heterosexual romantic relationships as egalitarian becomes difficult.

The key romantic relationships in Joss's worlds are not like that. In his 'verses, the strength of one romantic partner does not diminish the other. Thus, Angel encourages Buffy's growth and leadership while she relies on his strength and knowledge. Buffy helps Angel learn how to love while he teaches her about sacrifice. Zoe and Wash each appreciate what the other contributes to both *Serenity*'s crew and their marriage. Although Zoe's position as second-in-command creates a professional power imbalance, Wash speaks up when he views it as interfering with their relationship and both make changes so that the other feels comfortable. In every romantic pairing—Anya and Xander, Spike and Dru, Buffy and Riley, Fred and Gunn, Willow and Oz, Kaylee and Simon— both partners bring strengths (and weaknesses) to the relationship and value what the other has to offer.

There are aspects to Joss's 'verses that I would prefer to avoid; I don't really want to worry about vampires or start using the word "ain't." But because of the way Joss uses radical feminist ideals to help people be all they can be without artificial limitations, his worlds are places I would like to visit. I look forward to the day when I can.

MISTY K. HOOK, PH.D., first developed her love for all things Joss Whedon during her doctoral training in counseling psychology. After getting her degree, Dr. Hook spent five years as an assistant professor of psychology teaching classes on gender and family issues. Her students quickly learned about her love of both *Buffy* and feminism and often gave her *Buffy*-related items. Dr. Hook is now a licensed psychologist in private practice where she deals a lot with gender issues. In her spare time, she enjoys spending time with her husband and son, who she hopes will be as much of a feminist as Joss Whedon.

REFERENCES

Michael E. Addis and Geoffrey H. Cohane, "Social Scientific Paradigms of Masculinity and Their Implications for Research and Practice on Men's Mental Health," *Journal of Clinical Psychology* 61 (2005): 633-647.

Sandra L. Bem, "Gender Schema Theory: A Cognitive Account of Sex Typing," *Psychological Review* 88 (1981): 354-364.

_____, "Androgyny and Gender Schema Theory: A Conceptual and Empirical Integration," in *Nebraska Symposium on Motivation: Psychology of Gender*, ed. Theo B. Sonderegger (Lincoln: University of Nebraska Press, 1985), 179-226.

Christiane Brems, "Self-psychology and Feminism: An Integration and Expansion," *American Journal of Psychoanalysis* 51 (1991): 145-160.

Will H. Courtenay, "Constructions of Masculinity and Their Influence on Men's Well Being," *Social Science Medicine* 50 (2000): 1385-1401.

Toni Falbo and Letitia A. Peplau, "Power Strategies in Intimate Relationships," *Journal of Personality and Social Psychology* 38 (1980): 618-628.

Michelle Fine and Susan M. Gordon, "Effacing the Center and the Margins: Life at the Intersection of Psychology and Feminism," *Feminism & Psychology* 1 (1991): 19-27.

Goldberg, Herb. *The Hazards of Being Male: Surviving the Myth of Masculine Privilege.* New York: New American Library, 1977.

Lips, Hilary. *A New Psychology of Women: Gender, Culture and Ethnicity.* 2nd ed. New York: McGraw Hill, 2003.

Michael A. Messner and Jeffrey Montez de Oca, "The Male Consumer as Loser: Beer and Liquor Ads in Mega Sports Media Events," *Signs* 30 (2005): 1879-1909.

James M. O'Neil, Glenn Good, and Sarah Holmes, "Fifteen Years of Theory and Research on Men's Gender Role Conflict: New Paradigms for Empirical Research," in *A New Psychology of Men*, ed. Ronald F. Levant and William S. Pollack (New York: Basic Books, 1995),164-206.

Joseph H. Pleck, Freya L. Sonenstein, and Leighton C. Ku, "Masculinity Ideology: Its Impact on Adolescent Men's Heterosexual Relationships," *Journal of Social Issues* 49 (1993): 11-29.

Steinem, Gloria. *Outrageous Acts and Everyday Rebellions.* Owl Books, 1984.

Tajfel, Henri. *Human Groups and Social Categories.* Cambridge: Cambridge University Press, 1981.

Tong, Rosemarie. *Feminist Thought.* 2nd ed. Boulder, CO: Westview Press, 1998.

Brett A. Vicario, "A Qualitative Study of Profeminist Men," *Dissertation Abstracts International Section A: Humanities and Social Sciences* 64 (2004): 4234.

Whitehead, Barbara Defoe and David Popenoe, "The State of our Unions: The Social Health of Marriage in America: Who Wants to Marry a Soul-Mate?" The National Marriage Project, 2001.

As science fiction and fantasy fans, we're familiar with TV characters spouting multisyllabic science-speak. If you're like me, you can sometimes barely follow the rapid-fire pace (Stargate's Daniel Jackson, anyone?) let alone keep from wondering which part of "sci-fi" is more make-believe—the fictional plot or the science itself? Does the Whedonverse reflect the current state of knowledge in the biological sciences? We can thank future neuropsychologist Bradley J. Daniels for giving us a glimpse of the truth about Firefly *as he examines River Tam's surgical torment at the hands of the Alliance and her extraordinary behavior aboard* Serenity. *Whether that truth is reassuring . . . well . . . that's for you to judge.*

"STRIPPING" RIVER TAM'S AMYGDALA

Could the Alliance Create a Psychic?

BRADLEY J. DANIELS

WARNING: This chapter is about *Firefly* and *Serenity*. It's also about brains, and a field of psychology known as clinical neuropsychology, which specializes in knowing about brains, what they do, and how damage to them affects a person's behavior. But, first and foremost, this is a chapter about *Firefly* and *Serenity*, which means it's written by, and for, viewers of the *Firefly* 'verse. As such, it would not be complete without humor (or, at least, what I hope passes for humor), frequent references to the show itself, and the occasional Chinese word or phrase. If this doesn't sound like your cup of tea and you wish to skip this chapter and move on to the next one, I won't be hurt. I just wanted you to know what kind of ride you were in for with me for the next, say, three thousand words or so. *Dong ma?*[1] All right, let's get started.

Based on a thorough scientific (and, in all honesty, recreational) examination of both the television series *Firefly* and its accompanying major motion picture, *Serenity*, River's psychic abilities appear promi-

---

[1] Understand? ("The Train Job," "Out of Gas," "The Message," "Heart of Gold")

nently in nearly half of the fourteen episodes of the television show, and also play a central role in the motion picture. Some notable examples of her psychic abilities portrayed throughout the show included her ability to see the cause of a young child's mutism and just how it was that a backwoods religious village's patron acquired his post ("Safe"), her prediction of the presence of a shipboard fire ("Out of Gas"), the looming death of a hospital patient ("Ariel"), and the truth behind the lost planet Miranda in the major motion picture, *Serenity*.

But how exactly did she get this way? How was it that young River suddenly began to possess psychic abilities? This question was answered in the episode "Ariel," in which Simon discovered just what it was the Alliance did to his *mei mei*,[2] River:

> SIMON: They opened up her skull. That's a scalpel scar . . . they, they opened up her skull and they cut into her brain.
> JAYNE: Why?
> SIMON: The only reason to make an incision in someone's brain is to lobotomize them, to go in and remove damaged tissue. Why anyone would cut into a healthy brain is . . . they did it over and over. (shocked) They stripped her amygdala.
> JAYNE: What?
> SIMON: You know when you get scared, or worried, or nervous, but you don't want to be scared, or worried, or nervous, you push it to the back of your mind. You try not to think about it. Your amygdala is what lets you do that. It's like a filter in your brain that keeps your feelings in check. She feels everything. She can't not.

So, in essence, we learned that River possesses psychic abilities because the Alliance went in and "stripped" her amygdala. It probably warrants explanation here that when Simon referred to her amygdala being "stripped," what he actually meant was that the Alliance went in and ablated (a word that means damaged or removed) the area of River's

---

[2] Little sister ("Serenity," "Safe," "Ariel," "War Stories," "Heart of Gold")

brain which contains the amygdala. Could this work in real life? Could the Alliance (or the U.S. government, for that matter) create an army of psychics by removing people's amygdalae? (It is worth noting that you actually have two amygdalae in your brain, one in the left hemisphere and one in the right.) And does the amygdala even do what Simon said it does?

The answer to these last two questions, respectively, is no, and sort of.

What the Amygdala Does

So, if Simon sort of got it right, but sort of got it wrong, then what is the amygdala, and what does it actually do? According to Hal Blumenfeld's book *Neuroanatomy through Clinical Cases*, the amygdala (which is Greek for almond, since the amygdala is roughly almond-shaped in structure) is a group of nuclei located in the anterior (or front) portion of the temporal lobe in the brain. Before I go any further, let's review. The brain has four main areas, or lobes, known as the frontal, temporal, parietal, and occipital lobes. Though all of these lobes are heavily interconnected and work together to produce complex (or "higher order") functioning, certain lobes are more associated with certain functions than others. For example, the frontal lobe is heavily associated with personality, speech production, planning, attention, problem-solving, and other behaviors known in the scientific field as executive functions. The temporal lobe (located near your temples)—which is where the amygdala is housed— is heavily associated with processes like emotions, memory, auditory comprehension, and language processing. The parietal lobe (located just behind the frontal lobe and above the temporal lobe) is involved in processes like attention and somatosensory (body-sensation) functioning. The occipital lobe of the brain is almost entirely devoted to the processing of visual information, and is, oddly enough, located in the very back of the brain, as far away from the eyes as possible.

So, now that we have our bearings, let's get back to the amygdala. The amygdala is heavily involved in emotional processing and a vital process known as fear conditioning, which will be discussed in further detail a bit later. The amygdala, though, is actually one structure in a series of related structures throughout the brain that are interconnected and make up what is known as the limbic system. Together, the limbic system is heavily involved in four major functions, known by the mnemonic HOME: homeostasis (or the body's own natural balance, such as hormone levels, etc.), olfaction (or the processing of your sense of smell), memory, and emotions (Blumenfeld 762). Bilateral damage to the amygdalae (meaning damage occurring to the amygdalae in *both* hemispheres of the brain), and the anterior temporal lobe in general, has been associated with a neurological phenomenon known as Klüver-Bucy Syndrome.

Klüver-Bucy Syndrome

Klüver-Bucy syndrome is a series of symptoms associated with bilateral temporal lobe damage that was discovered by scientists Heinrich Klüver and Paul Bucy in 1937 in their work with rhesus monkeys. More specifically, Klüver and Bucy found that, after surgery to remove the temporal lobe (with the hopes of better determining its function), not only were previously overly aggressive rhesus monkeys completely tame, but they displayed a whole host of bizarre and unusual symptoms including visual agnosia (the inability to recognize previously familiar objects), hypermetamorphosis (the desire to explore everything), hypersexuality (including indiscriminant sexual behavior such as masturbation and heterosexual and homosexual acts), hyperorality (the tendency to explore everything in the environment with the mouth instead of the eyes, much as an infant does), and a significantly dulled sense of emotional functioning (known as placidity), including an almost total lack of fear (Wikipedia.org).

The monkeys in Klüver and Bucy's study, in addition to becoming tame and unafraid of humans, also became unafraid of other things that primates are instinctually afraid of, such as snakes. In fact, due to the hyperorality, some of the monkeys in the study were observed walking up to live snakes that had been placed in their cages, picking them up, and placing them in their mouths. *Da xiang beo zha shi de la du zi!*[3] I can't imagine the snakes must have liked that very much. These same monkeys were seen approaching snakes that had just previously bitten

---

[3] The explosive diarrhea of an elephant! ("Our Mrs. Reynolds")

them when they tried to approach, as though they somehow did not learn or remember the adverse consequences of their previous actions.

This is a perfect example of the role that the amygdala plays in fear conditioning, or the process of learning to fear. Fear conditioning is essentially the process by which fear is learned through classical (or Pavlovian) conditioning. In general animal studies, this process is often tested by placing an animal in a cage with a special floor that can deliver a shock. A light in the cage goes on, and a few seconds later, a shock is administered. Over time, the animals successfully learn to pair the presence of the light with the upcoming shock, and begin to show a startle (or fear) response to the presence of the light itself. Animals with damage to their amygdalae, however, do not show such a response, as was the case with Klüver and Bucy's monkeys and their inability to learn to associate the snakes with the negative consequences of being bitten when they approached them. Studies conducted by Elizabeth Phelps and her colleagues have shown similar impairments in fear conditioning in humans with damage to the amygdala. These types of impairments have also been postulated by some to be associated with individuals with antisocial personality disorder, as there may be some connection between the often destructive and antisocial behaviors exhibited by these individuals and their inability to have their behavior modified like most people would due to the possibility of negative consequences.

Klüver-Bucy syndrome is rarely ever seen in humans, as bilateral damage to the temporal lobes is not a commonly occurring phenomenon; however, the syndrome does occasionally occur, and some recent cases were documented by Jha and Patel. When the syndrome is diagnosed in humans, the clinician is required to document the clinical features of Klüver-Bucy syndrome (visual agnosia, hypersexuality, hyperorality, hypermetamorphosis, altered emotions, and memory deficits) and to "demonstrate the existence of a bilateral lesion in the anterior horn or amygdala," according to Carroll, Goforth, and Carroll (116).

How Klüver-Bucy Syndrome Was Discovered

Arguably just as fascinating as Klüver-Bucy syndrome itself is how exactly the scientists came to discover the phenomenon. At the time,

Heinrich Klüver had been experimenting (both scientifically and recreationally) with the hallucinogenic effects of mescaline and peyote (the dried tops of the cactus *Lophophorus Williamsii*) on human consciousness. He actually published detailed descriptions of his own experiences with the hallucinogens, and wrote a book on the topic called *Mescal, the "Divine" Plant and its Psychological Effects.* Over time, he began administering the consciousness-altering drugs to his monkeys, and studying the effects of mescaline on them. Now that must have been a fascinating research lab to be involved in! It was Heinrich Klüver's direct observations of his monkeys' behavior after being injected with mescaline that led to his subsequent interests in temporal lobe functioning and his future collaborations with Paul Bucy studying the behavioral effects of bilateral ablation of the anterior temporal lobe in primates. It is remarkable to know that some of Heinrich Klüver's most important scientific advances occurred directly as a result of his drug use!

What River Would Have Really Looked Like with a "Stripped" Amygdala

Though River did appear to be fearless at certain points during the television show and major motion picture (most often when her military combat training was being utilized or had been activated), she did not appear to have any of the other symptoms characteristically associated with bilateral damage to the amygdala. As our brief introduction to Klüver-Bucy Syndrome suggests, if she were to have truly had her amygdala ablated as the show surmises, her behavioral presentation would have been quite different. (In hindsight, however, it is probably best that she was portrayed as she was, since, if the show's creators had chosen to portray a character with this type of neurological damage accurately, they would have had to show River as a fearless, emotionally dulled, hypersexual adolescent girl with an intense desire to put just about anything she could get her hands on into her mouth. Frankly, that type of television programming description seems less likely to be found on the family friendly FOX network and much more likely to air on either late-night Cinemax—also known as "Skin-emax" in some circles—or the Spice Channel.)

So what, you ask? Are there other things that might better explain

River's overall behavior? Other than possessing psychic abilities, River's character also displays many behavioral traits consistent with post-traumatic stress disorder (PTSD). According to the *Diagnostic and Statistical Manual of Mental Disorders Fourth Edition, Text Revision (DSM-IV)*, PTSD occurs when a person has been exposed to a traumatic event in which he or she "experienced, witnessed, or was confronted with an event or events that involved actual or threatened death or serious injury, or a threat to the physical integrity of self or others," and responded with fear, helplessness, or horror (467). To be diagnosed as having PTSD, the person must re-experience the event through distressing thoughts, dreams, flashbacks, and psychological or physiological responses to stimuli that are similar in some way to an aspect of the traumatic event. The person must also avoid stimuli associated with the traumatic event, and have a general numbing of responsiveness (which often manifests in a loss of interest in activities, feelings of detachment from others, an inability to have loving feelings toward others, and a general restriction of feelings) and increased arousal symptoms such as sleep difficulties, hypervigilance, exaggerated startle response, difficulty concentrating, and general irritability that were not present before the trauma (*DSM-IV* 468). Lastly, these symptoms must occur for a period longer than one month in length. River's experience while under the control of the Alliance, including the involuntary medical procedures done to her, would undoubtedly qualify as a traumatic event involving the threat of death or serious injury, and the opening scene of the film *Serenity* clearly shows that she responded to these events with fear and horror. In addition, River's continued nightmares, avoidance of all things Alliance (such as her and her brother's active avoidance of Alliance-friendly central planets whenever possible), and increased arousal whenever they are near (as when *Serenity* is boarded and searched by the Alliance in the episode "Bushwhacked") suggest that River would probably be a very good candidate for a diagnosis of PTSD.

Since PTSD is a disorder heavily rooted in the experience of emotions like fear and anxiety, it is not surprising that, neurologically, it is also associated with the amygdala. Recent animal studies, as well as studies of humans with PTSD, have shown that increased activity in the amygdala, accompanied by decreased activities in other areas of the limbic system such as the anterior cingulate, is often found in patients with PTSD. This suggests that the Alliance's neural stripping of River's amygdalae would actually have made it *more* difficult for her to develop PTSD symptoms, since the most integral brain region associated with the experience of fear (central to the development of PTSD) would have been destroyed. In order for the Alliance to actually create symptoms similar to the behavioral symptoms of PTSD that River displays, they would have needed to stimulate, not ablate, River's amydgalae.

In Conclusion

I've given you a brief glimpse into the field of clinical neuropsychology, some of the basic functions of the amygdala, and symptoms of its dysfunction. It has also shown, I hope, that "stripping" someone's amygdala would no sooner make them a psychic than removing a crayon from Homer Simpson's frontal lobe would spontaneously make him a genius.[4] However, these are only two examples (believe me, there are many, many others) of times when the media has inaccurately portrayed the overall symptoms and behavioral presentations of someone with a neurological disorder or other brain damage. Whenever a major motion picture about war gets made, such as *Saving Private Ryan* or *Platoon*, the movie studios producing the films will, without fail, hire a technical advisor like retired U.S. Marine Corps Captain Dale Dye to assist with the production and train and educate the cast and crew on how to think, talk, and move just like a real soldier, or behave as a soldier would in battle. This is an excellent example of the media caring enough to "get it right" and portray things as accurately as possible. Unfortunately, this type of caring has not found its way into forms of media that portray psychological or neurological disorders as a dominant theme in their film or TV show, as was the case with River and her "stripped" amygdala. To my knowledge, clinical psychologists and clinical neuropsychologists are rarely, if ever, hired on as technical advisors to serve in this capacity. It is my sincere hope that, in the future, whenever a major motion picture or television

---

[4] For an excellent further look into this occurrence, I highly recommend Nelson Cowan, et al.'s chapter "Stupid Brain!: Homer's Working Memory Odyssey" in *The Psychology of The Simpsons: D'oh!*

series gets made that depicts persons with neurological or psychological disorders or conditions (especially if the disorder is a key part of the plot!), the Powers That Be associated with the production will care enough to "get it right" and hire a clinical psychologist or clinical neuropsychologist to serve as a technical advisor for the production, lest those Powers That Be risk being sent to the "special place in hell, reserved for child molesters, and those who talk at the theatre" ("Our Mrs. Reynolds").

I would like to thank Drs. Russell M. Bauer, Anna Bacon Moore, and Jay Brophy Ellison for their years of mentorship throughout my psychological education. It is people like you and your tireless guidance and encouragement that have made me the person I am today.

BRADLEY J. DANIELS, MS, (Brad, for short) earned his BA (*summa cum laude*) in psychology in 2003 from the University of Central Florida. He earned his MS in psychology at the University of Florida in 2005, and is currently a doctoral candidate there working on a Ph.D. in clinical and health psychology, with a specialization in clinical neuropsychology. He also teaches psychology courses as an adjunct assistant professor at Santa Fe Community College in Gainesville, Florida. He is an avid film and pop culture enthusiast, and regularly uses these media in the classroom as a tool to enhance the teaching of psychology. If you need to get in touch with him, you can find him on *Serenity*. He'll be in his bunk.[5]

---

[5] I couldn't very well end the chapter without one last show reference ("War Stories"), now could I? Seriously, though, feel free to contact me at danielsb@phhp.ufl.edu.

REFERENCES

American Psychiatric Association. *Diagnostic and Statistical Manual of Mental Disorders Fourth Edition, Text Revision*. American Psychiatric Association; Washington DC: 2000.

Blumenfeld, Hal. *Neuroanatomy through Clinical Cases*. Sunderland: Sinauer Associates, 2002.

J. D. Bremner, "Traumatic stress: Effects on the brain," *Dialogues in Clinical Neuroscience* 8.4 (2006): 445–461.

Brendan T. Carroll, Harold W. Goforth, and Lisa A. Carroll, "Anatomic Basis of Klüver-Bucy Syndrome," *The Journal of Neuropsychiatry & Clinical Neurosciences* 11 (1999): 116.

Nelson Cowan, Michael J. Kane, Andrew R.A. Conway, and Alexander J. Ispa-Cowan, "Stupid Brain! Homer's Working Memory Odyssey," in *The Psychology of The Simpsons: D'oh!*, eds. Alan Brown and Chris Logan (Dallas: BenBella Books, 2006), 49–64.

Sanjeev Jha and R. Patel, "Klüver Bucy Syndrome: An Experience with Six Cases," *Neurology India* 52.3 (2004): 369–371.

Klüver, Heinrich. *Mescal: The "Divine" Plant and Its Psychological Effects*. London: Kegan Paul, Trench, Trubner, and Company, 1928.

_____, "Mescal Visions and Eidetic Vision," *American Journal of Psychology* 37.4 (1926): 502–515.

Heinrich Klüver and P.C. Bucy, "'Psychic Blindness' and other Symptoms Following Bilateral Temporal Lobectomy in Rhesus Monkeys," *American Journal of Physiology* 119 (1937): 352–353.

Nahm, Frederick K. D. and Karl H. Pribram. "Heinrich Klüver." *Biographical Memoirs*. Washington, D.C.: National Academy of Sciences, 1998. 288–305.

National Academy of Neuropsychology. "Definition of a Neuropsychologist." 27 Feb. 2007. <http://nanonline.org/paio/defneuropsych.shtm>

Elizabeth A. Phelps, "Emotion and Cognition: Insights from Studies of the Human Amygdala," *Annual Review of Psychology* 57 (2006): 27–53.

Platoon. dir. Oliver Stone. Perf. Tom Berenger, Willem Dafoe, Charlie Sheen. MGM, 1986.

Saving Private Ryan. dir. Steven Spielberg. Perf. Tom Hanks, Tom Sizemore. DreamWorks SKG, 1998.

Sullivan, Kevin. "Firefly-Serenity Chinese Pinyinary." 27 Feb. 2007. <http://fireflychinese.kevinsullivansite.net/>

Wikipedia.org. "Kluver-Bucy syndrome." 27 Feb 2007. <http://en.wikipedia.org/wiki/Kluver-Bucy_syndrome>

Naficy and Panchanathan take an evolutionary look at Buffy's preference for predatory (but redeemable) men. I wonder, though—in this plausible and vastly entertaining analysis of why Buffy prefers cads to dads, bloodsucking vampires to mere pigs, and Angel /Angelus to Xander, I couldn't help musing about the casting of darkly delicious (and presumably redeemable) David Boreanaz as Angel. I mean, what hot-blooded woman wouldn't date David . . . Angel. . . David. . . . However, I digress . . . and, it seems, my own natural selections are showing!

BUFFY THE VAMPIRE DATER

Siamak Tundra Naficy and Karthik Panchanathan

The character of *Buffy the Vampire Slayer* has been heralded as an icon of modern feminism. Darker than ours yet still recognizable, Buffy's world is balanced on a knife's edge. Her constant vigilance is all that prevents hell's legions from overrunning the earth. Buffy resonates with feminists because vampires stand in for the old patriarchy, while mortals like Xander, Willow, and Giles represent a new hope for gender equality. At the same time, vampires are akin to powerful and capricious feudal lords like in a gothic medieval tale, riding down from time to time to slake their thirsts and take what they wish from the peasantry. In this way, Buffy becomes something of a Joan of Arc, a teenage girl called upon by destiny to war against the darker powers of the world.

Perhaps because its world bridges the reality of today and the promise of a better tomorrow, *Buffy the Vampire Slayer* presents us with starkly contrasting images of men. At one end, we have mundane men like Xander, and like Giles, one of the aptly named "Watchers," a passive and almost-neutered caste of males. At the other end of the spectrum, we have the monsters, creatures like Angel, primal and dangerous but (therefore?) sexy, and also like the Master, brutal, savage predators who are unsexy and (therefore?) unredeemable.

Given these choices, isn't it strange that Buffy, our modern-day Joan of Arc, has chosen to romance the very monsters she was born to destroy—vampires like Angel and Spike? Using evolutionary psychology, this essay explores Buffy's romantic choices. In the first section, we ask why Buffy fell in love with Angel and not Xander. In the second section, we explore the stormy nature of her relationship with Angel.

PART ONE
Tell Me about Your Father . . .

What do we make of Buffy's romantic choices? Specifically, how do we explain *Buffy the Vampire Slayer* falling in love with Angel the vampire? Why doesn't Buffy fall for Xander, who is nice and sweet, totally crazy for her, and, most important of all, not a vampire? If this were an exercise in literary criticism, we would allude to *Romeo and Juliet* or *Tristan and Isolde*. It's not, so we'll try to keep that to a minimum and, instead, seek a material explanation. In the tradition of traditional psychology, we can start by considering Buffy's relationship with her father. We know that Buffy's parents are divorced and that throughout the series, her father, Hank, was not a part of Buffy's life. Even when Buffy's mother died, Hank was not there for his daughter.

What does Buffy's dad have to do with her love life? If you were lying on a comfortable leather couch and giving us your hard-earned money, we'd be willing to play Doctor Freud with you. In this game, we might speak of the *Elektra Complex*, the female equivalent to the *Oedipus Complex*; we might argue that girls grow into the character of their mothers and seek out men who resemble their fathers. In another session, we could get into how Freud's concept of penis envy might, in part, explain Buffy's proclivity for impaling vampires.

Since you're probably not going to give us your hard-earned money, we'll repress the armchair analysis. Besides, current social science, for the most part, discounts psychoanalysis as a way of explaining human behavior. Still, there is a body of research that echoes one aspect of the *Elektra Complex*. It seems that girls who grow up in homes without a father are more likely to grow into women who have difficulty sustaining long-term relationships—who tend to date men similar to their father in commitment style (Belsky et al., Ellis et al.). Draper and Harpending make sense of this phenomenon by arguing that natural selection has shaped parenting styles to fit the local environment. When conditions are such that a father's investment can significantly improve his children's welfare (e.g., when resources are scarce such that children will starve unless they are provisioned by two parents), natural selection ought to favor males that settle down, form long-term monogamous relationships, and become good dads. But when paternal investment isn't crucial (e.g., resources are plentiful), natural selection ought to favor males that form short-term relationships with as many women as possible, thereby fathering as many children as possible.

Given this backdrop, what is a little girl to do? How can she best ensure her own reproductive success? Well, if environments are stable across generations (e.g., the conditions a prepubescent girl experiences are likely to be the same conditions she will face as an adult), then she can use her father's presence or absence as a clue as to what little boys are going to grow up to do. The prediction is that if her father is around, then on average, she can expect other guys to stick around. If, on the other hand, her father is not around, she shouldn't expect other guys to be good dads, and thus should plan accordingly.

It may seem odd to think of little girls scanning their environments and deducing strategies that will maximize their reproductive success as adults. It's important to note that we're not suggesting that little girls are, in any way, consciously deciding what kinds of adults they should grow up to be. Natural selection acts on organisms, across many generations, to produce adaptive preferences and behaviors. In this case, the developing organism (our fictional little girl) takes in information (presence or absence of father) to determine the appropriate developmental pathway (long- or short-term relationship orientation).

Don't believe us? Here's an experiment you can do in the privacy of your own backyard. (If you don't have a backyard, do what philosophers do and conduct this as a thought experiment.) Take a potted sunflower plant and reposition it so that it faces away from the sun. Over the course of a few weeks, you should notice that the sunflower's leaves have grown in such a way that they once again face the sun. Now, if you were to conclude that the sunflower "knows" that sunlight is good for it and so "chooses" to grow toward the sun, would you be correct? Well, it depends on what you mean by "know" and "choose." Obviously, sunflowers don't grow at a conscious level. Instead, natural selection has engineered plants in such a way that they adapt to their environment in appropriate ways.

So, knowing that Buffy's dad wasn't around, we might predict that she would have problems with establishing long-term relationships. Do we have any evidence to support this? During the course of the TV series, Buffy's romantic relationships were somewhat dysfunctional, to say the least. Whether plunging a sword into Angel or beating up on and, in turn, being beaten up by Spike, there were numerous acts of violence, vulgarity, and near rape. These behaviors seem unlikely to create a foundation for a long-term, stable, and happy relationship. But the focus of this section isn't why Buffy is bad at relationships. Here, we focus on why Buffy chose Angel instead of Xander.

To get there, let's first ask a more basic question: What do women want? Broadly speaking, there are two traits women are said to look for when choosing the father of their children: that they will be *good fathers*—they'll invest time and energy in kids—and/or that they will provide *good genes*—their kids will be healthier and better looking (Gangestad and Simpson). All else being equal, a woman should want both, seeking a man who will both provide her offspring with good genes and also invest heavily in them. However, because there isn't an infinite supply of men and, furthermore, because men have their own reproductive strategies (what men want), most women can't have both. Gangestad and Simpson argue that having good genes affects a man's willingness to be a good father. Men blessed with good genes eschew parenting and bed as many women as possible, while those without a favorable genetic endowment are more likely to form long-term, monogamous relationships and invest heavily in their children. For the sake of argument, let's assume this is true.

So, if women have to choose between *dads* (good fathers) and *cads* (good genes), what should they do? Pillsworth and Haselton propose that women can engage in a *dual mating strategy*, wherein a woman may pair up with a dad, but cheat on him with a cad, thereby getting the best of both worlds: paternal investment in offspring *and* good genes. While provocative, not to mention controversial, this model doesn't explain Buffy since she didn't date Xander and cheat with Angel.

Still, we now have enough pieces to put some of the puzzle together. We know that women can get two kinds of resources from men: parenting and/or good genes. We also know that if fathers are absent, girls grow up to expect men to be commitment-phobic. If a woman doesn't expect a man's help in raising her kids, then she should choose a man solely based on his genetic quality. By this logic, we predict that women like Buffy will prefer cads over dads. Now, let's compare Angel to Xander, Buffy's two suitors, and appraise their cad-ness or dad-ness.

To do this, we need to know what attributes a woman can use to tell a stud (cad) from a dud (dad). She obviously can't peek into his genes and tell. However, men with good genes often signal their quality through observable features. Folstad and Karter demonstrate that a masculine appearance (e.g., heavy brow ridge, overall musculature, large jaw) may be a cue to genetic quality—with testosterone acting as the mediator. We know that increased levels of testosterone correlate with an increased masculine appearance. We also know that, all else being equal, increased levels of testosterone compromise immune function, leading to increased risks of disease. The argument is that males of high quality remain healthy and vigorous despite "handicapping" themselves with increased levels of testosterone; lower quality males would surely suffer sickness and disease if they maintained such doses of testosterone. Because this differential cost keeps the signal "honest," females can metaphorically judge a book by its cover, knowing that healthy, highly masculine men are the ones with the good genes. A quick appraisal of Angel and Xander's looks should suffice in establishing who is the more masculine—Angel is larger, has a wider jaw, and his brow ridges cast shadows. (Fitting with our story, Joss Whedon chose to accentuate masculine features in vampires when they vamp out—Angel's brows get even heavier, his eyes get smaller, and his fangs grow.)

Now, when it comes to female preferences, several studies have found that the more masculine a man's face is, the more attractive women find him. Further, when women are asked to imagine themselves choosing men for short-term sexual relationships, this preference is even more pronounced (Johnston et al., Penton-Voak and Perrett). Women also consider more masculine men to be more dominant (Perrett et al.). At the same time, however, the study found that women thought more masculine men were colder, more dishonest, less cooperative—and worse at being dads. This fits with our story. Women seem to "believe" (again, at some unconscious level) that highly masculine men, while more attractive, are likely to be worse fathers.

However, beliefs aren't necessarily true; people believed the earth was flat before 1492. In a recent study, Roney et al. found that men's testosterone concentrations do not correlate with their interest in infants. This suggests that perhaps men are not simply arrayed along some dad-to-cad continuum. It would then seem that, at least to some degree, the quality of a man's genes are independent of his willingness to be a good father.

To recap: We began by noting the absence of Buffy's father in her life. We then suggested that this might have led Buffy to develop a pessimistic attitude about men's willingness to commit and help raise children. Making the best of a bad situation, Buffy might therefore have chosen to pursue masculine guys that could at least provide her kids with good genes. In this regard, Angel passes muster, while Xander does not. While we never used Freud's *Elektra Complex*, we seem to have reached a similar conclusion: because of her father's absence, Buffy may be doomed to seek out men that will tend to leave her the way her father did.

Note, however, that much of our story hinges on the putative causal relationship between the absence of the father and short-term relationship orientation in the daughter (Belsky et al., Ellis et al.). Now, any good scientist worth his tenure would tell you that correlation doesn't imply causation! If it's the case that some third (as yet undiscovered) variable causes both father absence and daughter short-term relationship orientation, then our case weakens.

The following research may have done just that. Using data from a twin study, Rowe found evidence that the same genes that influence a father's probability of abandoning his family might influence the relationship orientation of his daughter. This may indicate that a woman's development and, ultimately, her adult mate preferences may not be strategically determined by her father's behavior, but rather may simply be correlated with his behavior because of shared genes.

Why would we present data that weakens our story? Are we wasting your time? We suppose that depends on what else you could have been doing. Seriously, though, we believe that good science should entertain multiple, even contradictory, hypotheses. Only when there is competition do the best ideas emerge. And in this endeavor, let's not forget the fact that this isn't any ordinary girl, she's Buffy, the Vampire Slayer. As the titular character, Buffy excels, surpassing nearly every being she comes across. As the most powerful girl in town (since this is a science essay, we can ignore the role of Faith), whom should she date? In a study of medical students, Townsend found that women with high socio-economic status seek out men with equivalent or higher status. The same is not true for men. This difference in preference may mean that as a woman's status increases, her pool of acceptable partners decreases. Now, if we substitute power for status, we can assume Buffy would seek out men that can match her physical talents. Mortals, like Xander, aren't up to the challenge, while vampires, like Angel, might be. In the end, it is Buffy's status as the Slayer that may constrain whom she deigns a suitable partner.

PART TWO

Men Are Pigs, or Maybe Just Blood-Sucking Vampires

BUFFY: I—I don't understand. Was it me? Was I not good?
ANGEL: (laughing) You were great. Really. I thought you
  were a pro.

—"Innocence" (2-14)

Long before Joss Whedon provided such convincing evidence for it, women have had a notoriously pessimistic bias when it comes to men. The quote above comes from an episode in season two of *Buffy* called, appropriately enough, "Innocence." It is the episode after the perhaps more famous episode, again appropriately named "Surprise," in which Buffy lost her virginity to Angel, the dark, brooding, good-looking rebel vampire who plays by his own rules. Angel loved Buffy but became an ass (okay, lost his soul and became the soulless Angelus) after Buffy had sex with him, and thereby made manifest a common fear for women the world over—he isn't that into you, he just wants you for sex.

This all seems to demonstrate what Buffy's mother had probably long warned: women who are precautious when it comes to a man's intentions are almost always better off than women who are not. That is, psychologists have found that women who use a kind of "Men Are Pigs" decision-making rule seem to find more long-term mates than those who do not (Haselton).

So, good questions to ask are: Why is it that women overestimate a man's likelihood of abandonment? Why is this prejudice a good idea for her and not for him? And while Angel and Buffy do seem to love each other, why do they struggle against this love?

Making Hard Decisions Easy

First off, it may be necessary to point out that judgments result in consequences that affect survival and reproductive success. Therefore, these judgments are necessarily shaped by natural selection, and many of our decision-making mechanisms—from sensory perception to estimating the likelihood of future events—can be best understood from this perspective.

Given that humans are a social species, our interpersonal judgments are designed to help us avoid foes, find friends and form suitable partnerships. At the same time, as Kurzban and Aktipis explain, while the mind *is* constrained by what is plausible, it is *not* designed for the highest accuracy or even internal consistency *per se*. In certain contexts, accuracy is adaptive, whereas in others, what is adaptively useful might systematically misrepresent the "truth." For example, in the case of sensory perception, when a fast-moving object hurtles toward you—let's say a '95 Durango, real horror show—it's better to anticipate its arrival too early rather than too late. Too early and you're still safe; too late and you might be dead.

When it comes to courtship, Haselton and Nettle document differing kinds of biases in men and women. Specifically, women are significantly more skeptical of a partner's willingness to commit (see Haselton and Buss). This makes adaptive sense since the fitness costs of overestimating a man's interest in forming a long-term relationship are generally greater than the costs of underestimating it: the former could result in having to raise a dependent baby all alone, whereas the latter is likely to result merely in having to wait temporarily for another suitor.

Conversely, for men, since the costs of underestimating a woman's sexual interest (missing a sexual opportunity) are greater on average than the costs of overestimating her interest (spending fruitless effort on courtship), Haselton and Buss found a significant overestimation bias in men when it comes to a woman's sexual interest—commonly known as the "She Wants Me" mentality. So, the trade-off costs between overestimating and underestimating outcomes may be directing our differing romantic biases.

Another way to conceptualize all this is to consider the detector in smoke alarms. Smoke alarms are designed by engineers to sound when there is a fire. As in any decision problem, a smoke-alarm detector can make two different kinds of errors: a false positive (alarming when there is no fire) or a false negative (not alarming when in fact there is a fire). The costs of these two errors differ. Here, the more dangerous error is the false negative, when the alarm fails to signal a fire. While annoying, false positive alarms are unlikely to kill you. Why can't we engineer an accurate alarm, one that sounds only when there is a fire? Because the only way for the alarm to *know* for certain that there is a fire is if the alarm itself catches fire—and by then, of course, it's too late. To be effective, the alarm must detect a predictive signal like smoke.

Unfortunately, your alarm doesn't know the difference between the smoke of burnt toast and the smoke of a burning man. Engineers could reduce the likelihood of a false positive (alarming when there is no real fire), but only by increasing the likelihood of a false negative (failing to alarm when there is a real fire). When organisms are faced with analogous decision problems, natural selection may favor decision-rules that are not designed to maximize accuracy, but rather to minimize the more costly error (Haselton and Nettle).

I Love You, I Love You Not!

One of the more appealing elements of the show lay in the conflicted and doomed love that Angel and Buffy had for each other. So, why was it that Angel longed for Buffy, but the minute they consummated their relationship, he changed? Ignore the metaphysics for the moment

(Angel's curse, his soul, etc.): How can the same person feel opposite and contradictory emotions? Is this a kind of cognitive dissonance? Well, yes and no. Comforting as it may feel, the notion of a single unified self inhabiting the brain may be an illusion. No, not like Jack vs. the narrator in *Fight Club* or Smeagol vs. Gollum in the Lord of the Rings trilogy. Well, not exactly. This isn't about multiple-personality disorder, exactly. It isn't? No, it's not. Okay, we'll explain.

Why is it that Angel chased after Buffy one minute and then pushed her away the next? He may have been driven by separate and contradictory decision-making mechanisms. If you excuse the pun, it's like having the good angel on one shoulder and the evil angel on the other. Or as the comedian Jerry Seinfeld has discussed in his stand-up routine, within everyone there is a battle between "Morning Guy" and "Night Guy." Night Guy doesn't care that Morning Guy has to get up, soberminded and alert, to go to work; Night Guy wants to party all night, and Morning Guy hates him for it!

According to this view, Angel who had sex with Buffy and Angelus who he became after, can be one and the same. In fact, Angel's transformation to Angelus can be thought of as a metaphor for the way regular guys can turn from Dr. Jekyll into Mr. Jackass—as Joss Whedon likely intended. Does he love her, yes or no? If he ever loved her, how can he not love her now?

Social psychologist Leon Festinger is well known for his theory of cognitive dissonance, which argues that uncomfortable psychological tension often results from contradictory beliefs, in turn motivating people to look for resolutions to these contradictions. From Freud to Star Wars, much of Western religious thought, philosophy, fiction, and art seem to revolve around this kind of conflict, where the "self" is presented with mutually incompatible choices (good vs. evil) and must decide which path to take. In this view, the central assumption is that we all have a homunculus inside of us—a chief executive, a dictator, a real "self" or *ego*—that gets to decide for us.

However, another way to think about all this is that no "self" exists at all. Maybe then an unruly Roman senate is a better metaphor. We each contain myriad and sometimes contradictory drives, each with its own adaptive function. In this way, the drive that "screams" to us the loudest—the one that is currently the most relevant—is the one that is "heard." Say you're starving and you find some food by a tree. Your hunger should drive you toward it. But as you approach, you see a lion in the distance. Fear should now drive you to run away, leaving the food behind. In this case, fear of the lion trumps hunger. (For a similar model of the mind, see Barrett.)

Our strange and sometimes contradictory feelings result because natural selection doesn't want us to be happy. You're allowed moments of contentment, but you can't get no satisfaction! This is because selection favors traits that result in better and/or more resources, mates, etc. In this way, Angel can love Buffy, and still make decisions that seem to run contrary to that love—leaving her to go to Los Angeles, for instance. The same is true for Buffy, who, despite her love for Angel, was able to run him through with a sword to keep the world from being sucked into hell. The point is that there can be many different sides and decision-mechanisms in the same person. And in the end, the greatest mystery might be ourselves.

Seen in this way, these biased mechanisms are not design defects of the human mind, but rather design *features*. The point, ladies and gentlemen, is this: Men and women selectively navigate through the noisy buzz of cues, indices, and signals to find members of the opposite sex depending on their own gender-specific needs. Men gather clues to sexual possibilities and women hunt for signs of commitment. The errors in the rules of engagement in these early stages of courtship—long before we're even sure of the other's intentions—may appear to set us on an inevitable collision course of unmet expectations and emotional dissatisfaction. And yet each one of us is evidence that the sexes can and do in fact hook up. In the long view, men and women have overlapping, if not identical, goals: both want stable relationships in which they are able to raise dependent children. This is exactly what psychologist David Buss's famous thirty-seven-country study on mate choice reveals: around the world, traits that are predictive of successful long-term and committed relationships—traits like "mutual attraction" and "dependability"—are always in the top five, regardless of culture or gender.

Buffy, of course, hasn't gotten her happily ever after. As captured in the title, *Buffy the Vampire Slayer*, she is an amalgam of old-fashioned romance ripe with well-defined gender roles of femininity ("Buffy"), and modern feminism seeking gender equality through the absence of gender roles ("the Vampire Slayer"). Buffy's audience suffered with her as Joss Whedon toiled to honestly weave together within Buffy these seemingly contradictory ideologies. With the *Buffy*verse living on now in comics, perhaps someday he will.

SIAMAK TUNDRA NAFICY, PH.D., currently teaches classes in biological anthropology at Santa Monica College. His doctorate at UCLA explores the evolution of intelligence in dogs and wolves and what this work may say about the co-evolutionary processes that humans and dogs have shared. When he is not studying domestication and animal behavior, he makes a point of rescuing Siberian Huskies from certain death.

After scraping by as a financial analyst, KARTHIK PANCHANATHAN is currently pursuing a Ph.D. in anthropology at UCLA. His research investigates the role of reputation in the evolution of social behavior, inter-group psychology, and the perfect pork stew recipe for his dog, Savannah.

REFERENCES

H. C. Barrett, "Enzymatic Computation and Cognitive Modularity," *Mind and Language* 20 (2005): 259–287.

J. Belsky, L. Steinberg, and P. Draper, "Childhood Experience, Interpersonal Development, and Reproductive Strategy: An Evolutionary Theory of Socialization," *Child Development* 62 (1991): 647–670.

D. M. Buss, "Sex Differences in Human Mate Preferences: Evolutionary Hypotheses Tested in 37 Countries," *Behavioral & Brain Sciences* 12 (1989): 1–49.

P. Draper and H. Harpending, "Father Absence and Reproductive Strategy: An Evolutionary Perspective," *Journal of Anthropology Research* 38 (1982): 255–273.

B.J. Ellis, S. McFadyen-Ketchum, K.A. Dodge, G.S. Pettit, and J.E. Bates, "Quality of Early Family Relationships and Individual Differences in the Timing of Pubertal Maturation in Girls: A Longitudinal Test of an Evolutionary Model,"

Journal of Personality and Social Psychology 77 (1999): 387–401.

I. Folstad and E.J. Karter, "Parasites, Bright Males, and the Immunocompetence Handicap," *American Naturalist* 139 (1992): 603–622.

S.W. Gangestad and J.A. Simpson, "The Evolution of Human Mating: Trade-offs and Strategic Pluralism," *Behavioral and Brain Sciences* 23 (2000): 573–644.

M. G. Haselton, "The Sexual Overperception Bias: Evidence of a Systematic Bias in Men from a Survey of Naturally Occurring Events," *Journal of Research in Personality* 37 (2003): 43–47.

M. G. Haselton and D.M. Buss, "Error Management Theory: A New Perspective on Biases in Cross-Sex Mind Reading," *Journal of Personality and Social Psychology* 78 (2000): 81–91.

M. G. Haselton and D. Nettle, "The Paranoid Optimist: An Integrative Evolutionary Model of Cognitive Biases," *Personality and Social Psychology Review* 10 (2006): 47–66.

V. S. Johnston, R. Hagel, M. Franklin, B. Fink, and K. Grammer, "Male Facial Attractiveness: Evidence for Hormone-Mediated Adaptive Design," *Evolution & Human Behavior* 22 (2001): 251–267.

R. Kurzban and C.A. Aktipis, "Modularity and the Social Mind: Are Psychologists Too Self-Ish?" *Personality and Social Psychology Review* 11 (2007): 131–149.

I. S. Penton-Voak and D.I. Perrett, "Female Preference for Male Faces Changes Cyclically: Further Evidence," *Evolution & Human Behavior* 21 (2000): 39–48.

D. I. Perrett, K.J. Lee, I.S. Penton-Voak, D. Rowland, S. Yoshikawa, D.M. Burt, S.P. Henzi, D.L. Castles, and S. Akamatsu, "Effects of Sexual Dimorphism on Facial Attractiveness," *Nature* 394 (1998): 884–887.

E. G. Pillsworth and M.G. Haselton, "Male Sexual Attractiveness Predicts Differential Ovulatory Shifts in Female Extra-Pair Attraction and Male Retention," *Evolution & Human Behavior* 27 (2006): 247–258.

J. R. Roney, K.N. Handson, K.M. Durante, and D. Maestripieri, "Reading Men's Faces: Women's Mate Attractiveness Judgments Track Men's Testosterone and Interest in Infants," *Proceedings of the Royal Society, Series B, Biological Sciences* 273 (2006): 2169–2175.

D. C. Rowe, "On Genetic Variation in Menarche and Age at First Sexual Intercourse: A Critique of the Belsky-Draper Hypothesis," *Evolution & Human Behavior* 23 (2002): 365–372.

J. M. Townsend, "Mate Selection Criteria: A Pilot Study," *Ethology and Sociobiology* 10 (1989): 241–253.

Whedon fans are by nature attracted to strong, daring characters. A diehard fan myself, I have an unwavering admiration for those whose readiness to take a stand against evil is greater than their instinct to cower. As I read of Stephanie R. deLusé's face-off with her own intimate demons, of the brave sacrifices she made to save herself from a cult of emotional vampires, I became her fan, too. With shameless vulnerability, deLusé reveals her deep reflections upon the Jossverse as a self-healing crucible. How she learned to extract power from the psychic pain she might otherwise have kept buried away, and how similar reflection might confer power to any viewer, makes her tale as universally significant as it is moving.

MORE THAN ENTERTAINMENT

Notes on a Spiritual Recovery and What Jossverse Gave Me that Religion and Therapy Didn't

STEPHANIE R. deLusé

When I do good, I feel good; when I do bad,
I feel bad. That's my religion.
—ABRAHAM LINCOLN

It's been tough to write this essay. Many a word has already been written about Joss Whedon and his creations. Many, many a word. A bit of research would convince anyone that there is little left that is new to say, as Joss has inspired rabid fans in and outside academia such that, it seems, every laudatory and critical thing that can be said or theorized about him has been said or theorized (except as he unfolds new projects for us to consider). I had a potentially fresh idea or two, especially about *Firefly/Serenity*, but this is an essay for *The Psychology of Joss Whedon* so my preference was to somehow write about *him* and his impact rather than about a specific show or character or how some theory could be tied to yet another aspect of his work.

So I labored in the quarry of my mind, throwing the hammer of my pen to crack open this bit of ground, then that bit, to see if I'd hit a rich vein. I moved several mental rocks and then I had to push particularly hard against

155

an old stone that, I learned, was weighty with more than thoughts—there was emotion there. I finally craned it up to see moist earth, wet with tears and sweat, and a mess of worms and bugs. Out of respect for squirmy life that likes to live in the dark, I lowered the stone back to look for my angle in some other part of the landscape of my mind, my experience.

Then it came to me. If I felt that respected writers had already researched and written on most every angle on Joss and Jossverse then what was left for me to do was some me-search. What was left was to write what no one else could (though I know you each have your own story): a personal account of how Jossverse affected me. After all, in so doing, what is learned is still, really, about Joss. What was left for me was to lift that stone and let the worms see the light . . . and to show a few of those worms to you, dear reader. Because perhaps by sharing my tale, my process, I will encourage you to lift a few stones of your own.

It seems small, I know, but there's some heroism involved in being willing to move the stones and take a peek, in being willing to realize something, perhaps let something go, accept something else, or make a change. It's not necessarily easy. The stones can be heavy and what we see isn't always pretty. But by unearthing hidden issues and bringing the worms into the light, we invite a phase of growth that lets us take power from the very things we once hid, or hid from. And that's something that thoughtful entertainment, in the form of well-written characters and stories in television, books, and other media, can help us do if we let it. In gentle and not-so-gentle ways they invite us to move aside, crack open, or pulverize some stones by stimulating thought or offering examples of others making choices (good and bad) that we can learn from. Beyond just living vicariously through characters, we can—in the small-time parallel of our own personal universe—identify with and grow through some of their struggles.

Tips for Excavating Worms: What Shows Can Help Us Do

The proof is in the pudding, as they say. There is evidence that Jossverse can help heal, if one is mindful and open while watching, because I'm living proof of it. I'll not get heady or deep on psychology-speak here, as this is about what techniques I used personally. You can consider this a "phenomenological" account, of sorts, for phenomenologists generally believe (of course, there are divisions among them) that one's understanding of life, and of truth itself, comes from one's own, or others', life experiences—that meaning is developed by conscious consideration of the world in which we live. Thus, I'm talking to you as a person, who happens to be a psychologist (not as a psychologist who happens to be a person). But while I may not get technical or theoretical here, I trust you'll see the connections to terms many routinely associate with psychology, like "denial"—that's a big one, isn't it? Actually, let's start with that . . . with denial, and with make-believe.

Why is it good to use television for excavating versus, say, just talking it out with a friend or going to therapy? Well, I'd never advocate that we should avoid friends, counseling, or therapy as we know social support and counseling have real value. Yet many folks don't care to open up to others on some topics (preferring a private "catharsis," or emotional purging), can't afford counseling, or, like me (as you'll see shortly) don't even realize they have an "issue," or remnants thereof, to resolve. Thoughtful watching of certain shows can be of value in bringing buried skeletons to the surface and re-framing past events to bring greater awareness or peace. Truth may be stranger than fiction, but watching such realistic interactions in the clearly make-believe world that Joss and his team created allows us to suspend our disbelief at what we are seeing . . . to accept it as "real" long enough to pry up some of those rocks and see what's underneath, as long as we are also willing to suspend our disbelief about ourselves. That is, most of us live in some form of denial. We refuse to see things about ourselves or our relationships. We get comfortable with believing the status quo or, more often, we are afraid to question it. If, when watching Jossverse shows, we allow ourselves to momentarily suspend our comfortable denial and recognize ourselves in them, or momentarily question the tenets of our own world, we can use the material for personal growth.

I'll describe a few techniques that I used. As you read, see if they might also be of use to you.

Reflective Empathy for Compare and Contrast

Depending on what you read, some would call what I'm about to describe "reflexive empathy" (rather than "reflective empathy"), but really, in many places the terms are used as if they are interchangeable. I've seen both terms used to mean what I'd call, simply, good ol' "empathy." Empathy, in contrast to feeling compassion or pity for some struggle a character faces (which is sympathy and can keep us at a distance), is putting ourselves in that character's shoes and feeling what they feel. When I use the word "reflective," I mean it in the sense of your reflection in a mirror—catching a glimpse of oneself in the mirror of, for instance, a television show about a vampire slayer. I mean using that glimpse to understand one's own life better through thoughtfully considering the lives of others.

Let me expand. With plain ol' empathy we experience a character's emotions instead of just watching the character as a voyeur. Doing so helps us access our own hearts, our own feelings, which are often buried too deeply in the busy-busy, head-heavy society in which we live for us to easily reach them. But where the empathy gets *reflective* is in the way I have often watched Joss shows. When the commercial break came on (or after the show went off—or I hit pause, if watching a DVD), I'd let myself take a few minutes to process the story that had just unfolded and what the characters had just gone through. Sometimes I would see myself or my life reflected so clearly in the events of an episode that I couldn't help but think more about it. I'd remember a time when I, or someone in my circle, had been in a similar situation. And I'd imagine what I would do if I had to make a similar choice. I'd think back to the choices I'd already made and consider their wisdom or folly.[1]

If you are like me, you may find that your understanding of yourself or someone else starts to shift a bit. You may find that you decide to think, say, or do something a little bit differently based on what you've seen on your television screen, and thought or felt because of it. Which brings us to the most important part of what Jossverse helped me do, which was to heal.

Backstory and the Realization That I Needed Some Work

Put yourself in my shoes. I was raised in a strict fundamental Christian religion that I valued, and value, as lovely and important to my develop-

---

[1] Now, when I say "similar situation," I don't mean to imply that any of us know folks who are actually slaying demons and vampires. As "real" and ordinary as those demons and vamps were in the shows, as real as they were to Buffy and the gang, they were also metaphors or analogies for other things going on inside of them. So it is with us.

ment in many ways. That said, suffice it to say my religion had a very limited worldview. For instance, as a child, I was expressly forbidden to, among many other things, watch *I Dream of Jeannie* or *Bewitched* because of their connection to "the occult." We really didn't watch much television. All grown up (as if one ever is), a student of psychology, and having theoretically long since abandoned those beliefs, you'd think I'd have slain any fear I had of overexaggerated or fluffy entertainment versions of occult topics. Despite an admitted avoidance of devilish or ghost-related movies like *The Exorcist* and *Poltergeist*, I certainly thought I had. Though, really, I didn't watch many movies or much television at all, and had gone a full ten years without a television in my home.

So imagine my surprise when, not long after getting a television again, I accidentally tuned in to an episode of *Buffy the Vampire Slayer* and was watching some perky girl and her friends when, hello, there was suddenly some, to me, convincingly evil vampire violence and demon activity. I was taken aback but transfixed. Oops. Had I just fallen prey to the spell my lovingly overprotective, hypervigilant parents had warned about—had I just been pulled into an association with evil simply by watching it on a small screen in my living room? I felt some serious internal conflict even though I knew—of course, as I'm not given to breaking from reality—by the comic quips and commercial breaks that this was just a fun story, all make-believe. No worries. But still, I *was* worried in some ways. I remember having to leave the house for an evening appointment and walking with a false confidence through the very dark spaces between my apartment and my car. Despite my purposeful stride, my insides were fearful and tender from having just seen nasty vampires stalking prey and feeding in the dark. I couldn't believe how silly I was. I couldn't believe how powerfully intact my long-buried childhood belief systems still were. Never one to shy from growth, I tuned in the next week.

Watching *Buffy* was, after I got over my initial surprise, a safe way for me to explore in bite-sized portions not just my fears around religion and worldviews but also personal purpose and relationships with men, friends, and community. These issues—especially regarding the relationship between men and women in couples and as groups in society—hit close to home for most of us in some way or another. So, while I've alluded lightly to some beliefs about Bogey-Men and the occult that I started thinking about because of watching *Buffy*, permit me to expand, to share a more important and personal example to help illustrate how thoughtful television watching can help us grow and heal.

Re-Evaluating Past Events to Heal: Icky Fates, Patriarchy, and Choices

I'd been raised to believe that men are always right and that having their approval—having a man like you—is more important than liking yourself. From the day I was born I was taught that God was the head of Jesus, Jesus was the head of the Congregation of men, men were the head of households, and women were subservient to men. Watching *Buffy*, even years later, it made perfect sense to me that there would be a Watchers' Council (of men), that Giles (a man) would tell Buffy (a woman) what to do, and that she, following a long tradition of slayers (always women), should obey. When I was younger, that belief system was so ingrained in me that it was natural for my father to offer me only three choices when I came of age: serve the religion by being a missionary in a distant land, do full-time "pioneer" work as a local missionary, or marry—as women needed to be ruled by some rigid structure, or else have a man in charge. I married at the tender age of seventeen to a twenty-six-year-old man that my father didn't select, *per se*, but had pointed me toward—and limited me to, once mutual interest was detected.

Buffy resonated with me in part because she was a petite blond girl battling evil and figuring herself out. Hmmm . . . can you say "mirror"? Okay, not a perfect mirror—I was by that point a little bit older and a little bit more experienced than she was—but I too was once a petite young blond who had battled evil in the guise of severe patriarchy within the religion to which I'd been bound. And I was still nursing old scars from those battles, still figuring out my relationship to evil and good, to God and humankind, to others and self.

I'd had to turn into a slayer of sorts myself when my marriage turned out to be a twisted, oddly abusive sham and it came down to me or him (or them, as the case could be seen). I had tried to hold out and be subservient to my husband, and to the patriarchy of the religion, but when, due to abuse, I developed health problems from which I was warned I might not recover unless I left soon, I faced a choice not unlike the one Buffy faced as she struggled to accept her fate as Slayer. Buffy didn't want to be Slayer and leave

160

behind her normal life—she fought it as long as she could. I didn't want to leave behind the only belief system and social circle I'd ever known, and stayed as long as I could. Buffy had to accept her fate or suffer the consequences. I had to decide whether to stay faithful to my religion and succumb to the fate of dying both spiritually and, potentially, physically, or to fight for my own survival and create a different fate, which would require me to cross a line that, once crossed, would likely cost me both my friends and family (as divorce was forbidden except in cases of adultery). And though I'd ultimately seek a legal annulment, that didn't change matters in the eyes of the congregation, as "legal" did not mean "scriptural." If I left, ostracism would follow. I left. And, yes, good ol' fashioned shunning followed. Still does.

Now, while I didn't meet Buffy until after the crux of these events had passed, I was still wounded from them inside when I did. So it's no wonder I saw Buffy's situation as relating to my life. Buffy had her own male patriarchy to deal with and, for awhile, Giles wanted her to abandon the Scoobies and fight alone. (I had the Brothers—the elders in the congregation—and my father and husband telling me what to do.) Buffy was painfully aware of her obligation as Slayer and the danger she put her loved ones in, but bucked tradition anyway—and learned she was stronger with her support system than without it. Watching Buffy, I was able to see that while, no, I hadn't been chosen as a hero to save the world, I had saved myself; watching Buffy I was able to see how I'd chosen similarly and differently. That is, as Buffy chose to leave (in a manner of speaking) the system set up by the Watchers' Council, I too had chosen to buck the system and leave—ultimately getting officially kicked out for having the nerve to choose life. For Buffy, the whole slayer biz was new, so it was easier for her to deny the old traditions, and in so doing she got to keep her Scooby friends instead of ditch them. Unlike Buffy, my traditions were long held and cherished, and my choice cost me the only support system I'd ever known. I know, I was no Slayer—but each of us have our own demons we must slay and our own sacrifices we must make.

High-Tech Tools for "On-the-Fly" and "Post-Show Review"

The level of engagement that allows such serious emotional, mental, and behavioral worm-excavation can be aided by using two very high-tech tools: paper and pencil. I've used them in a couple key ways: First, for things I'd notice *on-the-fly*—a line or a quip that would catch my attention as funny, insightful, or worthy of more thought. I'd jot down a word or two to capture it (knowing my sieve-like mind wouldn't retain it otherwise), so I could remember to think about it later. After all, what catches our attention usually does so for a reason—even if that reason isn't immediately apparent. When we are drawn to a line, or character, or story, a little work can help us figure out why.

I caught an on-the-fly recently while re-watching the *Firefly* episode "The Message." An old friend of Mal and Zoe's resurfaced, and to keep him from harming the crew, Mal had to shoot. He said to Mal, "You just murdered me," to which Mal replied, "[You] murdered yourself. I just carried the bullet awhile." There's a number of places we could go with this interaction, beyond the obvious opportunity to ask ourselves if we are placing blame appropriately in our own lives (and there is often plenty of blame to share). We could consider broader issues of personal responsibility, personal agency, karma, or you name it. Indeed, what I'd consider might be different from what you'd consider. And what I'd consider could change depending on what sparks got fired in my mind or what was going on in my life at the time.

Which leads us to the second key way I've used my pencil and paper: *post-show review*. For me, post-show review involved taking the time after the end credits to think through the impact what I watched had made on me. It could involve putting some flesh on the bones of the word or phrase I caught on-the-fly; after all, I wrote it down for the express purpose of thinking about it later. But it could also include capturing some key point from the reflective-empathy style viewing described above—that is, actually writing down the lessons I'd learned or capturing the thread of a theme.

I know, I hear some of you moaning, "Is she actually suggesting I journal about *Buffy*?" Well, no and yes. It's better if you're writing about you rather than *Buffy*. Consider Jossverse as just the stimulus, or a prompt . . . an entry point of sorts to get you thinking about yourself through first seeing some aspect of your life in the mirror of the show. Our personal habits, and culture, of denial means it is often safer for us to first think about others in order to crack open the door to ourselves.

And I'm not suggesting a journal, *per se*, though that'd be cool. My personal favorite is sticky notes that I can stick on my dashboard, my mirror, or in my journal depending on if, and how, I want to think more about a particular insight. So, no, this doesn't have to be a tome, but don't be surprised if you try this technique and end up having moments of fluid clarity that encourage you to write more than you'd have guessed you would. Writing about how stupid Buffy was to make that choice or how sweet Spike was when he protected Dawn can get you going on the stupidities and sweetnesses (or absence thereof) in your own life, and before you know it, you've traversed into something more personal and meaningful for you.

Truly, length and approach are not as important as doing *something*, as it's still a personal gain to routinely capture even just a moment of thoughtful, mindful awareness. Sometimes one line (an on-the-fly scribble) will stick with me and haunt my reverie. Like Wash's, "I am a leaf on the wind," in *Serenity*. There is the obvious interpretation: it's his desperate attempt to be Zen-like under the pressure of having to outmaneuver Alliance and Reaver ships. But then, moments later, he dies, becoming yet another kind of leaf on another kind of wind—or is it really any different at all? That kind of thing can take my mind and heart down side-roads I'd never have traveled if I hadn't taken a snapshot of the phrase and made the time to reflect on it. Letting it go too quickly would have cost me ready opportunities for observations about myself—how I handle stress, how I handle the inevitability of death (Am I "ready"? Am I living the sort of life I want to live? What would I want the last words out of my mouth to be? What's my legacy?).

Realizing Leftover Biases and Introducing New Thoughts: Morality, Sacrifice, and Ethics

Jossverse raised questions in me on many fronts, including how one defines evil. I considered, for instance, the complex roles and various transformations of both Angel and Spike. I reflected on sacrifice: what Angel had to sacrifice in order to work out his redemption, what Spike went through to get to the point where he could sacrifice himself to save the whole world at the end of *Buffy*. Self-sacrifice came up in other ways, too, both big and small, and that brought up, for me, a lot of leftover thoughts about Jesus. *Buffy* let me think as well about what it meant to sacrifice others for a cause—through for example, how Professor Maggie Walsh sacrificed Hostile Sub-Terrestrials (like vampires and demons) in the service of her interpretation of a greater good. And even when sacrifice didn't come up in one of the stricter senses of the word, I still thought often about sacrificing beliefs. I had done this to some degree when I left, was cast out of, my childhood religion, but I was subtly sacrificing still more beliefs—or at least remeasuring them—along the way as I watched and processed Joss's shows. These were issues (evil and sacrifice and such) that, in my childhood religion, had always had pat answers. No form of true, expansive dialogue was encouraged or permitted.

Watching *Firefly* and *Serenity* blurred the lines of what I'd thought I'd known even further, continuing to open up broader ethical and social issues. I'd reflect on evil Niska's penchant for torture. I'd reflect on how Mal's behavior often demonstrated pro-social, altruistic, and ethical tendencies and then how it would not, at times, in sudden and spectacular ways. In one scene he would return much-needed medicine to the locals he'd stolen it from, and in the next kick a man into *Serenity*'s engine. Mal and his crew offered many opportunities to reflect on shifting meanings of ethics, selfishness, and compassion. Despite doing bad things to real people, Mal retained, it seemed, a moral compass of which many would approve. Every gray area I encountered in *Firefly/Serenity* reminded me of the black-and-white clarity I'd left behind, and made me question which way of being is better—if there is such a thing as "better." I'd reflect on how in all Jossverse shows, you are invited, if not forced, to make experience count for something; the best learning wasn't all from books and Bibles.

Firefly/Serenity made me think, too, about political ethics. It struck me as true, and offered another opportunity for reflection, when I heard River, in a real or induced memory of her childhood during her torture at the hands of the Alliance, reply to a teacher that the Independent planets didn't like the Alliance because they were meddling, because the Alliance told people "what to do, what to think, were in their homes and in their heads and they didn't have the right." I'd lived the Alliance in the guise of an oppressively "loving" organized religion for all too long.

I could especially appreciate Mal's loss of his ideals, hopes, and comrades when he lost the battle of Serenity Valley, and how that made the not-so-small victory at the end of *Serenity* more poignant: Mal revealing the Alliance's damaging secret about the Reavers, in helping to restore the balance in the political world, also helped restore some of Mal's serenity, and some of his hopes and ideals too. Even as recently as the movie, then, I used the material to allow little observations like these to remind me of the small ways I had restored serenity in my life, and to think, on a larger scale, about the influence of other powerful institutions, policies, and laws in all our lives.

Alternate Endings

Playing the "what if" game is something most of us have done in our day-to-day lives: "What if this happens?" Or, "What if that had happened?" Thinking of different possibilities can be useful; it allows us to consider how to respond to different outcomes, and inoculates us against the worst that could happen in addition to giving us a taste of the best. The process of thinking and feeling out those possibilities, and others in between, helps us identify and avoid, or even overcome, obstacles (thus increasing the likelihood of a positive result no matter what happens).

So it is with another tool for effective excavation: making up *alternate endings* for storylines. While I'd, say, brush my teeth (or perhaps weed the garden or run errands) after watching an episode, I'd think through various "what if" scenarios for key scenes. I'd imagine what would have happened had a character made a different choice, and think through how it might have affected the end of that episode or season-long plotlines. I'm not talking about trying to be as clever a plotter or as colorful a quipster as the Jossverse writers (could that even be done?). I'm talking about thinking through reasons and relationships, about our choices, and about how the way we communicate them (or fail to) can really impact outcomes. Blend that with the compare and contrast that comes with reflective empathy and, *voila!*, you've got the recipe for some good *self*-awareness (not just the ability to chat more thoughtfully on a Joss fan Web site, though you'll probably have that too). After all, most of our own heartaches and headaches—or at least mine—can be traced back to our failure to make better-informed decisions or to be clear and compassionate in how we speak to others. As you think about how the show could have gone differently, it's a short skip over to how *you* could do things differently.

For example, think about Buffy and Riley. I know, it would have spoiled other interesting plot twists if they'd stayed together, but it's still fun to think about what might have happened if they had. Which leads right to thinking about the reasons they broke up, and how they might have prevented it. Think about your own romantic relationships. Have you ever taken someone for granted, kept them out of the loop, or pushed them away (especially someone who is actually good to you or good for you)? Why? How did that serve you? Have you ever chosen to "cope" or tried to "prove" something by being self-destructive and risky (like when Riley let skanky vampire-chicks suck his blood) and told yourself some silly self-denial tale about it? As much as we can learn what to do from watching others, we can also learn what *not* to do. What can we learn about our own misunderstandings and missed opportunities by pretending that Riley or Buffy had done something more or different? What could they (or we) have said that might have helped?

I'm not suggesting we get caught in an over-analytical loop that causes us to question everything we've ever done, *ad nauseam*. I'm suggesting that a little fun, but thorough, thinking about alternate endings can lead to improved endings in our own relationships at work and at home.

Overcoming Fears: Prophecies, Prophecies Everywhere

During my childhood, watching world affairs was only deemed useful for showing us that prophecy was being fulfilled, that we were living in "the time of the end"—and the end would probably come tomorrow. The palpable "reality" of prophetic fulfillment was such that I was not raised with any long-term perspective. There wasn't any point in thinking past the immediate or near future, because Armageddon was just around the corner. My parents didn't believe in the benefits of long-term savings or accruing funds for college (which we weren't supposed to go to anyway because it took time from the ministry, exposed us to worldly people with crooked values, and encouraged faulty thinking with lessons in, for instance, evolution).

So when I started watching *Buffy*, it was comical and silly in some sense, yes, that the world came close to ending most every season. But in another sense, it spoke to my wormy, not-completely-discarded fears about the end of the world. Each apocalypse Buffy averted, each new one that arose, I'd revisit how far I'd come since the last time. I'd think about how those fears had affected my choices in the past and what remnants of those fears continued to affect my choices in the present. I still think about this (especially with 2012—which is when many consider the prophet Nostradamus's end-of-the-world scenario will play out—looming on the horizon), but not nearly as often or as much. That's good, but I have to wonder, is it because I'm pretty much over it, or because I'm not being as thoughtful about it anymore because I'm not watching *Buffy*, *Angel*, and *Firefly* as often as I did when they were first run? Yes, I finished the meat of my personal processing on these shows years ago and now can more or less watch them strictly as entertainment, but still, any one of us, if we allow ourselves to be receptive to our feelings, beliefs, and connections, can sit down with the DVDs and garner some good reminders and insights. I'd worked through my wormy Armageddon fears well before *Firefly* and *Serenity* came out but it's funny how I still thought about them when I considered *Firefly/Serenity*'s post-apocalyptic (of sorts) future where, while life was not ideal (and was downright bad for many), it went on in a passable way. I found it much more comforting than, say, Mad Max's world. I found myself thinking, too, about the tempering statements, like Zoe's to Wash in "Heart of Gold," that gently warned against losing time to fear. Wash felt that, considering the conditions under which they lived, it was too dangerous for them to have a child. Zoe agreed that their life was dangerous, but pointed out that they shouldn't be so afraid of losing something that they didn't even try to have it.

The Meritorious Evils of Being a Fan

So, then, I've given you a snapshot or two of some of the skeletons in my closet and cobwebs in my mind, by sharing a selection of topics and issues I engaged via Jossverse—issues that I don't think I would have otherwise engaged, or at least not as soon or as pleasurably. And I've shared some techniques for more effective thinking, my strategies for viewing that allowed me to turn watching Joss shows into real self-growth. But there's one last thing that bears discussing.

It wasn't until *Firefly* that I realized that, without even noticing, I'd slowly and surely become a fan of something, of some*one*, of Joss Whedon. I'd never been a fan before. The reason I'd never been a fan before was because, you guessed it, my childhood religion forbade that too (shocker!). We weren't, for instance, allowed to engage in politics or sports (or cheer for a team) because it encouraged divisions in the group, and to elevate a team or politician as such edged too close to idolatry. Similarly, we weren't allowed to celebrate birthdays because there were no positive examples of them in the Bible. (There were only two birthday celebrations mentioned in the Bible—one in the Greek scriptures/New Testament and one in the Hebrew scriptures/Old Testament—and both were accompanied by someone getting their head cut off.) But, mostly, we didn't celebrate birthdays because it was unthinkable to elevate oneself above our fellow human beings. And, thus, we weren't supposed to elevate anyone else either (say, by being a fan), as it took glory away from God (who was the only one worthy of fandom). So, there was another worm from under the rock: I was actually becoming a fan. No, I didn't join a club or spend any time on the Web posting to fan sites, and I've never gone hog wild or anything (though I am known to go, "Grrrrr. Argggh," like the Mutant Enemy logo now and then), but I was/am a fan, nonetheless.

Reflecting on how very much that would have been disapproved of (especially given the nature of Joss's work!), I realized that it was about power, the underlying theme of *Buffy*. My parents' religion feared what would happen if they let us followers have any power, whether through birthdays or fandoms or, say, thinking for ourselves. It was about power and how much of it I had reclaimed when I stood up, struggled, and left. It was about power and how much more I had yet to reclaim. And, perhaps paradoxically to some, it was about sharing power, as Buffy did with all the potential slayers in the series finale in order to conquer evil.

Yeah, so I'm a Joss fan. I'm a fan who watches his shows for the pure fun of them, yes, but as you now know, I also let them take me away into deeper thoughts. I know that those who like Joss or his work all have their own personal reasons. I read or hear a lot that suggests many are fans of his artistry . . . of the entertainment value of what he's done, his genius or creativity, or the impressive amount of quality work he can turn out in small periods of time. Others are fans because Joss wrote strong female characters (though certainly some disagree with this) and male characters that were happy to walk equally with, or even subordinately to, those women. He embodied this in his speech, kindly archived on several Web sites, when he was recognized at the Equality Now "On the Road to Equality: Honoring Men on the Frontline" conference:

> [E]quality is not a concept. It's not something we should be striving for. It's a necessity. Equality is like gravity; we need it to stand on this earth as men and women, and the misogyny that is in every culture is not a true part of the human condition. It is life out of balance. And that imbalance is sucking something out of the soul of every man and woman who's confronted with it. We need equality, kinda now.

Yep, having lived through several very personal soul-sucking experiences myself, I can see why folks would be fans of Joss for this. But while I appreciate all those things about him, and the casts and crews that helped bring his work to life, *Buffy*, *Angel*, and *Firefly/Serenity* were more, were different, for me. Like so many others who've no doubt experienced some form of personal growth through the work of Joss Whedon, these shows provided some tools—some opportunities for insight—to help me, with a straight-to-the-heart wittiness I so value, lift the stones and dig in the dirt, to excavate, to grow, to heal.

Many thanks to my friends and colleagues Dr. Stanley Parkinson, Dr. Linda Luecken, and Tracy Perkins—a subset of my own Scoobies without whom I'd be weaker and less happy—for commenting on drafts of this work. The patient support, wisdom, and good humor of these friends are priceless. Thanks also to the patient Leah Wilson, whose comments and suggestions most assuredly helped the final product.

STEPHANIE R. DELUSÉ, PH.D., psychologist, researcher, author, and teacher, is also associate faculty director of the Bachelor of Interdisciplinary Studies (BIS) program at Arizona State University. Her graduate training focused on social and personal issues that affect most of us at one time or another—issues around individual/group interactions, family and divorce, and health and wellness. Her most recent academic efforts have earned her recognition for her teaching, including selection as one of ASU's Featured Faculty in 2006 and an Outstanding Faculty Award in 2005. In her sparse free time she communes with nature most frequently in the guise of her cat, her trees, and her herb garden replete with insect life and lizards. As she edits this essay, she is teaching in London for the summer and getting acquainted with all manner of new flora and fauna—and seeing some very spooky, ancient cemeteries where the likes of vampires, rogue-demon hunters, and the Slayer must surely roam.

Like ice cream, psychotherapy comes in many flavors and colors, and most practitioners mash it up a bit, eventually dishing out multi-hued swirls rather than pure chocolate or vanilla. Yet psychological theories are often taught as if their conversion into practice was pristine; chocolate theory yielding chocolate cones, vanilla yielding vanilla, and so on. While that may not be so in clinical work, nevertheless, Mikhail Lyubansky allows us a glimpse of pure strawberry: existential theory and therapy unsullied, as applied to Buffy Summers. Considering the unimaginable responsibilities and undeniable confrontations with death that Buffy must endure year after year, Lyubansky views an existential approach to making sense of it all as just the right flavor.

BUFFY'S SEARCH FOR MEANING

Mikhail Lyubansky

The hardest thing in this world . . . is to live in it.
— Buffy Summers, "The Gift" (5-22)

I'm just going to go ahead and say it. Buffy Summers, the blond former cheerleader and long-time vampire slayer, is the most psychologically well-developed character on television. Ever. Her character, like the show itself, probes deeply into life's biggest questions: the nature of good and evil, the meaning of love, the weight of responsibility, the fear of death. In this essay, I approach Buffy as an existential therapist, using existential theory and therapeutic principles to make sense of Buffy's motivations, worries, and behaviors.

The therapeutic lens is not intended to imply that Buffy is "crazy."[1] She most certainly is not; for delusions cannot be shared by so many people. The fact that Willow, Xander, Spike, and the rest of the Scoobies all share Buffy's reality indicates that Sunnydale and all its monsters and

---

[1] "Crazy" is not a psychological or psychiatric term, but the popular connotation of the word suggests a thought disorder, like schizophrenia in which a person experiences a different reality than other people (e.g., hallucinations, delusions).

171

slayers are real and not delusional.[2] So, why therapy? It is almost certain that Buffy would meet diagnostic criteria for depression during most of season six, but that's really not the point. Existential therapists don't generally see people as sick but as sometimes needing guidance in their efforts to negotiate the challenges of life.[3] We could all use this sort of guidance occasionally, but it would be of particular benefit to Buffy, whose daily challenges are epic in nature.

But why existential therapy? It is not the most popular (that would be Cognitive Behavioral Therapy) and it is not the latest new treatment, like Dialectical Behavioral Therapy. In all honesty, it may be difficult to even find a practicing therapist who works primarily from existential theory.[4] I don't myself. And yet, if Buffy asked me for a referral during any period of her life after becoming the Slayer, this is the specific type of psychotherapy I would recommend, for it is the only therapy developed to explicitly deal with those big life issues that Buffy seems to confront on a daily basis. Consistent with existential principles, I prioritize depth over breadth, and focus exclusively on just two existential themes: *responsibility* and *death*.

The Weight of Responsibility

"How did I get into the world? Why was I not asked about it, why was I not informed of the rules and regulations but just thrust into the ranks as if I had been bought by a peddling shanghaier of human beings? How did I get involved in this big enterprise called actuality? Why should I be involved? Isn't it a matter of choice? And if I am compelled to be involved, where is the manager—I have something to say about this. Is there no manager? To whom shall I make my complaint?"

—The Young Man, *Repetition*

[2] The other possibility is that, as shown in "Normal Again" (6-17), all the episodes actually reflected Buffy's delusional world. However, there was ample evidence in "Normal Again" that it was the mental hospital that was delusional, not Sunnydale.

[3] This is also true of many other types of psychotherapies, including Adlerian, Rogerian, and Cognitive Behavioral.

[4] Existentialism is a philosophy that argues that individual human beings have full responsibility for creating meaning in their lives. Existential therapy was developed to guide people along this meaning-making path.

One of the fundamental assumptions of the *Buffy*verse is the element of free choice. Almost everyone, dead or living, has the ability to choose what they become.[5] Spike and Angel chose the hard road of redemption for their evil pasts, the vampires have all chosen (by drinking their sire's blood) their immortal but also inhuman existence, and even Buffy, "the Chosen One," had the ability to either accept the role of Slayer or turn her back on it. Similarly, all of the Scoobies made a conscious choice to join Buffy in her fight against evil, even at the cost of pursuing other interests, including attending a prestigious university. Willow described this process in "Choices" (3-19):

> The other night, getting captured and all, facing off with Faith . . . things just got kind of clear. I mean you've been fighting evil here for about three years, and I've been helping out some, and now we're supposed to be deciding what we want to do with our lives, and I realized that's what I want to do. Fight evil. Help people. I think it's worth doing, and I don't think you do it because you have to. It's a good fight, Buffy, and I want in.

It is, to be sure, not a one-time decision but a lifelong process. Thus, even though Buffy chose to accept her responsibility as Slayer in season one, she hid from her responsibility in season three ("Anne," 3-1) and confided in Giles in season five that she was "thinking of taking a break . . ." and "not get[ting] into full Slay mode" ("Intervention," 5-18[6]).

As in the *Buffy*verse, free choice is also an important assumption of existential therapy. Like Alfren Adler before them, existential therapists believe that it is neither genes nor environment (nor even the gene X environment interaction) that determines our behavior, but *how we choose to respond* to our genes and environment.[7] According to existential tenets, people are often afraid of freedom (to choose) because with freedom to choose comes the possibility of choosing poorly. With free-

---

[5] There are notable exceptions, including Spike's killings and sirings when under the influence of the First.

[6] I examine this episode in depth later in this essay.

[7] This is not to suggest that genes and environment are unimportant. They are just not seen as deterministic.

dom, in other words, comes responsibility.[8] Existential therapists point out that many individuals, at some point in their lives, struggle with accepting this responsibility and, therefore, deny or limit their own freedom. Some displace the responsibility onto other people (e.g., "My boss made me work late"); others think of themselves as helpless victims of life circumstances (e.g., "They only want to hire someone with a college degree"); still others absolve themselves of responsibility by a sort of temporary insanity, as when they attribute a behavior to their drinking (e.g., "It was the beer talking") or to their unconscious drives[9] (e.g., "I don't know what happened; I would never do something like that) (Yalom and May). The existential philosopher Jean-Paul Sartre referred to these types of excuses as statements of "bad faith," and argued that it is inauthentic to assume that our existence is controlled by forces external to ourselves. To live an authentic and meaningful life, existentialists would have people take personal responsibility for their lives, honestly evaluating the kind of person they are and mindfully choosing the kind of person they wish to become (Corey). This is the focus of existential therapy: to help clients "own" their feelings, desires, and actions and find meaning in their lives.

Accepting responsibility is something that Buffy learned early on, with a particularly crucial lesson coming at the end of the first season, when a prophesy of her death caused her to quit her slayer duties, resulting in the deaths of several classmates. These deaths convinced Buffy to resume slaying, and, with the exception of the previously mentioned lapses, by season three, her willingness to take responsibility for her behavior stood in stark contrast to Faith's unwillingness to do so. As a slayer, Faith had her own way of giving up responsibility. When she accidentally killed the deputy mayor, she blamed her supernatural powers—"Something made us different. We're warriors. We're built to kill" ("Consequences," 3-15)—and much to Buffy's dismay, she seemed to feel no remorse or distress.

The freedom to choose and, therefore, to accept responsibility, accord-

---

[8] Viktor Frankl in 1978 recommended that the Statue of Liberty on the East Coast be complemented by a Statue of Responsibility on the West Coast. Money is currently being raised to turn Frankl's vision into reality (see http://www.sorfoundation.org/).

[9] "Whose unconscious is it?" the existential therapist might inquire.

ing to existential therapists, requires a combination of wishing and willing. Although the first part may sound easy, wishing, or being in touch with what one really wants, is closely connected to feeling, and individuals disconnected from their emotions often have trouble experiencing or expressing a wish. Faith, who lived under the motto, "Want. Take. Have," provided a good example of a person struggling with wishing, as existential therapists believe that impulsive persons avoid wishing by acting impulsively on all urges rather than prioritizing their wants and acting accordingly.

Once a person connects to his/her wishes, it is necessary to choose how to act on the wish. Here again, some people have trouble—delegating the decision to someone else or passively allowing circumstances to control what happens.

Buffy had to make a series of hard choices over the years. When she first arrived at Sunnydale, she chose to befriend the geeky Willow and Xander rather than the popular Cordelia, to disclose her identity as Slayer to her friends but not her mother, and to avoid normal boys because dating them would be a hazard to their health. Later, she chose to sleep with Angel, and later still, to kill him in order to seal the entrance to hell. Buffy's choices did not always end up serving her own best interest, as when she hid her Slayer identity from her mother, who most likely would have been supportive, nor were they always righteous, as when she chose to emulate Faith's lifestyle and rob a gun store. But in making her choices, Buffy also showed a willingness to take responsibility for the consequences. Thus, she blamed only herself for her estranged relationship with her mother and stood up to Faith when Faith refused to take responsibility for accidentally killing the deputy mayor.

Buffy, it turned out, became rather good at taking responsibility, and eventually her friends learned to do so as well, for responsibility and accountability were part of the show's underlying themes. In episode after episode, we were reminded that our actions always have consequences. This was probably best exemplified in "Bargaining" (6-1 and 6-2), when the Scoobies, overwhelmed by grief (following Buffy's death) and slayer responsibilities, decided to bring Buffy back from the dead. It was not a choice they made lightly, but none of them were fully prepared for the consequences of their decision: Buffy resented having her life back, and a new demon was created to balance out the good energy (in the form of Buffy) that should not have been on the Earth. The existential message is not that Buffy's friends should have foreseen the consequences (there was no way to do so), or that they should have made a different choice. To the contrary, the message is that even though none of us can know for certain how our actions will impact the world around us, we still have to wish and decide, and then take responsibility for those decisions. There may be free choice, but there is no free lunch.

Some choices, to be sure, are harder than others—for Buffy, as well as for the rest of us. At the top of this list is how to cope with the death of loved ones and, more importantly, with our own sense of mortality—an issue at the very center of existential theory.

The Gift of Death

> "As death, when we come to consider it closely, is the true goal of our existence, I have formed during the last few years such close relations with this best and truest friend of mankind, that his image is not only no longer terrifying to me, but is indeed very soothing and consoling! And I thank my God for graciously granting me the opportunity . . . of learning that death is the key which unlocks the door to our true happiness."
>
> —Wolfgang Amadeus Mozart

To existential psychologists, death is a gift. By definition, it provides an awareness of our mortality, which, in turn, may produce a profound shift in perspective and lead to personal growth. It kills us, but without death, we would not know that we are alive. Without death, life would have little urgency, and there would be little to live for. It is the inevitability of death, existential psychologists argue, that forces us to find meaning in our lives. The specific meaning can only be determined individually, but Rollo May and Irvin Yalom argue that a confrontation with death persuades individuals to count their blessings and become more aware of how their relationships impact their life. In the words of novelist Paul Theroux, "Death is an endless night so awful to contemplate that it can make us love life and value it with such passion that it may be the ultimate cause of all joy and all art."

Of course, death, or actually the fear of death, can also produce intense anxiety. This death anxiety can be so crippling that it becomes intolerable, causing the afflicted to live their lives in such a way that they practically eliminate all alone time, which is when thoughts of death and mortality tend to intrude. In their desperation to avoid isolation, individuals sometimes form unhealthy relationships, which leads to other problems.

Buffy confronted death[10] (and also the dead) on a daily basis and in many different forms, including dealing with the death of her mother ("The Body," 5-16), maintaining relationships with the long-dead vampires Spike and Angel, and ultimately, confronting her own death ("The Gift," 5-22) and eventual resurrection ("Bargaining," 6-1 and 6-2). In each instance of death, the associated existential questions came to the forefront.

Perhaps the *Buffy* episode that is most difficult to watch (but also among the best!) is the one in which Joyce died. In "The Body," there was no playful humor, no witty wordplay, and until the very end, no supernatural creatures. As Jana Riess wrote in her spiritual guide to the vampire slayer, "the monster that has taken her mother so abruptly . . . [is] the one monster that Buffy cannot overcome" (25). In this episode, Buffy was like the rest of us, helpless against the unpredictability and permanence of death. In the course of the forty-eight hours following her mother's death, Buffy experienced shock, self-blame, denial, and confusion. Her friends also struggled to deal with the loss, each reacting differently, but always with more intensity than when they faced supernatural death. It is an episode about grief—real grief!

May and Yalom point out that grief is experienced differently depending on the individual's relationship to the deceased, with the loss of a parent particularly linked to feelings of personal vulnerability. "If our parents could not save themselves, who will save us?" they ask, adding, "When parents die, nothing remains between ourselves and the grave. At the moment of our parents' death, we ourselves constitute the barrier between our children and their death" (288).

---

[10] She literately confronted Death in season two's "Killed by Death" (2-18) when she fought the demon Der Kindestod, whose German name means "the child's death."

Consistent with existential theory, her mother's death reminded Buffy of her own mortality and set off a new search for meaning. Buffy became concerned with the possible negative impact that slaying was having on her life, worrying that it may have been hardening her emotionally and preventing her from experiencing love and intimacy. For Buffy, existential therapy[11] came in the form of a spirit (of the First Slayer), with whom, at the recommendation of Giles, she decided to consult. Much to her dismay, the spirit informed her that death is a gift:

> FIRST SLAYER: Death is your gift.
> BUFFY: Death . . .
> FIRST SLAYER: Is your gift.
> BUFFY: Okay, no. Death is not a gift. My mother just died. I know this. If I have to kill demons because it makes the world a better place, then I kill demons, but it's not a gift to anybody. ("Intervention," 5-18)

As it turned out, the vision of the First Slayer is right. In "The Gift" (5-22), Buffy made the ultimate sacrifice, plunging to her death in order to save the world and, not incidentally, Dawn. It was her gift to them, but it was also her gift to herself, for in dying, she found purpose in her life (to save the world and her sister). For existential therapists, the discovery of life's meaning is gift enough, and, by all appearances, Buffy's last moments were content, for she not only reaffirmed her purpose in life but in her final selfless act also absolved herself of the responsibility of slaying. Her life's work was done. But upon her death Buffy received yet another unexpected gift, for she found herself in what she assumed to be heaven:

---

[11] In this context, the word "therapy" is used to convey the idea that the spirit's words serve a therapeutic function. I do *not* wish to create the impression that this benevolent spirit is functioning as a psychotherapist, existential or any other. A real therapeutic relationship is one that both therapist and client enter consciously and deliberately, and it brings with it a series of obligations for the therapist—among them a commitment to help the client. Disappearing after a few wise words, as this spirit does immediately after the exchange below, would be unethical.

> Wherever I was, I was happy. At peace. I knew that everyone
> I cared about was all right. I knew it. Time didn't mean any-
> thing. Nothing had form. But I was still me. . . . And I was
> warm, and I was loved, and I was finished, complete. I don't
> understand theology or dimensions, or any of it really, but I
> think I was in heaven. ("After Life," 6-3)

It is noteworthy that, despite her ongoing fight against evil, Buffy never really aspired to reach heaven. Rather, she grew to embrace her role as Slayer because it was what she needed to do. If heaven is the ulti-mate measure of success—a life well lived—then Buffy's ascendance to heaven can also be seen as consistent with existential principles. As Viktor Frankl admonished in *Man's Search for Meaning,* "Success, like happiness, cannot be pursued; it must ensue . . . as the unintended side-effect of one's dedication to a course greater than oneself" (xiv). He might as well have been talking about Buffy.

To be sure, death in the *Buffy*verse is not quite as permanent as it is in our reality, and Buffy was soon brought back to life by her friends ("Bargaining," 6-1 and 6-2). She told them she was grateful to them for giving her the world, but she later confided to Spike that she was happy in the heaven-like place and actually resented that her friends tore her away from it:

> Everything here is . . . hard, and bright, and violent. Everything
> I feel, everything I touch . . . this is hell. Just getting through
> the next moment, and the one after that . . . knowing what I've
> lost. . . . ("After Life," 6-3)

Following her resurrection, Buffy experienced her greatest existential crisis yet. Not only did she have to deal with life's mundane responsibil-ities (finding a job, paying the bills), but her Slayer responsibilities were a violent and jarring contrast to her former peaceful existence in para-dise. Although she had previously struggled to face the inevitability of her own death ("Prophecy Girl," 1-12), she now, for the first time, strug-gled to face life, going through the motions of slaying and living, not feeling anything, not knowing if it would ever get better. "Will I stay this way forever? Sleepwalk through my life's endeavor?" she sang in "Once More, With Feeling" (6-7).

Buffy recognized that she was stuck in a rut. She knew that she had lost not only the will to live, but along with it, her sense of self:[12]

> I don't want to be
> Going through the motions
> Losing all my drive.
> I can't even see
> If this is really me. ("Once More, With Feeling")

Although she had earlier found meaning and purpose, these were torn from her when she was brought back to life[13]—after all, she had already fulfilled her life's purpose. What reason could there possibly be for her to live now? "I don't understand . . . why I'm back," she confided to Giles ("Grave," 6-22).

According to existential therapists, the solution to the problem of meaninglessness is engagement, "wholehearted engagement in any of the infinite array of life's activities" (Yalom and May 290). The goal of existential therapy, then, is to remove the obstacles to engagement, to explore what prevents the person from loving another or from gaining satisfaction from work or creativity.

In Buffy's case, the main obstacle seemed to be her social isolation from her friends. She resented them for bringing her back to life but cared enough about them to want to shield them from the knowledge that they had torn her away from heaven. She felt that, not having had the experience of dying (and being raised from the dead), they could no longer understand her. Moreover, her desire to protect their feelings prevented her from doing anything that might increase their understanding. This isolation was devastating for Buffy, who earlier made a point of turning her back on the slayer tradition of working alone[14] in order to

---

[12] Frankl called this sense of emptiness "the existential vacuum."

[13] As Anya put it, "She came back from the grave much graver" ("Once More, With Feeling").

[14] This tradition is evident in season one's opening voice-over: "She alone will stand against the . . . vampires."

enjoy the emotional and instrumental support of her friends. In her desperation to control her psychological torment, Buffy shut down emotionally, not feeling anything—positive or negative. Fortunately, Buffy was once again offered some sound existential advice, this time by Spike, who explained (in verse) that her pain would only diminish if she could reengage in living life.[15]

Simple though this advice may be, removing the obstacles to engagement is often far from easy. To the contrary, May wrote that "one does not become fully human painlessly."

For Buffy, the first step of reengaging in life was being honest with her friends about how they "rescued" her from heaven, which she finally revealed in the song "Something to Sing About" ("Once More, With Feeling," 6-7). Even then, however, her journey toward engagement was long, hard, and, as far as her sexual relationship with Spike was concerned, degrading.[16] Although she had told her friends about being in heaven, she still maintained a psychological distance from them by hiding her relationship with Spike. As he did before, in "Normal Again" (6-17) Spike offered an astute existential analysis, reminding Buffy that she, like all of us, had the ability to make choices about how to live life:

> You're addicted to the misery. It's why you won't tell your pals about us. Might actually have to be happy if you did. They'd either understand and help you, God forbid . . . or drive you out . . . where you can finally be at peace, in the dark. With me. Either way, you'd be better off for it, but you're too twisted for that. (pauses) Let yourself live, already. And stop with the bloody hero trip for a sec. We'd all be the better for it.

At this point, Buffy was in no psychological condition to follow Spike's advice. Even disregarding her temporary bouts of delusions and halluci-

---

[15] Part of the charm of this advice on living was that it came from a vampire who, by definition, was dead.

[16] Although many fans, as well as Sarah Michelle Geller herself, disliked the sixth season's dark storyline, Buffy's compulsive sexual relationship with Spike was consistent with how individuals often respond to terrifying isolation: using another person to meet a specific need (in Buffy's case, to feel something emotionally), rather than getting to know and relating to the whole person.

nations, she was simply not yet able[17] to reengage in the emotional intimacy that she had shared with her friends prior to her death.

Existential therapists would acknowledge both her wish to find meaning in her new existence and her "stuckness" in making that wish a reality. As Abraham Maslow wrote, "If we wish to help humans to become more fully human, we must realize not only that they try to realize[18] themselves, but that they are also reluctant or afraid or unable to do so. Only by fully appreciating this dialectic between sickness and health can we help to tip the balance in favor of health."

Interestingly, the person who finally allowed Buffy to tip toward health was not Spike but Dawn. When Buffy finally emerged from her depression and despair at the end of season six, it was because watching Dawn fighting demons stirred within Buffy a combination of parental pride and sisterly love. With tears of joy, she told Dawn,

> Things have really sucked lately, but that's all going to change, and I want to be there when it does. I want to see you grow up, the woman you're going to become. Because she is going to be beautiful and she is going to be powerful. I got it so wrong. I don't want to protect you from the world. I want to show it to you. ("Grave," 6-22)

This was a fundamental paradigm shift for Buffy. Whereas before she found her life's purpose in her calling as Slayer and in her fight against evil, now she found it in sharing the beauty of life with her sister. Thus, with the help of her friends, her sister, and some well-placed existential guidance, Buffy managed to overcome a crisis of meaning and, once more, to reengage in life.

In *Man's Search for Meaning*, Viktor Frankl writes that the categorical imperative of logotherapy[19] is to "live as if you were living already for the second time and as if you had acted the first time as wrongly as you are

---

[17] An existential therapist would say "not yet willing."

[18] This second "realize" refers to the humanistic notion that humans are constantly striving to improve themselves.

[19] This is a specific type of existential therapy, developed by Frankl, which focuses on finding meaning in life.

about to act now" (131–132).[20] It's a rather tricky thought-experiment, at least for most of us. But Buffy, who has died not once, but twice, embodies its very essence. We all have to grapple with existential issues in our lives. To the extent that living a meaningful (by existential standards) life is truly possible, Buffy has shown us the way.

MIKHAIL LYUBANSKY, PH.D., is a lecturer in the department of psychology at the University of Illinois–Urbana-Champaign, where he teaches psychology of race and ethnicity and theories of psychotherapy, does research on immigration and race relations, and writes an occasional essay for BenBella. He loves the "Statue of Responsibility" idea and can't wait to talk about both the statue and Buffy the next time he teaches the psychotherapy course. Much to his surprise, but possibly not to his students', one online test revealed that he had "a complex, multi-faceted personality, kind of like Glory-Ben-Glorificus."

REFERENCES

Corey, Gerald. *Theory and Practice of Counseling and Psychotherapy*. Belmont: Wadsworth, 2001.

Frankl, Viktor E. *Man's Search for Meaning*. Boston: Beacon Press, 2000.

May, Rollo. *Love and Will*. New York: W. W. Norton & Company, Inc., 1969.

Riess, Jana. *What Would Buffy Do? The Vampire Slayer as Spiritual Guide*. San Francisco: John Wiley & Sons, Inc., 2004.

Sartre, Jean-Paul. *Being and Nothingness*. New York: Bantam Books, 1971.

Irvin Yalom and Rollo May, "Existential Psychotherapy," in *Current Psychotherapies*, eds. Raymond J. Corsini and Danny Wedding (Belmont: Thomson, 2005).

---

[20] Here's an example: Imagine that you are thinking of doing something unethical, like taking credit for someone else's work. Frankl's categorical imperative would have you pretend that you carried out this unethical action and had to face all of the corresponding consequences (which also have to be imagined), and then had the opportunity to live your life again. Would you make the same choice with the benefit of such "hindsight"?

Philosophy, religion, and science have wrestled with the question of mind/body dualism since Aristotle's time. In the seventeenth century, Rene Descartes framed what has become the mantra of dualism, Cogito ergo sum (I think, therefore I am). Though he identified mind with consciousness and self-awareness, he perceived it as an immaterial substance with properties independent of the brain. Though dualism has fallen from scientific favor, the true nature of consciousness remains a conundrum in the Whedonverse, where inserting a chip in Spike's head or returning a vampire's soul can whisper of dueling philosophies of mind. Ed Connor explores Whedon's casting of neuroscience as the villain in Firefly, *while making his case that, in the Whedonverse, the brain and the self are one and the same.*

PSYCHOLOGY BAD

Why Neuroscience Is the Darkest Art in the Latest Whedonverse

ED CONNOR

In the *Buffy*verse, the bad guys are arch-demons and their minions. Their most potent and fearsome weapon is magic. In the *Firefly* 'verse, the bad guys are Alliance government higher-ups ("key members of parliament") and their operatives. What is their most powerful and frightening weapon? It's not military—armed conflict is fairly conventional, the unsuccessful war for independence is over, and the government maintains only an occasional military presence near the border planets. It's not information technology—Captain Malcolm Reynolds and the crew of *Serenity* fly beneath the government's radar and neatly elude detection at every turn. It's not genetics or cybernetics—Joss's vision of the future is refreshingly free of aliens, mutants, and robots (all the characters are very recognizably human). Instead, the really scary stuff in the series *Firefly* and the movie *Serenity*, the homologue to magic, the most insidious weapon, is neuroscience.

The two central mysteries that drive the larger story arc are the madness of a young girl on the run from Alliance agents (River) and the existence of the savage, demonic "Reavers" on the outskirts of known space. As it turns out, both of these story elements arise from abuse of neuroscience by the government. Neuroscientific manipulation is the most devastating form of personal mutilation (River) and the most destructive source of mass mayhem (Reavers). Like magic, it can also be used for good, but with unpredictable and mixed results, as exemplified by River's largely unsuccessful treatment by her physician brother Simon, using neuroactive drugs and neuroimaging.

By adopting neuroscience as a superweapon and dramatic engine, Joss follows a long tradition of extrapolating from current scientific frontiers to dystopian extremes. Nuclear physics, genetics, and computer/robotics technology have been mainstay dramatic devices since the 1950s. Joss's choice of neuroscience is relatively novel and very timely—brain research is on the verge of revolutionizing our world and our understanding of what it is to be human. *Firefly* and *Serenity* dramatize this revolution by making neuroscience seem nearly magical, personifying its power and peril in the character of River.

The reality of brain science is, of course, much less mystical and dark—modern neuroscience provides a biological basis for understanding human psychology and leads to unprecedented cures for neurological diseases. But it takes mystery, danger, and strife to construct a gripping story, and in *Firefly* and *Serenity* neuroscience provides those ingredients. That's okay—as in most dystopian fiction, Joss's dark vision of science still inspires a sense of wonder along with the dread. River makes us marvel at how our very essence depends on the neural mechanisms of the brain—a central truth emerging from current neuroscientific research with ever-increasing clarity (Crick). Most philosophers of mind now believe that human consciousness will be explained at its most fundamental level by neuroscience—that perceptions, beliefs, desires will be precisely identified with specific brain states (Dennett, Chalmers). We will need to reconcile and integrate that scientific revolution with our understanding of what we are, so that neuroscience enlarges rather than diminishes our humanity. In *Serenity*, River epitomizes this synergy of neuroscience and soul, by taking control of her own explosive neural potential and turning it into something miraculous and powerfully human.[1]

---

[1] There is a natural tendency to view scientific explanations of human psychology as somehow incompatible with our status as unique, individual human beings possessed of free will. If we are simply complex neural networks whose characteristics and actions are determined by physical processes, how can we also be loving, suffering souls, free to choose right or wrong, wisdom or folly?

1. How Joss Makes Neuroscience Seem Like Magic

In *Firefly* and *Serenity*, Joss draws on his considerable dramatic powers to make neuroscience seem as dark, mysterious, and potent as magic seems in *Buffy* and *Angel*. Throughout *Firefly*, Joss deftly juxtaposed River's beauty, grace, and innocence with bouts of violent madness and flashes of preternatural power, the aftereffects of her psychic mutilation in a government research facility. Even in lighter episodes focusing on Mal's semi-comic heroism, we got troubling hints of the terrible force that River represents. In the beginning of "War Stories," Kaylee and River chased each other around the ship, fighting over an apple and laughing gaily like the young girls they should have been. Kaylee won the apple away from River and exulted that, "No power in the 'verse can stop me." Late in the episode, Kaylee was left alone to guard the rear in a gunfight. She looked horrified and lost, unable to do anything but hide behind a barrier. Then River, barefoot and clad in a flimsy shift, walked dreamily into the frame and gently took away Kaylee's huge revolver. River briefly scanned the scene, muttered some nursery rhyme-like mnemonic, stood up, and calmly shot three men dead in quick succession, with her eyes closed. When she then said to Kaylee, in her little girl voice, "No power in the 'verse can stop me," the effect was chilling. River is a frail young girl, but neural manipulation had made her into a

---

I believe this longstanding philosophical dilemma arises from an impoverished conception of what a complete scientific explanation of human psychology would look like. We imagine that the brain works like a desktop computer or a B-movie robot, with simple input/output behavioral patterns and no internal life. But in fact our brains contain on the order of 100 billion neurons, each making on the order of 1,000 to 10,000 connections with other neurons. This makes the human brain by far the most complex system in existence, with a number of possible states on the order of $2^{100,000,000,000}$ or $10^{30,000,000,000}$—unimaginably greater than the number of particles in the entire universe (which is on the order of 10^{100}).

Thus, our physical embodiment is not a constraint on human freedom, but instead a virtually infinite substrate that supports the ineffably rich and subtle variety of human experience. We should celebrate the brain as a miraculous source of human power, not bemoan it as a physical prison. River's story explores both the physicality and human power of the brain. She dramatizes how the brain is part of the material world—and thus subject to physical mutilation that can cause madness—but also how it is rich enough to embody love, courage, sacrifice, genius—all the personal qualities that are most essential to our concept of humanity. (Ed.'s Note: See Thomas Flamson's essay on free will, pages 35–49.)

187

homicidal monster, and Kaylee stared at her, aghast. As River said (in the episode "Trash") to the formidable fighter Jayne, after his previous betrayal of her and Simon was revealed: "I can kill you with my brain."

River's outbursts in other episodes ranged from the comic and relatively harmless (cutting up Preacher Book's Bible and trying to rearrange it into something more sensible) to the clearly dangerous and seemingly demonic (suddenly slashing Jayne across the chest with a kitchen knife, declaring that "he looks better in red"). Her genius is not only for violence; in various episodes she showed off hints of an unguessable range of abnormal talents. In "Safe," she grasped a complex local Maypole dance in just seconds and joined in seamlessly, then elaborated, eventually becoming the center of the dance as everyone else clapped appreciatively. In "Shindig," she seduced the petty criminal boss Badger by suddenly adopting a brash Cockney persona that convinced him she was a kindred spirit from the same slums. In "Objects in Space," she outwitted and humiliated a Boba Fett–like bounty hunter named Jubal Early. Like River, Early was psychologically twisted in a way that gave him great power. He quickly and quietly overcame the crew one by one with his spooky ability to assess a person's weak point and apply the right kind of cruel, irresistible pressure. But River was spookier and more subtle—a spirit who seemed to take possession of the ship itself, and finally to inhabit Early's own mind.

In fact, River is a psychic. Perhaps this is innate, like much of her other genius, although Simon hinted that this too could be a "gift" from the Alliance—when Mal said, "I think she's a reader," Simon replied, "They've definitely altered the way she reacts to things, even the way she perceives." Her demonstrations of psychic ability earned her the label "witch" at several points, especially in "Safe" (where she was nearly burned as one), making the connection to magic explicit. By the beginning of the movie, the rest of the crew is clearly frightened of her and her unpredictable powers.

In the opening to *Serenity*, Joss treats us to a dizzying first-person taste of River's psychological dislocation. He steps the audience back through four levels of reality in a sequence that would do credit to Philip K. Dick (the master of layered realities, whose fiction gave rise to the movies *Blade Runner*, *Total Recall*, *Minority Report*, and *A Scanner Darkly*). We begin with the familiar Universal logo unfolding to announce the feature. Next is the startling realization that we are already in the movie itself, looking at a computer display of the real planet Earth. We pull back to see River's childhood classroom lit in saturated nuclear white. That scene briefly establishes her youthful genius and conflict with authority, then subtly sours into a bad dream foreshadowing the holocaust on Miranda. We are violently jerked into the next reality—a densely equipped laboratory in dim blue light, our first glimpse of the scientific nightmare hinted at so darkly throughout *Firefly*. Here the adolescent River we know is restrained, struggling but still dreaming, with a steel probe inserted into her forehead. We are introduced to her chief tormentor, an Alliance scientist who describes his manipulation of River's brain with cold-blooded relish and obvious pride. This scene evolves into a thrilling (and deliberately parodic) rescue. At the height of the action, Joss pulls the rug out from under us again (and laughs at his own action sequence starring the more typically inept Simon) by freezing the frame, then rewinding. We are finally in current time, watching a holographic tape with the Operative, a Bond/ninja-like government agent in pursuit of River. As punishment for a serious breach of security, the Operative executes the sniveling scientist in a poetic and brutal fashion calculated to satisfy our thirst for revenge against River's captors. By the end of this opening sequence, we have an intimate sense of River's disordered mind, and we are left in no doubt about the movie's attitude toward neuroscience. It is the government's most insidious and powerful tool.[2]

How insidious, and how powerful, we will not fully realize until the neuropharmacological holocaust on Miranda is revealed. Miranda is neurosci-

---

[2] It is worth noting that, while neuroscientists are unsavory characters in *Firefly* and *Serenity*, in reality they are mostly a decent lot, more interested in curing disease and understanding the mind than in world domination. The technologies employed for evil purposes in Joss Whedon's fiction are beneficial or promising therapies in the real world. Neuroactive drugs provide our best approach to controlling depression and other debilitating or life-threatening psychological disorders. Brain stimulation is used to ameliorate movement deficits in Parkinson's disease and to relieve intractable pain (Perlmutter and Mink). Prosthetic sensory implants in deaf patients can support auditory perception up to the level of speech recognition (Wilson, Lawson, Muller, Tyler, and Kiefer). Neural implants in the frontal cortex can be used to read the brain's movement commands, and are expected to someday give paralyzed patients and amputees precise control over real or prosthetic limbs and hands (Barton). I imagine Joss appreciates much of this himself, and has no more real antipathy toward neuroscience than James Cameron (writer/director of *Terminator*) does toward computers.

entific mind control writ large and gone catastrophically wrong. It is the ultimate in disastrous utopian experimentation. It is the deepest explanation of River's madness, and her confrontation with the awful reality of it brings about a Freudian release that restores her sanity.[3] Most surprisingly, it is also the explanation for the demonic Reavers. They turn out to be the tiny fraction of the Miranda populace with paradoxical reactions to the "Pax," the neuroactive drug spread by the Alliance government through the water supply to control all hints of violence and rebellion. The Pax made everyone else simply "lie down" (as River's teacher commands in the dream), becoming so apathetic that they simply wasted away in place. As River says of the Reavers, "They never lie down."

2. How Joss's Vision Relates to Neuroscientific Reality

In *Firefly* and *Serenity*, Joss has constructed a wonderfully human story, with the kind of emotion, action, and detail that makes us believe in, laugh with, and cry over a family of human characters. Yet this story points up a scientific truth that some find to be disconcertingly inhuman—that we are essentially neural creatures, nothing more and nothing less than our brains. In fact, referring to the brain as something we possess is inappropriate. We do not own brains, we *are* brains. That fact is vividly dramatized by the profound neural alterations to River's perception, cognition, behavior, and personality. Yet scientific reality can be even more bizarre. Brain lesions can strike at the heart of what it is to be human.

The one brain structure specifically mentioned in River's case is the amygdala, an almond-shaped nucleus in each hemisphere near the base of the brain that is involved in emotions and memory formation. Simon explained that repeated "stripping" of River's amygdalae had made it impossible for her to filter or control her emotions: "she feels everything . . . she can't not" ("Ariel"). In reality, selective damage to the amygdalae, which is very rare,

---

[3] Freud's classic conception of hysteria involved repression of a traumatic event into the subconscious. The psychic energy associated with that trauma manifested itself as the hysterical symptoms afflicting the patient. The cure, according to Freud, was to relive the event, bringing it into the light of consciousness and thus releasing the psychic energy once and for all. River's experience on Miranda follows this pattern quite explicitly. The mystery that Joss then teases his audience with is whether, in losing her madness, River has also lost her genius and power.

has the opposite effect, blunting emotional reactions.[4] Wider damage to the amygdala and other structures in the medial temporal lobe, including the hippocampus, produces amnesia, the inability to form new long-term memories. This condition (dramatized in the movie *Memento*) was first clinically described in a patient known as H.M., who underwent bilateral surgical removal of the medial temporal lobes in order to control debilitating epilepsy. As a result, H.M. lost the ability to form new long-term memories (memories that last beyond the point at which we are deliberately holding them in consciousness, over the course of seconds or at most minutes). H.M. lives in an eternal present, unable to extend his own personal narrative beyond what he remembers from before the surgery (Squire and Kandel).

Other brain lesions due to surgeries, mechanical injuries, strokes, or tumors can impact perception, cognition, and selfhood even more dramatically. Perceptual agnosias can be strikingly specific, eliminating a narrow slice of conscious experience and leaving the rest intact. For example, patients with lesions confined to the "fusiform face area" of the brain have perfectly normal vision, but can no longer identify individual human faces. Other specific lesions can selectively eliminate color or general form vision. Lesions of the parietal lobe (one of the four major divisions of each brain hemisphere) affect spatial cognition. Most brain functions are "crossed," and thus lesions of the right parietal cortex impact perception of the left half of space. Awareness of the left half of objects or even the left half of the body can be wiped out. In a famous series of self-portraits, an artist who suffered a parietal stroke began by drawing only half his face; the other half was added gradually in subsequent portraits as he recovered over a period of months. Parietal patients sometimes fail to groom or dress the affected half of their bodies, feeling that they belong to someone else. It is hard to believe that a thinking, functioning human being could cognitively disown half their body, but this goes to show that everything we experience and believe depends on some kind of neural information processing. When you destroy that neural process, you take away a piece of reality (Rapp).

Even the unity of consciousness can be disrupted by brain lesions. The two hemispheres of the brain, which are largely redundant in function, communicate via a thick bundle of fibers called the corpus callosum. In some

---

[4] Ed.'s Note: See Bradley J. Daniels's essay, "Stripping' River Tam's Amygdala" 131–140.

cases of intractable epilepsy, the corpus callosum is surgically severed to pre-vent the spread of seizures between hemispheres. Experiments on these patients have shown beyond doubt that the two hemispheres have separa-ble conscious experiences and behavioral responses. If the two hemispheres are presented with conflicting cues in a visual recognition test, the patient will point to one answer with the right hand (controlled by the left hemi-sphere) while simultaneously pointing to a different answer with the left hand (controlled by the right hemisphere) (Gazzaniga, Ivry, and Mangun).

These scientific observations present us with an inescapable truth: the brain and the self are one and the same. There is nothing about us that does not depend on some kind of neural processing somewhere in the brain. That is the reality dramatized by River's condition throughout *Firefly*. How can Joss reconcile this scientific reality with his own moral framework, defined as always by human individuality and self-determination? For the answer, we have to examine the climactic battle in *Serenity*.

3. River Triumphant

We can see in retrospect how the entire *Firefly* story was always building toward the final battle in *Serenity*. This is where Joss weaves together all the longer threads of his story—Mal's cynicism, Alliance oppression, River's madness, the nightmarish Reavers. The setup occurs on Miranda, where River exorcises her madness by unearthing her searing memory of the holocaust, and Mal rediscovers his idealism when confronted by an Alliance crime too heinous to ignore. Both characters, internally conflicted throughout the series, are at last themselves again, Mal a hard-bitten free-dom fighter, River a delicate teenage girl, though with a difference.

Many of Joss' final battles in *Buffy* and *Angel* take place on two planes, one physical, the other magical.[5] In *Serenity*, Mal fights the straightfor-

---

[5] In the Buffy season seven finale, for instance, the powerful fighters (Buffy, Spike, Faith) opened the Hellmouth and took on the First Evil's army of übervamps. Elsewhere, the magically gifted Willow was performing a spell to activate an army of Potentials as full-blown slayers, providing essential support in the physical battle. Willow had previously described this spell as the most powerful magic she had ever attempted and given instructions that she should be destroyed if the spell failed. Everyone fought bravely, but final victory again depended on magic, in the form of an amulet worn by Spike, through which the enemy was destroyed, though at the (temporary) cost of Spike's own life.

ward physical battle, going one on one with an invincible opponent, using gun, blade, and fists, and calling on every combat trick and ounce of stubborn courage he's got. River must fight a battle that is physical but also entails another plane of reality, not magical this time but neuropsychological. The Reavers are transformed on this plane, gutted of human personality and inflamed into virtual demons by an accident of Alliance neuropharmacology. River herself has been transformed by Alliance neuroscience, into the ultimate warrior, a murderous automaton triggered by a subliminally broadcast Alliance signal in the bar on Beaumonde, unstoppable until Simon utters a safe word and she collapses. Her transformation into the perfect fighter cost River her sanity. After Miranda, she seems to have recovered her sanity, but as battle commences, she unfortunately seems to have simultaneously lost her will and ability to fight. She weeps over her fallen brother like a child losing a parent, plaintively crying, "You always take care of me." Then, she straightens, and Joss turns the scene on its head with just two words: "My turn."

Like any good Whedon apocalypse, this one forces the heroes to face imminent death under hopeless circumstances. Mal is run through with a sword, expiring on the floor, while the Operative dusts his hands off and walks away. River sacrifices herself to protect the rear, sealing the blast door but dragged into a pit of raving demons. On first viewing I believed at one point that Joss had really killed off both characters (okay, I'm gullible). But Mal drags himself up off the floor for one more round of punishment, and he has one more *ruse de guerre* up his sleeve. And River, miraculously, is dancing in a Reaver inferno, a slim wraith dealing death with balletic martial grace. This is the scene where Joss brings together everything Alliance neuroscience has created: the inhuman ferocity of the Reavers, the supernatural power of River's transformed mind.[6] When the blast door opens again at last, it reveals River standing over a roomful of slain Reavers, eyes

---

[6] Joss professes to choose his character names with great care. The phonetic similarity between "River" and "Reaver" is no accident—the girl and the madmen are two sides of the same coin, both products of Alliance meddling with minds. I think of "River" as a reference to the "stream of consciousness," psychologist William James's famous description of the continuous succession of states in one mind that we think of as the self or the soul. A "Reaver" can be one who plunders or pillages (from Middle English *reven*, to plunder) or one who tears things apart (from Middle English *riven* and Old Norse *rifa*, to rend, cleave, split, or break)—both apt descriptions for the savages in *Firefly* and *Serenity*.

smoldering, blade dripping, the apotheosis of girl power. The awesome potential of her neural transformation is unleashed, but it is now hers to command. Her sword hand is retightening, in readiness to mow down the Alliance soldiers who have swarmed behind her, but when they are given the order to stand down, she exchanges a glance with Mal and drops her blade. The epilogue shows her whole again, a naturally curious teenage girl, innocently spying on Simon and Kaylee's lovemaking. But she is also the genius and the warrior, ready to take her place beside Mal at the helm of *Serenity*, in full control of herself and her power.

Thus endeth Joss's neuroscience lesson. Humans are neural creatures; they can be destroyed at the neural level, they can be twisted at the neural level, they can even be enhanced at the neural level. But, as River exemplifies, those neural circuits contain a core of humanity, a kernel of self-determination that can overcome the agony and madness to assert itself as a courageous and loving human being. Science confronts us with the fact that our essential selves are neural—we are brains, nothing more. But that does not make us one bit less human.

———————————

ED CONNOR, PH.D., is an associate professor of neuroscience at Johns Hopkins University, where he earned his Ph.D. He lives in Baltimore with his wife Amy and their fiercely independent two-year-old son Malcolm.

REFERENCES

Samantha Barton, "Neurological Disorders: Mind over Machine," *Nature Reviews Neuroscience* 7 (2006): 682–683.

Chalmers, David J. *The Conscious Mind: In Search of a Fundamental Theory.* New York: Oxford University Press, 1996.

Crick, Francis H. C. *The Astonishing Hypothesis: The Scientific Search for the Soul.* New York: Scribners, 1994.

Dennett, Daniel C. *Consciousness Explained.* Boston: Little, Brown & Co., 1991.

Gazzaniga, M. S., Ivry, R. B., and G. R. Mangun. *Cognitive Neuroscience: The Biology of the Mind.* New York: W.W. Norton, 1998.

James, William. *Principles of Psychology.* New York: Holt, 1890.

J. S. Perlmutter and J. W. Mink, "Deep Brain Stimulation," *Annual Review of Neuroscience* 29 (2006): 229–257.

Brenda Rapp. *Handbook of Cognitive Neuropsychology: What Deficits Reveal about the Human Mind.* Philadelphia: Psychology Press, 2000.

Squire, L. R. and E. R. Kandel. *Memory: From Mind to Molecules.* New York: W.H. Freeman, 2000.

Blake S. Wilson, Dewey T. Lawson, Joachim M. Muller, Richard S. Tyler, and Jan Kiefer, "Cochlear Implants: Some Likely Next Steps," *Annual Review of Biomedical Engineering* 5 (2003): 207–249.

Our relationships are our mirrors, and the truth of our nature is revealed in the glimmer of their refracted light. Through our intimate unions we birth ourselves, define ourselves, destroy ourselves, and sometimes even redeem ourselves. In Angel's unbreakable bond with Darla, Whedon gives us our passions amplified and our nightmares multiplied. Yet, in testing that bond, he shows us two empty vessels transformed, newly pulsing with purpose and life. In Angel and Darla, Whedon shows us our most selfish and venal selves—and then reveals what it means to become something far more.

"THERE'S MY BOY . . ."

JOY DAVIDSON

Since the first episode of *Buffy*, I've been a captivated fan, easily losing myself in the alternate universe where every dark remnant of the psyche lives vibrantly in the flesh. Perhaps that's because as a psychologist and sex therapist, I come from what some might consider an alternative universe, too, where passions are living creatures, both wanted and feared, and the demons of shame, guilt, and regret can keep us chained for a lifetime. In my universe, curses are often self-made, knitted from the wool of our own histories: our families, our lovers, and our beliefs about ourselves. To the degree that my universe intersects with the *Angel*verse, I view Angel as far more than a creature tormented by blood cravings, past horrors, and mystical forces. In his hulking handsomeness, Angel may be one of the small screen's most sexually confused heroes. He's torn by sadistic impulses, terrified of the consequences of intimacy, and driven to redeem tortured women—all because a consuming relationship with one of them framed his destiny.

We could easily mistake Buffy for the most important femme in Angel's life, considering that they had "the forbidden love of all time." But another relationship was better than forbidden, it was formative. Of course, I'm speaking of the same relationship that is central in most men's lives—the one with Mom. Except, in Angel's case, Mother did not spit him from her womb, but bit him into bloody being.

To say that Darla "made" Angel is to tell only a fraction of the story. She made him, yes, but more than that she shaped him, molded him into her perfect consort. She directed his slaughter of his own family, wowed him with sadomasochistic thrills and showered him with otherworldly wisdom. When she abandoned him, he trailed her across continents and decades. Later, ensouled and divided against himself, Darla cast him off to suffer alone, yet Angel sought her reflection all over again in another preternatural little blond.

Now that's a doozie of a relationship!

And then there's the part where he dusted her, and where she rose from oblivion to have his baby. But I'm getting ahead of myself. Let's go back to the beginning. . . .

Angel/Angelus began life as Liam of Galway, Ireland. The son of a harsh and punitive patriarch, Liam failed to cull even a lick of warmth or approval from his self-righteous father. No surprise, then, that the rejected young man turned to rebellious womanizing, drinking, and brawling. Who can help but wonder about his mother's role in his fate? Given her husband's iron will and the subservience expected of eighteenth-century women, she would have been powerless to stand between Liam and his father. We can only speculate about how unprotected young Liam felt, and how he might have resented his mother's helplessness.

Enter Darla, a delicately beautiful, anything-but-helpless 150-year-old seductress, magnetized by lovely Liam's recklessness and bawdy charm. Before her own vampire-birth in 1609 Darla had been an "independent" woman—a prostitute—accustomed to the fragile power that comes with belonging to no man. From the moment of Liam's "rebirth," the two cruelly kindred spirits are bound together, and remain so for centuries.

As a vampire, Liam finally triumphs over his nemesis, his father, when he drains his lifeblood: "Now I've won!" Liam boasts. But Darla, older and by far the wiser, reminds Liam that his brief victory pales beside his father's longstanding defeat of him. With deceptive gentleness, she imparts a truth so elegant, so pregnant, that its echoes reverberate throughout Angel's existence. "What we once were informs all that we have become," she tells him. "The same love will infect our hearts even if they no longer beat" ("The Prodigal," 1-15).

Arrogant, stubborn Liam sneers at her words. He doesn't yet understand the tug of the past or the power of unresolved yearning. It will take him another 250 years to absorb this very first lesson of his making.

Liam's denial of the longing that drives him lies at the heart of his character, for Liam the Man had possessed little more soul than Liam the Vampire. We only need explore the similarities between "soul" and "Self" to see through the entrancing darkness that envelops both Liam and his vampire alter ego, Angelus, and to comprehend Darla's power.

In vampire literature, "soul" is often equated with human conscience, but it may be more fitting to compare soul with what many in my profession refer to as an integrated or "solid" sense of Self.

Let me explain.

A solid Self is believed to evolve when caregivers consistently respond to and reflect a child's wholeness and uniqueness as he grows. In the light of this accepting gaze, a child becomes grounded in an ineffable essence of "me." This consciousness of Self allows him to appreciate the sheer "not me-ness" of another, which imparts the capacity for emotional and sexual connection, and, in turn, yields empathy. Liam never developed these qualities. His father regarded him as a derivative creature, a disgustingly flawed "mini-me" rather than a treasured other. Though Liam fought against his father's indicting perceptions of him, he absorbed them too, leaving him developmentally impoverished and empty inside.

In the absence of solid Self, a person will struggle to divine a set of illusions, a trusted fiction to fill his inner void. Liam was doomed to seek in others this reflected, idealized vision of himself—or the opposite, a devalued, repudiated image of his shriveled Self, huddling beneath his polished veneer. This hunger for reflection made him vulnerable to Darla's über-femme predations. Ironically, on becoming a vampire, he lost whatever sense of self-observation he might have acquired in time, symbolized by the absence of reflection in the mirror. A damaged, invisible Self does not empathize; others exist only to fill his needs and make him seem real.

One word describes this embodiment of selflessness: narcissism.

Most of us harbor some narcissistic traits, if only because we are raised in an obscenely narcissistic culture. But the pathological narcissist virtually hemorrhages from his developmentally incurred narcissistic wounds. He is both great and puny; he is one moment indomitable, entitled by his specialness to pillage and use, and the next so lowly as to be unworthy of sucking air.

As a mortal, Liam was selfish, self-indulgent, and given to grandiose displays of machismo. Once his soul was extracted, his excesses became gluttonous to the point of psychopathic extravagance. Just as Liam once searched his father's visage for a reflection he could love, Angelus seeks that reflection in his new mother's smile—and finds it. He basks in her admiration. Cruelty fills the emptiness within him that might have flowed with compassion had he experienced a different sort of upbringing.

Angelus and Darla's relationship accelerates quickly in intensity, fueled both by Darla's attachment to the boy she can shape and mold, stunningly packaged in the body of a pleasure-seeking adult demon, and Angelus's fascination with Darla's strength, beauty, and lustiness. At first it seems they might love each other, but at second glace it becomes obvious that neither is capable of such generous emotion.

Before being turned, Darla had been dying of a syphilitic heart condition—perfectly symbolizing her corrupted capacity for loving. As a human she had been too desperate and self-serving to love. As a vampire, she might display loyalty or the desire to merge with a mate, but she could no more love than walk freely in sunshine. Like Darla, Angelus could love only to the extent that Liam was able—suggesting that his feelings for Darla were something else entirely.[1] In light of their damaged psyches, it would seem that love's doppelganger—obsession—held Darla and Angelus in thrall.

However, obsession can be an even more demanding taskmaster than love, for it positions compelling need above reason or good sense.

---

[1] We have evidence that vampires can and do love—but not more or better than they did as humans. James and Elizabeth had what Cordelia called the "big, forever love" (*Angel*, "Heartthrob," 3-1). Spike felt love for Buffy long before he was ensouled. But all of them had been love-struck as humans, too.

Obsession is trouble enough in a human. In a vampire it's . . . well, demonic. As a result, Angelus's universe collapses into a mere pinpoint of ferocious desire. Nothing matters but Darla and the satisfaction of his demented cravings.

During their first dozen years together, Angelus and Darla tear across Europe, easily besting any adversary in an escalating reign of destruction. Finally, one vampire hunter, Holtz, traps them in his barn, nearly costing them their lives. But Darla's cunning survival instincts kick in and she escapes, abandoning Angelus to near-certain torture and death. Her ever-resourceful son does get away—intact if not unscathed—and eager to extract his revenge upon mommy dearest. We never actually see what happens when Angelus finds Darla, but years later they both relish spinning a tale of her betrayal and subsequent punishment to the young vamp lovers, James and Elizabeth ("Heartthrob," 3-1): "She hit me with a shovel, wished me luck and rode off on our only horse," Angelus announces.

Delighting in his recollection, Darla reminds Angelus that when he finally caught up with her in Vienna, she was made to pay for her sins, again and again. Can James and Elizabeth even begin to fathom the things that he did to her, Angelus wonders—leaving both the horrors and pleasures to their innocent imaginations. Naturally, they can't, because James and Elizabeth are "in love" and vampires in love don't brutalize one another—do they?

Even if Angelus had harbored love for Darla prior to her betrayal—twisted though it might have been—the emotion would likely have died in that barn anyway, leaving Angelus with an unquenchable, ever-soaring thirst: to find her, punish her, and then have her again. Obsession is sustained by the urge to gain power over another, and here we glimpse a climactic turnabout in the power-relationship between Darla and Angelus. The son gains control; mommy luxuriates in baring her throat. Watching, we feel a mingling of disgust and erotically tinged wonder as we ponder the things Angelus did to his lover . . . his mother . . . his betrayer.

As years pass, Angelus becomes ever more artfully depraved, the legendary master of psychological torture. And Darla continues to provide fresh flesh for their sexual sideshows. True to Darla's prophecy, the past continues to inform all that Angelus becomes, as the rage of Liam builds upon itself and is unleashed upon their victims in a whirlwind of mayhem.

In the making of their own vampire child, Drusilla, Darla and Angelus's sexual sadism reaches a high point—or a low, depending on one's outlook. In a scene depicting the two preparing to bring Drusilla into their fold, Darla and Angelus thrash about on the floor of a convent as Dru cowers in a corner, awaiting her fate:

"This one's special. I have big plans for her," Angelus taunts. Dru watches them, alert to the sexual repartee. "Snake in the woodshed. Snake in the woodshed!" she recites, sing song. Is she referring to Angelus's snake in Darla's "woodshed"?

"So are we going to kill her during, or after?" Darla inquires, as they continue wrestling on the floor. Darla's question reminds us that Angelus now utterly dominates in their predatory marriage, while Darla submits to his whims.

"Neither," he says. "We turn her into one of us."

Darla's eyes widen, for Dru is incontrovertibly "a lunatic," and even she is startled by the incomparable evil of subjecting Drusilla to eternal life. For Angelus, that's the beauty of his plan. "Killing is so merciful at the end, isn't it? The pain has ended." He prefers to prolong his victims' suffering. The idea, itself, is an aphrodisiac, and Angelus forcefully rolls on top of Darla, pinning her beneath him as Dru looks on ("Dear Boy," 2-5).

This scene is thick with the syrup of passion and dependency in Darla and Angelus's relationship. A more potent elixir than love alone, their obsession thrives on this intoxicating coalescence of lust, power, and insane violence.

The terrible two might have continued cutting a crimson swath across the continents if Darla hadn't one day outdone herself in procuring damsels for their erotic bloodbaths. On Angelus's birthday she surprises him with the perfect gift: a glassy-eyed gypsy girl, bound and gagged in front of the fire.

"She's not just for you," Darla teases. "I get to watch."

As Angelus lifts the trembling girl's skirt, we see the couple at their most intimate, sharing a last moment of gleeful depravity, unaware that their destiny is about to change irrevocably.

The gypsy-girl's tribe soon exacts revenge against Angelus by casting a spell to restore his lost soul, condemning him to everlasting remorse over his ugly past. What's more, the curse carries an unknown tripwire: should he ever experience a moment of true bliss, he will lose his soul and any small measure of redemption he might have earned.

Darla is incensed by the curse. She rails, ". . . they gave you a soul. A filthy soul! No!" and attacks Angelus wildly, scratching his cheek until he bleeds. "You're disgusting!" ("Five By Five," 1-18).

Angelus is consumed by the horror of his past barbarism and despair over Darla's rejection. Once more he is the spurned and loathsome off-spring, abandoned and bereft. But, Darla, too, is lost, and for a century and a half ingrains a ragged need not easily slaked. She beseeches the gypsy elders to "remove that filthy soul so my boy might return to me." However, the curse remains intact and Angelus, broken and tormented, wanders alone, living on vermin to appease his agonizing craving for human blood. However, nothing can appease his longing for Darla, and in a few years he returns to her, begging to be taken in. Tempted as she is, Darla can't trust that a vampire with a soul could still be "her boy."

"I don't know what you are anymore."

"You know what I am. You *made* me, Darla. I'm Angelus."

"Not anymore," she counters, though she desperately wants to believe otherwise. Obsession is not easily burnt out, and the barest flicker of hope can reignite it in an instant.

"I can be again," Angelus promises. "Just give me a chance to prove it to you. We can have the whirlwind back."

Darla's longing supplants her better judgment. They both want to believe that their naked desire for one another will overshadow the glare of his defective soul.

"We can do anything," Darla whispers, as their trembling lips meet. And when they kiss, Angelus morphs into his primal vamp-face—for this is not just his killing face, it is his lustful face . . . the face of passion for the woman who has been at his side nearly forever. A dark romanticism infuses the scene, and it seems for an instant that love between them is not so impossible after all.

Before long, Darla discovers Angelus has failed to keep his promise.

Although he has been drinking human blood, he confines his kills to "rapists and murderers, thieves and scoundrels." For Darla, his cowardly acts strike her as merciless betrayals. Yet, she can't help offering him one final opportunity, one last test through which he can atone for his moral collapse by sinking his fangs into a missionary's baby.

Angelus—now the "Angel" we know so well—is unable to consummate the awful deed, and he bolts with the baby ("Darla," 2-7).

The lovers do not see each other again for nearly 100 years.

If the first phase of Angel's "life" as a vampire is an exotic free-for-all under Darla's tutelage, the second phase is a nightmare of stagnation. Angel no longer feeds on even the most repugnant of humans, but subsists on subterranean vermin. Isolated from both humanity and demons, devoid of attachments or connections to the world, he hovers ghost-like among the living, unchallenged, psychologically still as stone. We see the human Liam in him—a Liam whose bravado has been knocked out—wasting away in a bed of pain and self-hatred. As self-centered as ever—even if consumed by sins rather than caprices—Angel wallows in worthlessness as he once swelled with grandiosity. He may have a soul, but he still lacks a core Self; a crippling conscience is not enough to make him whole.

Joss Whedon has suggested that Angel's need for blood is a metaphor for addiction, and that he is always one drink away from reverting. But I question the actual substance of Angel's addiction. Is it blood? Or is he hooked on something from which he cannot abstain without effecting an inner transformation: his own self-loathing?

A century after his exile from Darla, the Powers That Be finally break through Angel's desolation by assigning him a mission. The new Slayer is in danger from the Master, and Angel is entrusted with her protection. Unknown to Angel, Darla has become the Master's new hit-woman and when she threatens Buffy, her own dear boy is forced to drive a stake into her breast.

Darla is finally lost to him, it seems. Will his lingering obsession be stilled? Not quite—for he seeks her again in another little blond spitfire. The advice of a "faux Swami" on how to cleanse Darla from his psyche comes to mind: "Go out and find some small blond thing. You bed her, you love her, you treat her like crap!" ("Guise Will Be Guise," 2-6). And this he did . . . in spades.

Although his longing for Darla contaminates Angel's attraction to teenage Buffy, the relationship is just what the doctor ordered for the 250-year-old vampire. Angel and Buffy are not quite the May/December pairing they seem; emotionally, they may be closer to the same level of adolescent development. So, together they grow up, through trials and heartache and the crucible of deep caring for one another. For a while it appears that Angel might have finally begun to mend Liam's wounds. But things don't quite work out the way either of them planned, and Angel eventually leaves Sunnydale.

When Angel arrives in LA, he resumes his brooding isolation. But the Powers again intercede. (Obviously they have big plans for this accursed boy!) Flush with the new mission imprinted upon his business cards— "we help the helpless"—he becomes the paterfamilias of Angel Investigations. More than ever haunted by his deeds as Angelus, he craves redemption as he once craved human blood. And hope springs eternal when an ancient prophecy foretells that a vampire with a soul, after saving the world from apocalypse, will be made human again. Unlife is good. Sort of. Except for the fact that Angel's new obsession— his quest for redemption—sweeps him into a claustrophobic labyrinth of his own making. Convinced that asceticism is the path to salvation, he accepts a joyless, passionless existence in the service of his Sisyphusian struggle. How ironic that love at its most intimate and con- nected—the experience that makes the rest of us most human—deprives Angel of his strongest link to humanity.

Meanwhile, the senior partners at the evil law firm of Wolfram & Hart, in the hopes of drawing the powerful "Angelus" into their orbit, invoke magic to bring Darla back from the dead as a mortal—with a soul. As Lindsey says to Darla: "We don't want Angel dead. We want him dark. And there's no better way to a man's dark side than to awaken his nastier urges . . ." ("Dear Boy," 2-5).

Darla's return raises some hopelessly romantic questions: Could Darla and Angel have a real chance at love? Could they be "soul mates" after all? Not likely. For a soul's installation can't wipe away hundreds of years of per- sonal history, nor heal a damaged psyche. A soul, alone, can't sweeten a hardened, selfish heart. Darla is no more a being of innocence in her second incarnation than she was on the day she was turned by the Master.

The folks at Wolfram & Hart are certainly on the right track if they want to nab Angelus. Like any good therapist, they know that a desire buried in shame and shadow will eventually rise feverishly to the surface. And because Angel embraces the celibate path to sustained goodness, he is ever so ripe for Darla's plucking.

Darla quickly rekindles Angel's neutered sexuality, spinning irresistible tales of their past debaucheries. She croons of taking the gypsy in front of the fire until the girl was nearly drowning in her own blood, and Angel's animal nature leaps to life uninhibited, unashamed. How different are these dreams from memories of times shared with Buffy, when the "good boy" remained ever cautious. His feelings for Buffy may have elicited true happiness, but he always restrained the full measure of his lust. As Darla conjures her hypnotic dreamscape, she slowly isolates Angel from his team, replacing the bleakness of his daily existence with a tempting illusion and leaving his waking hours choked with remorse.

In Angel's world, intense sexuality is associated with dark forces that taint love. It's a world bloated with Christian guilt, and Angel's masochistic self-hatred is rooted in the very human dilemma of being simultaneously consumed with sexual tension and terrified of its release, of yearning for love yet mistrusting its carnal expression.

Angel's reaction to his curse reflects the dynamic tension operative within the majority of modern males who wrestle with extremes of connection and separation, of merging and thriving independently. To love without fear is daunting. Fear of being enveloped, suffocated, of losing one's Self, may keep love at arm's length. Men are often caught in the wasteland between polarities, unable to achieve a balance that enables them to hold on to themselves and another.

I suspect that Angel's desire to connect, to extend himself fully, may one day lead him to the completion of his heroic journey. I'd like to imagine that love will become the antidote to his curse, and cease to be the evil potion that inevitably invokes Angelus. Of all the trials that Angel confronts season after season, his final trial, and the road to triumph over the gypsy magic, may be (almost) as simple as a commitment to love fearlessly.

Angel's relationship with Darla allows him to brush closely up against this very possibility.

The first time that a wakeful Angel encounters the human Darla, his pent-up feelings quickly ignite and he bursts into vamp-face with one passionate kiss.

"There's my boy . . ." Darla coos.

Desire ripples off the screen in almost palpable waves. The raw eroticism Angel has been holding at bay oozes through, just as it does in his dreams. Angel tries to halt the momentum, but Darla pushes him up against a pillar, nuzzling close. He grabs her arm and shoves her away as she continues to entice him. "You're hurting me," she whispers. "And I like it."

So does Angel—but his concern for Darla's precious soul takes precedence. When he warns her of the toll her guilty memories will soon take she offers a means of easing his troubled conscience: allow her to give him one delirious moment of happiness—and then give her life eternal.

Angel won't bite. "You blew the top off my head," he says. "But you never made me happy."

Infuriated, Darla strikes back. "There was a time when you would have said I was the definition of bliss! Buffy wasn't happiness. She was just new!"

Angel continues preaching. "Darla, I couldn't feel that with you, because I didn't have a soul. But then I got a second chance—just like you have."

Angel is deluding himself about the soul being his handicap, but at least he believes his own lies. And who can blame him for harboring just a flicker of a fantasy that if Darla aligns with the good in the world, they could be together again and, if not happy, perhaps the next best thing.

Darla will have none of Angel's moralizing, and once again reveals her disdain for the idea of the "soul."

"What a poster child for soulfulness you are. . . . Before you got neutered you weren't just any vampire, you were a legend! Nobody could keep up with you—not even me. You don't learn that kind of darkness. It's innate. It was in you before we ever met. . . . My boy is still in there and he wants out!" ("Dear Boy," 2-5).

Centuries earlier, Darla had recognized in Liam the very qualities she sought in a mate—ruthless cruelty and daring self-indulgence. However,

Liam's darkness wasn't "evil," it was merely his own pathetically human pain turned outward, savagely visited upon the world.[2] In the grip of soulless excess, however, he became her monstrously dear boy. Now, even Darla's wiles fail to sway Angel from his redemptive path, and he holds fast to the conviction that her salvation is his as well.

Soon after their confrontation, Angel learns that Darla is dying of the very disease that nearly took her before the Master made her a vampire. To save both her life and her soul, he embarks upon a tortuous series of trials. Despite his efforts, the Powers refuse to grant her another chance at humanity, and Angel resigns himself to the idea that turning her into a vampire is the only way to spare her.

"Maybe it would be different. We don't know . . . because, you know, I have a soul. If I did bite you . . . ."

He is reaching, searching, but Darla, too, has been changed by her short mortal life. She has been so deeply moved by Angel's sacrifices, his willingness to die to save her, that she refuses.

"Angel, I've seen it now . . . everything you're going through. I felt how you care. The way no one's ever cared before—not for me. That's all I need from you."

Darla is willing to die as she was meant to die all along, and Angel promises to remain at her side until the end. "You're never going to be alone again."

For the first time, Angel and Darla realize a depth of unselfish caring for one another that transcends obsession. They are on the verge of the healing they need, and there is a chance, finally, for a resolution to their dramatic relationship. If only this tender moment could last. However, in the mythopoetic universe created by Joss Whedon, almost as soon as love blooms, tragedy strikes.[3] So it is really no surprise that black-ops specialists burst in, subdue Angel, and force him to watch helplessly as his own spawn, Drusilla, gives Darla the eternal life she had been seeking ("The Trial," 2-9).

---

[2] Angel also acknowledges this point when he tells Faith that he once tried to bury his pain, "but you can't get the hole deep enough. You know there's only one way to make the pain stop. Hurt something else" (*Angel*, "Salvage," 4-13).

[3] Think of Buffy/Angel, Giles/Jenny, Willow/Tara, Darla/Angel, Cordelia/Angel, Lilah/Wesley, Fred/Wesley. . . .

In the aftermath, Angel unleashes decades—centuries—of fulminating rage. His old obsession with possessing Darla gives rise to an urgency to destroy her—and, it seems, himself. His behavior becomes erratic, driven: giving the Wolfram & Hart staff over to Darla and Dru's blood lust, setting fire to the two vampires, and finally launching his own Kamikaze mission into the bowels of Wolfram & Hart's home office to wipe out the senior partners. He has lost hope, lost belief in anything except vengeance upon the evil that he can no longer abide—especially as it lies concealed within him. To the team at AI, he is almost unrecognizable.

"I don't even know what you are anymore," says Cordelia, noting that Angel is neither evil vampire nor good "helper of the helpless," but some curious hybrid.

"I'm a vampire. Look it up!"

Angel has no illusions about the side of the divide from which he's drawing energy. This scene is starkly reminiscent of the one between Angel and Darla when she says nearly the same words after Angel returns to her, ensouled, promising to prove himself.

When Angel fails to annihilate either his own misery or the world's, he returns home, defeated, more disconnected from life than ever before. And there is Darla, waiting. Too lost to wonder why she is there, Angel violently pushes her up against a wall, devouring her with his mouth.

"I just want to feel something besides the cold."

But in the midst of passion, Darla begins to giggle.

"Why are you laughing?" Angel snarls.

In spite of herself she continues to laugh, perhaps at the improbability of it all, the single turn she hadn't anticipated. Angel strikes her viciously across the face, sending her crashing through the glass doors that lead to his bedroom. Slowly, he approaches her, a predator stalking prey. Light bounces off the jagged shards of glass that surround them, reflecting his own shattered sense of meaning. He reaches for her, gently pulling her up off the floor.

"What are you doing?" She seems genuinely puzzled.

"It doesn't matter," he replies, stroking the marked side of her face where he'd struck her. "None of it matters." He kisses her again and she matches him eagerly. They fall back onto the bed, ripping at each other's clothes . . . tearing at each other . . . mouths locked tightly. Angel pulls back and looks into her eyes with such blatant desire it borders on amazement . . . and, of course, the screen goes black ("Reprise," 2-15).

Finally, we see the wreckage of 250 years of psycho-emotional torture (350 if we count the century-spent-in-hell's timeline). If Angel wakes up as Angelus, so be it. Angel has ceased to care, and like any of us when pushed beyond our capacity to bear the burden, he reverts to the most familiar and predictable form of comfort. Darla is Angel's touchstone. And for a while he is—in every way that counts—her boy.

Angel awakens with Darla beside him in an agony of "perfect despair," yet his soul is intact and he feels illuminated. While he may not have had a chance to see Darla through her illness, or been able to give her a shot at redemption, her presence in his life has both incited and helped resolve his crisis of meaning. Later, he shares his epiphany with Kate Lockley—shortly after preventing her suicide. (Angel is still run by the axiom, "If you can't save one little blond, rescue another.")

He tells Kate that he knows there is no grand plan to life, no big win. But, "if there is no great, glorious end to all this, if nothing we do matters, then all that matters is what we do—'cause that's all there is. What we do, now, today. I fought for so long. For redemption, for a reward—finally just to beat the other guy, but . . . I never got it."

Now, all Angel wants to do is help, "Because if there is no bigger meaning, then the smallest act of kindness is the greatest thing in the world" ("Epiphany," 2-16).

Angel's epiphany is the first real step in his psyche's resurrection, drawing him back to Angel Investigations where he humbly apologizes to Wes, Gunn, and Cordy. He is willing to relinquish his quest for power and do what ordinary folks do . . . reach out, share, cooperate. Once again, his involvement with Darla breeds his transformation.

It also . . . well . . . breeds!

Darla discovers that she is impossibly, yet quite assuredly, carrying Angel's child. How two undead could create life is a mystery even to the shamans and mystics Darla consults to try to put an end to the pregnancy. The fetus seems magically protected, and as her due date approaches, Darla appears—where else?—but on Angel's doorstep, seeking help. As if Angel's "perfect despair" was itself a dream, the two reminisce almost longingly about the last time they were together. Angel says he can't help thinking about the episode, in spite of trying to forget. Darla needles him with her rendition of events:

"So, you threw me through those glass doors, slammed me against the wall, pushed me onto the bed, and took what you wanted?"

"It seemed like the thing to do—at the time" ("Quickening," 3-6).

The wry playfulness of their banter is charming in spite of its dark underpinnings. With Darla, and only with Darla, Angel is fully realized, completely present in all his aspects. Whatever he feels, whatever he needs—be it a trick of the light or the shadows—he embodies with absolute commitment. Though Darla lies and deceives, Angel reveals to her, and thereby to himself, the truth within. He might not have a reflection, but Darla is still his pure mirror.

As Darla prepares to give birth, she realizes that she is sharing more than a belly with her baby. She is sharing a soul—his soul—and its presence infiltrates her with such maternal love that she fears letting him leave her body.

"I love it completely. I-I-I don't think I've ever loved anything as much as this life that's inside of me."

"Well—you've never *loved* anything, Darla," Angel reminds her.

"That's true. Four hundred years and I never did—'til now. I don't know what to do."

"You'll have it. You'll have it and then . . ." Angel begins.

"What?" Darla interrupts. "We'll raise it?"

"Why not?"

Darla's dear boy is momentarily quite mad with paternal joy and the rush of hope that arises whenever Darla reveals even a hint of vulnerability. Clearly, the embers of Angel's obsession with Darla will not die. Try as he might to snuff them out, Darla's slightest exhale wills them into flame.

Darla, as usual, is the practical one.

"It's impossible. . . . What do I have to offer a child, a human child, besides ugly death?"

She knows that she has not been nourishing the baby, that the feelings she's having are not coming from her; they're coming from him.

"You don't know that," Angel argues, hopeful of her capacity to love—logic be damned. But Darla's strength is her ability to appreciate the harshest of history's legacies. Her very first lesson to Liam echoes here: what we were informs all that we become. Darla knows who she was—and what she will become once her body no longer envelops her baby's soul.

"I won't be able to love it. I won't even be able to remember that I loved it," she sobs, as Angel holds her close, stroking her hair and crooning "Shhhhh . . . shhhh."

Darla knows intuitively that her body is not a life-giving vessel, and that she can't carry the baby to term. But because the child is protected, it can't be C-sectioned from her, either. As long as the baby remains inside, he will die. When Angel begs her to fight for the baby, he is just as desperately begging her to fight for them. Darla swears she doesn't know how.

"My boy," she murmurs, stroking her belly. "My darling boy." Is she speaking of the child in her belly, or the "child" by her side—or both? "I told you I had nothing to offer this kid. Some mother. . . . I can't even offer it life."

Darla is wrong, she can and will give life.

Lying in an alleyway amidst the debris of club Caritas, Darla feels the child's life-force ebbing away. Angel squeezes her delicate hand between both of his and lovingly presses her fingers to his lips.

"This child—Angel, it's the one good thing we ever did together. You make sure to tell him that."

She reaches out with her free hand to grasp a pointed chunk of wood from the rubble and swiftly buries it in her chest. Angel looks as if his heart will break as Darla's hand disintegrates within his . . . and she turns to dust.

Where Darla had been, a naked human infant lies squalling in the rain ("Lullaby," 3-9).

Angel carefully gathers the infant in his arms. He will later learn that he is holding the "new life" that he had heroically battled to win for Darla during the Trials—a "gift" from the Powers That Be.

Angel has kept his promise to see Darla through to her death. With her final act of unselfish love, she achieves a sort of redemption, and certainly Angel's forgiveness. Angel once told Darla that if he could redeem her—the vampire who made him—he could redeem himself. Perhaps, in forgiving her, he can finally begin to forgive himself.

The team at AI rallies around the newborn. With Darla put to rest, Angel's relationship with Cordelia deepens. But, before anyone can grow too chipper, the child is abducted by the revengeful Holtz and lost to a demon-infested world where time moves at a different pace. Soon afterward, the "baby" reappears through a dimensional portal in the lobby of the Hyperion Hotel. Trouble is, he's now an angry eighteen-year-old, hell-bent on killing the father he has been raised by Holtz to detest.

Despite Angel's efforts to bond with his beloved son, Connor is driven by the hatred and bitterness instilled by his adoptive father. Just as Cordelia is about to declare her love for Angel, Connor imprisons him in a metal box, welds it shut, and drops it into the sea ("Tomorrow," 3-22). Connor is anxious to see Angel suffer for the agonies of Holtz's lost family, and his death. He might have succeeded if not for Wesley, who, a few months later, drags Angel out of his watery grave.

When Angel sees Connor, his sadness seems to overwhelm any vestiges of anger. Time below has given him perspective—an M.C. Escher perspective, he admits, but, hey, he'd weathered worse when his girlfriend, Buffy, stuck him in a hell dimension for a hundred years.

The events of the last year had demanded that Angel grow in ways surpassing anything evident in the previous two centuries. We see his identity, his Self, taking shape. We see his unconditional love for his offspring shining through his pain. We see his strength, his honor. His trials have forced him to mature, and now his task is to guide his son. Weakened, blood starved, near unconsciousness after his ordeal in the sea, he confronts Connor.

"What you did to me was unbelievable," Angel says. "But I did get time to think. About us, about the world. . . . Nothing in the world is the way it ought to be. It's harsh, and cruel. But that's why there's us. Champions. We live as though the world was what it should be, to show it what it can be. You're not a part of that yet. I hope you will be." Angel moves closer to his son, looking him square in the eye.

"I love you, Connor," he says quietly. "Now get out of my house" ("Deep Down," 4-1).

Angel may retain some of his old grandiosity, but he is now dedicated to ideals instead of indulgence, to loving rather than loathing. His indelible relationship with Darla has completed itself. Life has emerged from her ashes; Angel, the father, has taken the place of Angel, the son. Again, Darla's first lesson to her own dear boy ripples down through time. We feel sure that Angel's pure love for Conner will inform all that each is yet to become as their intertwined destinies unfold.

And so it does.

In the wake of Jasmine's ascension and Connor's vicious rampage ("Home," 4-22), Angel sacrifices himself again to save his son, his love proving as deep and boundless as the very sea to which Connor would have abandoned him. For his child's physical and psychic security, he makes a pact with the devil, and, taking the helm of Wolfram & Hart, he delves into the magma core of the evil he once sought to destroy.

As Angel's saga draws to a close, the apocalypse that had been prophesied bears down upon the new team at Wolfram & Hart. Connor, his memories restored and cleansed of Holtz's pestilent imprint, acknowledges his father's love on the very day that could well become Angel's last. As the final battle begins, Connor appears at Angel's side—an angelic savior himself—and we see that Darla and Angel, through their extraordinarily selfless love and Angel's tenaciously forgiving efforts, have indeed brought forth a champion. Whatever cruelties Angel may have perpetrated in the past, he has redeemed himself in the fire of this singular creation, this brave and stalwart son.

However, in the Whedonverse, redemption is not an end. Even an apocalypse—that "nowish" concatenation of events—is not an end. These are merely harbingers of cycles yet to be. So, as Angel and his valiant troops gather—tragically, minus one—in exhausted celebration of a world that they hope is finally as it should be, they discover that nothing, nothing at all is as it ought to be. There is no grand resolution, no "big win."

Hideous, shrieking demons swoop down upon the wounded, weary troop, so many creatures that the odds are surely impossible. Yet, raising their weapons, fervor burning in their eyes, the team attacks the resurgent evil. Angel's words of epiphany ("Epiphany," 2-16) seem to echo silently in the darkness: "If there is no great, glorious end to all this, if nothing we do matters, then all that matters is what we do. Because that's all there is. What we do now . . . today."

JOY DAVIDSON, PH.D., is a psychologist, certified sex therapist, author, and video-maker based in Manhattan. She is a familiar expert guest on national television and radio, including *Oprah, 20/20, CNN News, NPR, Prime Time Live, Entertainment Tonight,* and *Montel.* Dr. Davidson is the author of or contributor to six non-fiction books, and the creator of multi-volume self-help videos for women and couples. She is well known as a magazine and Web advice columnist and appears frequently in publications such as *Glamour, Cosmopolitan, Marie Claire, Esquire, Redbook,* and *Men's Health.*